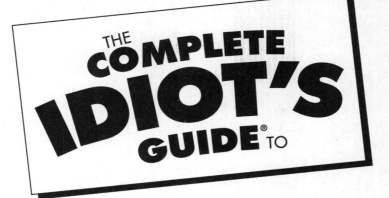

THE COMPLETE IDIOT'S GUIDE TO

Good Food from the Good Book

by Leslie Bilderback, CMB

ALPHA

A member of Penguin Group (USA) Inc.

ALPHA BOOKS

Published by the Penguin Group

Penguin Group (USA) Inc., 375 Hudson Street, New York, New York 10014, USA

Penguin Group (Canada), 90 Eglinton Avenue East, Suite 700, Toronto, Ontario M4P 2Y3, Canada (a division of Pearson Penguin Canada Inc.)

Penguin Books Ltd, 80 Strand, London WC2R 0RL, England

Penguin Ireland, 25 St. Stephen's Green, Dublin 2, Ireland (a division of Penguin Books Ltd.)

Penguin Group (Australia), 250 Camberwell Road, Camberwell, Victoria 3124, Australia (a division of Pearson Australia Group Pty. Ltd.)

Penguin Books India Pvt. Ltd., 11 Community Centre, Panchsheel Park, New Delhi—110 017, India

Penguin Group (NZ), 67 Apollo Drive, Rosedale, North Shore, Auckland 1311, New Zealand (a division of Pearson New Zealand Ltd.)

Penguin Books (South Africa) (Pty.) Ltd, 24 Sturdee Avenue, Rosebank, Johannesburg 2196, South Africa

Penguin Books Ltd., Registered Offices: 80 Strand, London WC2R 0RL, England

Copyright © 2008 by Leslie Bilderback

THE COMPLETE IDIOT'S GUIDE TO and Design are registered trademarks of Penguin Group (USA) Inc.

International Standard Book Number: 978-1-59257-728-6
Library of Congress Catalog Card Number: 2007937238

10 09 08   8 7 6 5 4 3 2 1

Interpretation of the printing code: The rightmost number of the first series of numbers is the year of the book's printing; the rightmost number of the second series of numbers is the number of the book's printing. For example, a printing code of 08-1 shows that the first printing occurred in 2008.

Printed in the United States of America

Note: This publication contains the opinions and ideas of its author. It is intended to provide helpful and informative material on the subject matter covered. It is sold with the understanding that the author and publisher are not engaged in rendering professional services in the book. If the reader requires personal assistance or advice, a competent professional should be consulted.

Most Alpha books are available at special quantity discounts for bulk purchases for sales promotions, premiums, fundraising, or educational use. Special books, or book excerpts, can also be created to fit specific needs.

For details, write: Special Markets, Alpha Books, 375 Hudson Street, New York, NY 10014.

Publisher: *Marie Butler-Knight*
Editorial Director: *Mike Sanders*
Managing Editor: *Billy Fields*
Senior Acquisitions Editor: *Paul Dinas*
Development Editor: *Julie Bess*
Production Editor: *Megan Douglass*
Copy Editor: *Nancy Wagner*

Cartoonist: *Steve Barr*
Cover Designer: *Bill Thomas*
Book Designer: *Trina Wurst*
Indexer: *Tonya Heard*
Layout: *Ayanna Lacey*
Proofreader: *John Etchison*

Contents at a Glance

Contents

Appendixes

Introduction

In modern America we are faced with many challenges. Families, economics, politics, and culture surround and bombard us with demands. Many of us turn to the Scriptures for guidance, insight, and peace of mind. Religions throughout the world incorporate daily activities as integral elements of worship, including meals. But Christian spiritual life often does not include such mundane daily activities as eating. By looking closely at the Bible, the food we feed our loved ones, and ourselves, we can extend our spiritual life to touch not only the soul but also the body.

Our country is technologically advanced and culturally sophisticated, yet our health is deteriorating rapidly, and this is in direct correlation to the food we eat. This book presents a straightforward discussion of the biblical dietary laws, explains why they are sound, and shows you how you can follow them to build a healthier family.

Part 1, "Not by Bread Alone …," takes a look at the Old Testament through modern eyes, bringing to light the good sense behind the dietary laws. An overview of ancient food and cooking methods will lead into an investigation of modern nutrition, and the problems we face individually and as a nation. Armed with the power of nutritional knowledge, you can then sift through hundreds of recipes designed to fit your modern lifestyle while addressing your nutritional needs. You'll find all your favorite foods for every meal, as well as menus to help you plan special events.

Part 2, "Breakfast and Baking," includes recipes for the most important meal of the day, plus all your favorite breads, sweet and savory.

Part 3, "Snacks and Starters," keeps entertaining in mind, with lots of nibbles and favorite first courses, suitable for casual get-togethers or more formal affairs. Here, too, you'll find an abundance of soups and salads to serve either as a first course or light meal.

Part 4, "Main Dishes," provides dozens of ideas for dinner. Whether you're craving meat, poultry, fish, or a comforting casserole, you'll find something here to satisfy you.

Part 5, "Accompaniments," helps you put it all together with side dishes including vegetables, grains, potatoes, and pasta.

Part 6, "Celebrating," includes sweets to share on special occasions, as well as menu ideas for special meals throughout the year.

Extras

Scattered throughout these pages you'll find several sidebars that dive a little deeper into the topic at hand.

Biblical Culture
This sidebar gives a historical reference to the subject.

def•i•ni•tion

This sidebar explains terminology, both historical and culinary.

 Kitchen Tips

This sidebar gives you heads up with warnings, hints, and shortcuts designed to make your cooking experience more enjoyable.

At the end of the book, you'll find more terminology in the glossary and a handy listing of Internet sources for specialty foods.

Acknowledgments

Thanks to my wonderful family for their continued support. Thanks to Rev. Anne Tumilty for her insight, and everyone at Saint James for giving us a foundation of faith from which to grow. I hope you enjoy your spiritual quest for a healthier lifestyle. Good health!

Special Thanks to the Technical Reviewer

The Complete Idiot's Guide to Good Food from the Good Book was reviewed by an expert who double-checked the accuracy of what you'll learn here, to help us ensure that this book gives you everything you need to know about healthy eating. Special thanks are extended to Lisa Vislocky.

Trademarks

All terms mentioned in this book that are known to be or are suspected of being trademarks or service marks have been appropriately capitalized. Alpha Books and Penguin Group (USA) Inc. cannot attest to the accuracy of this information. Use of a term in this book should not be regarded as affecting the validity of any trademark or service mark.

Part 1

Not by Bread Alone ...

The laws extolled by Moses are not difficult to follow and can have a lasting effect on overall health and well-being. These chapters explain and champion these ancient laws, showing how they make sense in our chaotic lives today.

Life in the twenty-first century has many conveniences that have impeded our overall health. Lack of exercise and increased food refinement are on the top of the list. But modern life makes getting healthy easy, too. Good food is just as easily attainable as bad, at supermarkets, health-food stores, and over the Internet. Products that were once limited to one side of the globe now hop from continent to continent, enhancing our pantries. And clever tools and equipment make formerly arduous tasks a piece of cake.

Modern Wisdom and the Ancient Hebrew Dietary Laws

In This Chapter

- ◆ Clean and unclean
- ◆ Leviticus and the dietary laws
- ◆ Mammals, fowl, and fish

Many religions carry dietary laws with them. Jewish and Muslim dietary laws are similar; one follows the Laws of Moses, while the other keeps in step with the notion of clean and unclean. Hindus are mainly vegetarian as are Buddhists, although by following strict guidelines, believers are allowed meat and fish. Early Christian food rules banned the ingestion of meat offered to idols, the blood of animals, and animals that had been strangled. Roman Catholics abstained from eating meat on Fridays until the Second Vatican Council (Vatican II) in the 1960s.

So why should we pay attention to what the Bible says about what we eat? Initially, these laws were meant to draw a distinction between those who worshipped one God and the pagan-idol-worshipping rest of the world. The intent, in part, was to help people grow spiritually. These laws became, in a world of nonbelievers and temptation, a daily exercise in self-discipline and self-control. In this way, the laws were meant to promote ethical and moral behavior because, as now, civilized existence relied upon the ability of man to curb some of his basic natural desires.

Those who followed the laws of Moses eventually became the Israelites and are today members of the Jewish faith. But what about Christians? Why do they need to follow these rules? After all, no religious edicts regulate Christian meals.

As it turns out, the Bible's dietary guidelines promote a sensible, healthy diet. And while, for most Christians, serving God has little to do with what we serve our families for lunch, we may find some wisdom in these ancient ideas. Moreover, regardless of one's spiritual beliefs, these Old Testament laws make good nutritional sense.

Food in the Bible

The first mention of food appears in Genesis:

"Then God said, 'I give you every seed-bearing plant on the face of the whole earth and every tree that has fruit with seed in it. They will be yours for food.'" (Genesis 1:29)

The fruits were meant to be eaten. So, in the beginning, Adam and Eve were vegans. But after they compromised their integrity and begat several generations who displeased the Lord, God instructed Noah to build an ark, and a great flood occurred.

Biblical Culture
In the first century A.D., Christian believers gathered regularly for meals of fellowship, which they called *agape*, which denotes love, not of a romantic nature, but of a spiritual one. The poor were invited to these agape in which all celebrated the meals of Jesus. These feasts included elements of the Passover Seder, but the *Eucharist*, a Greek word meaning "giving of thanks," was detached, as such gatherings would deteriorate into drinking parties. As Christianity grew, the Eucharist became an adaptation of the Lord's Supper used at the conclusion of public meetings and reserved for the baptized believers. A form of the agape is still practiced in many churches in the form of a fellowship or coffee hour.

"Take with you seven of every kind of clean animal, a male and its mate, and two of every kind of unclean animal, a male and its mate." (Genesis 7:2)

This is the first reference found to clean and unclean animals. Clean animals were intended for food and for sacrificial offerings (a common practice in which a life was given in atonement for one's sins, later demonstrated to the extreme in the crucifixion). But which animals were clean and which were unclean? The Bible doesn't tell us until Leviticus 11, but we can assume Noah, who was tight with the Lord, knew the difference.

> **Biblical Culture**
>
> The destruction of the Temple of Jerusalem in 70 A.D. marked the end of ritual sacrifice in the Jewish tradition because exile to Babylonia afforded the Jews no opportunity to perform sacrifices. Thereafter, prayer replaced sacrifices.

The Leviticus Contract

Moses received the rules for God's people at Mt. Sinai. Leviticus itemizes these rules, much like a how-to book on attaining, and maintaining, holiness. The book is full of regulations regarding not just food, but also sacrifices, sickness, priesthood, conduct, holy convocations, blessings, curses, and vows. It is meant as a covenant, or contract, between God and man.

Such contracts were commonplace at that time, especially between servants and masters. If the servant was loyal and obedient, he was guaranteed protection and benefits. This is precisely the point of Leviticus. If one listens to the word of God, obeys His commandments, and does the right thing in all aspects of life, God will protect him.

"I will put none of the diseases on you which I have put on the Egyptians; for I, the Lord, am your healer." (Exodus 15:26)

By following the laws of God, man displays will, morality, obedience, and loyalty. At first glance, these laws seem like a random set of rules. But upon deeper study, it becomes clear that in regard to the sanitary and dietary laws, the covenant protected man through good health and cleanliness. Dietary laws are a prophylactic against disease, and throughout history observance has led to longevity, physical power, and moral integrity.

The Dietary Laws

The book begins with the LORD saying to Moses and Aaron, "Say to the Israelites: 'Of all the animals that live on land, these are the ones you may eat.'" (Leviticus 1:1-2) And then for several chapters, the Lord gives instructions to his people.

The only animals that may be eaten by man are those deemed clean. Clean animals include quadrupeds that chew their cud and have completely split hooves, fish with fins and scales, domesticated birds, locusts, and grasshoppers.

There is little restriction on vegetation, but certain restrictions apply to first fruits, meant for worship and charitable offerings. Fruit may not be eaten within the first three years of growth, but must instead be offered as sacrifice. This is to acknowledge that it is not only man's labor that produces food, but God's. There are also rules associated with sowing seeds in mixed crops.

Slaughter and preparation of food is regulated. Animals must be killed in a clean and humane manner, remembering always that the sanctity of every creature's life is not to be taken lightly. Kosher slaughter is meant to limit the animal's suffering and demonstrate the responsibility that comes with having power over life and death. In preparing meat, body fat and sinuous tendons must be removed, and the body must be drained completely of all fluids. Through this careful ritual cleaning and dressing of meat, man is given time to reflect on the meaning of life, and to thank God. The fat of clean birds is acceptable.

Specific food combinations are prohibited. An animal may not be seethed (boiled), in its mother's milk. The intention of such an act is indeed horrifying. This is seen as symbolic combination of life and death, and has come to be interpreted that meat and milk in any form may not be cooked or consumed together, whether in a particular dish, or within the same meal. Fish and meat are also not to be consumed together, and there are certain holidays that require specific foods.

Unclean animals should not be touched. They are thought to be literally unclean, and if contact is made, special washing must take place. Also restricted is anything that comes out of an unclean animal, which includes animal products like milk or eggs. Only eggs of clean birds are acceptable, if free of blood.

Clean animals found to be diseased are forbidden. Clean animals that die naturally, or are killed by others, are forbidden.

There are specific foods that are forbidden by name, and others that are inferred.

Animals forbidden by name:

Bat	Heron	Ossifrage
Camel	Kite	Owl
Chameleon	Lapwing	Pelican
Coney	Little Owl	Raven

Cormorant	Lizard	Snail
Cuckhow	Mole	Stork
Eagle	Mouse	Swan
Ferret	Nighthawk	Swine
Gier Eagle	Osprey	Tortoise
Glede	Ostrich	Vulture
Great Owl	Weasel	

Animals not specifically mentioned, yet considered unclean, based on characteristics mentioned in Leviticus and Deuteronomy:

Abalone	Crow	Lobster	Shark
Alligator	Dog	Lynx	Shrimp
Ape	Dolphin	Magpie	Squid
Bear	Donkey	Monkey	Squirrel
Cat	Eel	Mussel	Snake
Catfish	Elephant	Parrot	Starfish
Cheetah	Fox	Penguin	Tiger
Clam	Gecko	Prawns	Turtle
Cockatoo	Gibbon	Raccoon	Wolf
Crab	Hedgehog	Rat	Worm
Crayfish	Lion	Scallop	Zebra
		Seal	

Some believe these laws are based on hygiene, sanitation, and health. Others think they originated as a national law, to separate the Israelites from their neighbors: the Egyptians, the Canaanites, and the Arabians. These are both logical explanations.

Many of the dietary laws seem reasonable, while others take some further investigation for us to understand. But the underlying motive is the same: these laws promote physical and spiritual health.

A Closer Look

As we explore the regulations, we find that the criteria for clean animals is far from random. The animals that appear on the clean list are as close to the bottom of the food chain as possible.

At the bottom of the food chain are organisms that can create organic substance from inorganic material with the help of an energy source. These organisms are called *autotrophs*, and autotrophs are plants, bacteria, or algae that use the sun to create food via the process of photosynthesis.

The next level of the food chain contains primary consumers. These are creatures that consume the autotrophs. We call land creatures that do this *herbivores*. These veggie eaters transform the sun's energy, stored in plants, to food that can be eaten by carnivores and omnivores up the food chain.

We refer to animals that eat animals as secondary consumers. As we move higher up the food chain, further and further from the primary food source, animal meat contains more and more of the unknown. Carnivores do not distinguish fresh meat from old, spoiled, toxic, or diseased meat, and once ingested, such impurities are then carried by the secondary consumer.

def•i•ni•tion

Trophic levels are the different levels of the food chain.

In addition to harboring the unknown, each position, or *trophic level*, of the food chain incurs a decrease in biomass. Biomass is organic matter converted to energy by the body. The biomass transfer from vegetation to animal is 100 percent; however, the biomass transfer from prey to predator is just around 10 percent. So the closer to the primary source one eats, the more bang for the buck one gets.

What's on the Menu?

Now, let's look at the specific foods more closely.

Land Mammals

"You may eat any animal that has a split hoof completely divided and that chews the cud." (Leviticus 11:3)

What distinguishes these animals from all the others? They are herbivores, for one thing. But while other animals are herbivores, these split-hoofed animals share a similar, and remarkable, digestive system.

Animals with hooves are called *ungulates*. These mammals developed elongated bones between the nail and the wrist, which means they are essentially walking on their tip-toes because a hoof is just a modified toenail. This allows for swift locomotion, particularly important when evading predators across a grassy plain. Several species exist, including even- and odd-toed ungulates. Those with split hooves are cows, sheep, goats, and deer. The giraffe is a split-hoofed ungulate, and although technically clean, it is rarely hunted.

These animals evolved in the grasslands, where the vegetation has low nutritional value for most creatures. But this family of ungulates, called *ruminants*, developed a unique digestive system that allows them to extract maximum nutrients from the vegetation.

Ruminants are the cud chewers. Cud chewing is a mechanism used to break down fibrous vegetation for digestion. This process, in conjunction with a four-chambered stomach, allows for the extraction and purification of all the available nutrients in food. This amazing process allows these animals to efficiently live off foodstuffs that humans and other animals cannot.

Biblical Culture

Why not include camels in this list? They chew their cud, but their hooves are only partially split. Why should this matter? We do know that a camel's stomach has only three chambers, and a camel has no gall bladder, which stores bile that contributes to the breakdown of fat in the stomach. Additionally, the camel was a valued mode of transportation.

The majority of mammals, including you and me, has one stomach called a mono-gastric digestive system. In this system, digestion begins in the mouth, moves to the stomach where it is acidified, and is then sent through the intestines, where nutrients are absorbed. This system cannot break down plant fiber, or cellulose. But ruminants can. In a ruminant's digestive system a lot more goes on. The first stomach chamber, called the ruminum, contains bacteria and symbiotic organisms that break down cellulose. These protozoa actually eat the digested cellulose, too, helping it ferment, and releasing a unique enzyme specifically for the breakdown of cellulose. Most of the ruminant's protein intake is generated by these organisms.

Once cellulose is fine enough, it will move into the next chamber, the reticulum, where it is broken down and fermented further. If the matter is still too course, it goes back out as cud to be chewed further by the animal. The third chamber, the omasum, absorbs liquid and filters food into the fourth chamber, the abomasum. This last chamber is often called the true stomach because it acts like stomachs of other mammals, secreting acids and enzymes to digest the incoming food. By this time, everything useful has been digested and absorbed.

As you can see, this specific family of ungulate ruminants ingests the primary food source in a highly efficient manner. Impurities and toxins are removed over a period of 24 hours, before they can be absorbed into the animal's tissues Anything t hat is foreign is passed out.

When an animal ingests food off of their natural diet, diseases occur. An example of this is *mad cow disease*, or Bovine Spongiform Encephalopathy. Mad cow is a fatal prion disease, called spongiform because it causes the brain to become spongy and riddled with holes.

Most prion disease is caused by ingestion of animal products that are not a natural food source. In the case of cows and sheep, both herbivores, the major cause is feed tainted with animal by-products, which is added to feed to increase the muscle and weight of the animal. Unfortunately, it can also kill them. Humans contract mad cow from eating tainted meat. The practice of feeding animal by-products to mammals was banned in the United States in 1988. A strain of prion disease called Kuzu originated in humans but was contained within a Papua New Guinea tribe that practiced ritualistic cannibalism of its dead. The practice, and accordingly the disease, stopped in the 1960s.

Pork

Although pigs have split hooves, they are not ruminants. You can see by their short legs that they were not grassland creatures. Modern pigs descended from wild pigs native to woodlands across Europe, Africa, and Asia. They adapted easily to, and thrived in, a variety of terrains because of their omnivorous eating habits. Their indiscriminant diet includes vegetation, small animals, eggs, carrion, and manure.

Pigs do not need a complex digestive system because they consume a variety of foodstuffs allowing them to obtain sufficient nutrients from their food. It requires only four hours for a pig to digest and absorb its food, while ungulate ruminants require 24 hours to do the same. Without that ingenious filtering system of a ruminant's stomach, every impurity an animal eats is absorbed into its tissues and muscles, and then into the tissues and muscles of the animal that consumes it.

Some believe the law against eating pork was imposed as protection against the trichina parasite. But trichinosis, and infectious diseases in general, were unknown in ancient times. It is more likely that the notion of *you are what you eat* is older than we think. Simply observing a pig and what it eats was enough for folks to determine its culinary rank. Just as most Americans react to the thought of people eating dogs and cats, so, too, do the observant react to eating unclean animals.

It is interesting to note that pork consumption universally leads to health problems and has been shown to cause stress and poisoning, especially in tropical regions. Pacific Islanders consume an unusually large amount of pork and have an historically high rate of obesity. Native Hawaiians and Samoans, among the world's most obese people, have a high rate of diabetes, hypertension, cardiovascular disease, and stroke.

Physically, it is harder for humans to digest pork, and that, in turn, leads to chronic diseases of the digestive system. We know that animal fat contains cholesterol, a well-documented contributor to heart disease. But even today's leaner pork causes danger because, unlike herbivore meat, the fat is found in great quantity within the cells and not simply marbled throughout the muscles.

Consuming fat in moderation is not necessarily bad. The human body needs fat for insulation, as padded protection for our organs and as a stored source of energy. Most animal fat, when consumed, undergoes *hydrolysis*, an enzymatic process that breaks down the fat and stores it as energy. However, because of the pig's diet and digestive system, pork fat does not undergo hydrolysis. Without hydrolysis, humans cannot utilize pork fat as energy, and it is simply stockpiled, which contributes to obesity.

Fowl

"These are the birds you are to detest and not eat because they are detestable: the eagle, the vulture, the black vulture, the red kite, any kind of black kite, any kind of raven, the horned owl, the screech owl, the gull, any kind of hawk, the little owl, the cormorant, the great owl, the white owl, the desert owl, the osprey, the stork, any kind of heron, the hoopoe and the bat." (Leviticus 11:13-19)

These laws clearly indicated what the people could not eat but did not give clear rules about what they could. This omission still keeps many a rabbi busy, deciding what does and does not fall into the clean category.

We know that birds of prey and most waterfowl are unclean. This makes sense if we follow the same logic applied to land mammals. Animals that eat other animals are further up the food chain, and so the nutrition they provide us is less pure and the biomass less available to the LV human body. Birds of prey routinely eat diseased meat and carrion, thereby carrying the disease themselves. We also know that scavengers, like many of these birds, serve us by cleaning our environment. If we were to use these animals as food, we would ingest what they had scavenged and prevent them from doing their cleanup job.

def•i•ni•tion

Kashrut is the body of Jewish law, based on the Torah (the first five books of the Bible), that governs diet.

The Bible does not address the issue of domesticated fowl, which *Kashrut* allows. Poultry is a vital component of many cuisines worldwide and is allowed because they are not birds of prey.

When allowed to roam and forage as nature intended, these birds eat a diet that consists mainly of vegetation and insects. They are not naturally cannibalistic but will fight and eat each other if aggravated. This might occur due to poor living conditions and in preparation for cockfighting, both situations put upon them by man. And contrary to popular belief, chickens do not willingly eat manure but look for insects within it.

Native to China and India, chickens were domesticated as early as 7000 B.C., and their bones have been found in Egyptian tombs dating to 2500 B.C. Chickens have no teeth, and they are not ruminants. But their digestive system is special because it contains a multichambered stomach which includes a gizzard. The bird swallows small stones and grit, and in the gizzard these particles help break down food.

Man has fattened chickens throughout history. In biblical times they were routinely fed bread soaked in milk to improve the flavor of their meat. But birds raised today are much different. Kept in close quarters, medicated, and physically altered for their own safety, today's chickens have little in common with their ancestors. Feed typically does not consist of vegetation and foraged insects, but manmade chicken feed, antibiotics, pesticides, and hormones.

Creeping Creatures

"All flying insects that walk on all fours are to be detestable to you. There are, however, some winged creatures that walk on all fours that you may eat: those that have jointed legs for hopping on the ground. Of these you may eat any kind of locust, katy-did, cricket or grasshopper. But all other winged creatures that have four legs you are to detest." (Leviticus 11:20-23)

Creeping things were forbidden, including rodents, reptiles, and bugs. The exceptions were insects of the suborder *orthoptera*, which include grasshoppers, locusts, crickets, and katydids, all herbivore insects with hopping back legs.

Considered unpalatable to most Americans, these highly nutritious insects are commonly consumed in other parts of the world. In Nigeria, locusts are a popular snack. Lured by flashlight at night, they are captured, de-winged, and fried in oil. Dipped in a chili-based sauce, they are fondly referred to as Desert Shrimps. Fried grasshoppers, called *capulines*, are popular in Oaxaca, Mexico, with a squeeze of lime.

Eating insects, known as *entomophagy*, has many proponents because insects pack a bigger nutritional punch. They are high in protein and low in fat. Insects have twice the calories and much more protein compared to an equal size serving of beef, while beef has four times the fat. More importantly, they are a readily available food source that imposes little impact on the environment.

Locusts and grasshoppers have sensitive leg and mouth hairs that taste, and then avoid, pesticides. And they are naturally finicky eaters, always seeking out a healthy balance of protein, carbohydrates, and salts. They can eat their body weight (about 2 grams—just under a half ounce) in food. If their diet is lacking, they will compensate at later feedings. All this makes them a good, healthy choice to help fulfill our protein requirements.

Biblical Culture

"And the same John had his raiment of camel's hair, and a leathern girdle about his loins; and his meat was locusts and wild honey." (Matthew 3:4)

This passage, telling of John the Baptist preaching in the wilderness, is entirely plausible. Locusts are on the clean list, and contain all the essential amino acids humans need. Yet some scholars believe the locust referenced here is fruit from the locust tree, a species of carob. Still more controversy surrounds this passage and its Greek translation. "Locust" in Greek is *akris*, while "pancake" in *Greek egkris*. This similarity has led some scholars to believe that the food John ate was a grain. The debate rages on.

Fish

"Of all the creatures living in the water of the seas and the streams, you may eat any that have fins and scales. But all creatures in the seas or streams that do not have fins and scales—whether among all the swarming things or among all the other living creatures in the water—you are to detest. And since you are to detest them, you must not eat their meat and you must detest their carcasses. Anything living in the water that does not have fins and scales is to be detestable to you." (Leviticus 11:9-12)

The limits on fish revolved around the cleanliness of their environments. Swift-moving currents naturally filter the water, while calm waters harbor impurities.

Scholars have made no discoveries of fish with scales that do not also have fins. Because of this, those looking to adhere to biblical dietary guidelines put the emphasis on determining the presence of scales.

Several types of scales are found on seafood, but the only type acceptable are those that are easily seen and easily removed without tearing the flesh of the fish. This type of scale is called a cycloid. Fish that have a few of these scales, or had them at one time in their life cycle, are deemed acceptable.

Fish without fins, which include crustaceans (like shrimp and lobster), mollusks (like oysters and clams), and cephalopods (like squid and octopus), are off limits. Absence of fins keeps these creatures from moving swiftly. Settled at the bottom of the sea, on rocks, reefs, under piers, or crawling slowly on the ocean floor, they are susceptible to all the toxins of the sea. Fish that swim use their movement as a filter for the debris and waste of the ocean. Motionless, slow-moving, and bottom-feeding creatures absorb these toxins. This action filters the ocean for the rest of us, but it also transfers the impurities to whomever, or whatever, consumes them. Consider, too, that much of what pollutes the oceans these days is runoff from civilization.

Scientists, fishermen, and chefs have known for years that shellfish can be toxic. Red tide, a discoloration of the water caused by algae bloom (technically a rapid growth of phytoplankton), is filtered by shellfish and transferred to humans who eat it. The specific problem with red tide is *saxitoxin*, a neurotoxin that causes paralysis and eventually death. Saxitoxin has been isolated and designated by the United States military as a chemical weapon. This danger has given rise to popular belief that one should never eat shellfish in months that end in "r". Unfortunately, red tide can, and does, occur around the globe throughout the year.

In addition to being the filters of the sea, shellfish cause allergic reactions in many people and is one of the top five food-related allergies in humans.

The following list contains only commonly consumed seafood:

Clean Fish—Albacore, Bass, Buffalo Fish, Carp, Cape Capensis, Char, Cod, Flounder, Goldfish, Grouper, Haddock, Halibut, Herring, Mackerel, Mahi Mahi, Orange Roughy, Perch, Pike, Pollock, Salmon, Sardines, Snapper, Sole, Suckers, Tilapia, Trout, Tuna, Walleye, Whitefish, Whiting

Unclean Fish—Catfish, Eels, Grayfish, Marlin (except the Blue Marlin), Octopus, Shark, Snake Mackerels, Squid, Sturgeons, Swordfish

Other Rules and Regulations

Other food-related rules that appear in Leviticus revolved around the preparation and handling of these foods, and human cleanliness in relation to handling food. They make good sense to us now, knowing as we do about bacteria, contamination, and disease. But until the twentieth century, only Jews practiced such careful handling. Today, meat processors who are certified kosher are not subject to the United States Department of Agriculture (USDA) guidelines because they are already much more sanitary than the USDA requires.

Leviticus discusses what to do if contact is made with unclean animals, alive or dead. Humans can easily transfer the uncleanliness, and specific steps must be taken to cleanse and purify oneself after such an encounter. If an unclean animal falls into a pot of clean food, the pot must be discarded. There is no three-second rule in the Bible.

Clean animals can only be eaten if killed for that purpose. Natural or predatory, death by any other means makes an animal unclean.

The most difficult of these laws to explain scientifically is the prohibition on the combination of dairy and meat. Symbolically it makes sense. Boiling an animal in its mother's milk is cruel and unusual. As compassionate beings with a reverence for the sanctity of life, we are repulsed by that notion. But in today's world, the cheese or yogurt or milk is certainly no relation to the steak on the grill. Sure, we know both foods are loaded with saturated fat and that limiting our fat intake in general is a good idea. But is that reason enough to forgo the occasional cheeseburger?

Perhaps of all the dietary laws, this ban of dairy and meat is the most important. This is the one law that we must take on faith alone. After all, man has been following these regulations for thousands of years, yet it wasn't until the last century that science could confirm the sound reasoning. As modern humans, we are accustomed to explanations. But here, we may need to simply believe that God knows what's best. So far, He's batting 1,000.

Who Are These Rules For?

Many cultures follow dietary guidelines, but only the Jewish tradition specifically follows the Laws of Moses, set forth in the first five books of the Bible, known as the Pentateuch. So why did Christianity abandon the Old Testament's dietary laws? Most people point to a certain passage in the Book of Acts as proof that God wants us to eat everything. (Acts 10:1-11:18)

In this story, God prepares Peter, a Jew, to enter the home of a gentile, a thing Jews did not do because they considered such places unclean. On the day before this visit occurred, Peter was waiting for a meal to be prepared when he had a vision that included the appearance of all the animals of the earth. In this vision, a voice commanded Peter to kill and eat these animals. As a Jew, Peter knew these animals were unclean and would not eat them. But the voice assured him that God had cleansed them and they were no longer unclean. Peter saw this as a test and as a sign that entering the home of a gentile was okay.

This story reveals a deeper message, one of tolerance and acceptance. Although Jesus was a devout Jew and rabbi, he accepted everyone into his fold, regardless of background or affiliation. Here, within this deeper message, we can find an explanation for Christianity's dismissal of dietary law.

Because the followers of Jesus were not just Jews but also gentiles, with no laws guiding their diet, early Christians might have simply overlooked these elements of the Mosaic Laws as an act of forbearance. And as the movement grew, such laws could have only been seen as a hindrance. One imagines the early Christians had enough on their plates. Being asked to not only accept the story of the Resurrection but also to change their lifelong, even generations-long, eating habits, would have simply been too much.

This history, coupled with the abundance of food we enjoy in the modern era and the giant steps modern medicine has taken in the past century, has led even the most fastidious Christians to become complacent. But if one follows the Bible's teachings in other aspects of life, why ignore the culinary ones? If God has something to say about the way we should treat one another, don't you think he might care about the way we treat ourselves?

Remember, we find the first reference to clean and unclean in the story of Noah. The Jews wrote these scriptures while in exile in Babylon, as a way of understanding their own cultural identity. Gathered from tales passed through generations, this story took place about 900 years before Moses descended from Mt. Sinai with the Laws of God. Noah was aware of clean and unclean animals before there was a Moses or commandments or Israelites or the dream of a promised land. So the knowledge of clean and unclean was not necessarily meant for Jews alone but for all people who wished to lead a good and clean life.

Perhaps these rules have more to offer than a complicated shopping list. Perhaps they provide a healthier mind and body.

The Least You Need to Know

◆ The Book of Leviticus lays out the Laws of Moses, including dietary guidelines.

◆ The dietary laws of Moses make good nutritional sense.

◆ Living as a Christian should include knowing and following the healthful, nutritional awareness of our biblical forebears.

2

Life of the Ancients

In This Chapter

- ◆ The Fertile Crescent
- ◆ Culinary evolution
- ◆ Food of our forebears
- ◆ Modern nutrition
- ◆ Recommended food quantities

A specific spot on earth has been witness to the evolution of civilization, from nomads to tillers, herdsmen, city dwellers, traders, craftsmen, businessmen, the industrial and technological revolution, and beyond. This special place is called the Fertile Crescent.

Civilization and the Fertile Crescent

The Fertile Crescent, essentially a bridge between Africa and Eurasia, forms an upside-down "u" of territory that runs from Egypt in the southwest, up the eastern edge of the Mediterranean, swings out to Mesopotamia in what is now eastern Jordan, Iraq, Iran, and Saudi Arabia and then down to the Persian Gulf. Between the fertile lands of Egypt and Mesopotamia was the Holy Land; in today's world, it is modern Israel and Palestine.

The rivers of the region, the Nile, Tigris, Euphrates, and Jordan, extend the fertile area north of the Syrian desert into modern Southeastern Turkey and as far south as Southwestern Iran. Today, about 120 million people, or one fourth of the population of the Middle East, live in the Fertile Crescent.

Biblical Culture
While people were migrating into the Fertile Crescent, civilizations were simultaneously springing up in China, India, and Mesoamerica.

Nomads to Farmers

Mesopotamia, a Greek name that means "land between two rivers," is an area of great archeological importance. Scholars have unearthed skeletal and cultural remains of early humans, including agricultural artifacts. Here we find evidence of the evolution of civilization.

Early man lived in nomadic tribes that followed herds and foraged for vegetation. Clever hunters knew it was easier to kill an animal if they could box it into a canyon or trap it in a cave or a hole. The first domesticated animals were dogs, which appeared around 14000 B.C. and were trained to help with the hunt. With a dog's help, man experimented with controlling herds of goats and then sheep. Young males of the herd were slaughtered for food, leaving the females and older males for breeding.

The first signs of agriculture appeared around 8000 B.C. Wild strains of wheat, barley, legumes, and beans grew wild along the riverbanks, and it probably didn't take man very long to discover that seeds grew and could be controlled for his benefit. People began to migrate out of the caves in the mountains and foothills into the well-watered plains and build huts. Finding they were safer in groups, they built their huts closer together in villages. And in the center of the villages they erected corrals for goats and sheep.

The selection of suitable plants and animals happened over hundreds of years, and eventually people found foods that suited their needs. Planted areas would be fertile for decades, but as water dried up and fertile soil was washed away, farmers moved on to new fields. Returning years later, they found those fields productive once more. This custom gave rise to fallow fields, the practice of leaving a field dormant or planting it with animal fodder in alternating years. Farmers soon discovered the waste from animals grazing on infertile fields improved crops the following year, which led to experimentation with crop rotation.

The abundance of food brought about by agriculture resulted in increased population. Because food was plentiful, it was no longer necessary for every member of the family to spend the day in search of it. Consequently, people used their time to develop skills, and so began the development of towns and cities.

In Jericho, the world's oldest continually inhabited city, the first examples of axes and knives appeared around 6000 B.C. Goods such as these, as well as pottery and textiles, led to trade. Sumerian excavations unearthed goods from India and Egypt. Seafaring communities eventually spread trade technologies as far as Spain, France, and England.

Dry years signaled the need for irrigation, as evidence found along the Nile and Euphrates as early as 5000 B.C. indicated. Such complex engineering would have required the organization of large groups of people, giving rise to the first forms of government. To facilitate this, means of communication were developed, and the first form of writing, cuneiform, showed up in Sumeria around 3300 B.C.

This awakening led not only to prosperity but also to warfare. The Sumerians, first a group of fighting villages, were united by a series of rulers. But efforts to extend the kingdom through warfare weakened the civilization, and it eventually split. Several strong city-states sprang up, among them Babylon, and Hammurabi, whose code is the first known written law, was its ruler. The Hittites overthrew the Babylonians; then the Assyrians, whose armies built roads, had iron weapons, and were known to be cruel and violent, overthrew the Hittites. In the sixth century B.C., several neighboring city-states joined to crush Assyria, and under King Nebuchadnezzar, Babylon was returned to its former glory, complete with hanging gardens. But then the Persian armies of Cyrus the Great defeated them a century later.

During these centuries of war and expansion, many tribes migrated from one land to another. The Hebrews left Ur in Mesopotamia for the land of Canaan, today's Palestine. Later famine drove them to Egypt, and Moses led them back again to Canaan. Once established, King David ruled the kingdom of Israel, then his son Solomon, who made Jerusalem the capital. Ambitious building projects weakened the state through forced labor and taxes, and it eventually split, with Israel in the north and Judea in the south. Nebuchadnezzar destroyed Jerusalem and sent the Hebrews into exile in Babylon. When Cyrus of Persia gained control of Babylon, he released the Hebrews, who returned to Palestine to rebuild. They lived there under a series of foreign rulers, including the Persians, Greeks, and Romans.

The following timeline is an approximate synopsis of culinary evolution, with some historical events added for context.

38000 B.C.

Homo sapiens evolve from Neanderthals and begin to hunt and gather.

25000 B.C.

Hot embers line pits for cooking.

14000 B.C.

Dogs are domesticated for hunting.

12000 B.C.

Grinding stones are used for cereals along the Nile.

11000 B.C.

Flint-edged tools are first made.

10000 B.C.

Almonds are discovered in Crete.

Goats are domesticated.

9000 B.C.

Sheep are domesticated.

Bows, arrows, and spears are discovered.

Figs are domesticated in the Fertile Crescent.

8500 B.C.

Hunter-gatherers make encampments to utilize wild grains.

8000 B.C.

Pigs are domesticated in China.

Farmers use digging sticks to plant wild grass seeds.

7000 B.C.

Pig domestication in the Fertile Crescent fails, as these animals compete with mankind for food.

Wild emmer wheat is domesticated in Kurdistan.

6500 B.C.

People begin settling in Mesopotamia.

Aurochs (wild cattle) are domesticated.

The wheel shows up in Sumeria.

6000 B.C.

Chickens are domesticated in Asia.

Axes, chisels, and knives are first used in Jericho.

Fired pottery allows for new forms of cooking.

5000 B.C.

Irrigation begins along the Nile.

Chinese cultivate rice.

Egyptians domesticate donkeys.

4000 B.C.

Olive trees are cultivated in the Fertile Crescent.

Irrigation begins along the Euphrates.

Egyptians use yeast as a leavening agent.

Horses are domesticated in the Ukraine.

Honey bees are domesticated in Egypt

3500 B.C.

Sumerians move into Mesopotamia and develop civilization. Animals harnessed for agricultural power means less manpower is needed. Man turns his attention to religion, government, business, craft.

First cuneiform writing appears, including *The Epic of Gilgamesh*, which mentions barley, caper berries, cucumbers, figs, flat bread, grapes, honey, meat flavored with herbs, sesame, and onions.

Bronze objects are made.

3000 B.C.

Pigeons are domesticated in Egypt.

Dromedary are domesticated in Arabia.

Chickpeas are used as rations for Egyptian pyramid builders.

2500 B.C.

Egyptians sun-dry meat and fish.

Iron plow revolutionizes farming.

2000 B.C.

Egyptians give up domestication of oryx, gazelle, and antelope.

Water is purified by boiling and filtration.

Onions are eaten in Sumeria.

1800 B.C.

Pork is first considered unclean.

Hammurabi rules Babylon Empire and creates first written code of law.

1700 B.C.

Babylonians harness wind power for irrigation.

1600 B.C.

Egyptians create large oven capable of baking multiple loaves of leavened bread at once.

1500 B.C.

Coriander is used as culinary spice in Egypt.

1470 B.C.

Rising sea water creates famine in Egypt.

1450 B.C.

Cinnamon is used as a culinary spice in Egypt.

1275 B.C.

The Israelites migrate for 40 years from Egypt to the Promised Land.

1100 B.C.

Tables and chairs are first used.

800 B.C.

Phoenicians plant chickpeas and olive trees.

700 B.C.

Aqueducts appear throughout the Near East.

600 B.C.

Coins replace grain as a basis for exchange in Greece.

The Israelites transcribe Deuteronomy.

500 B.C.

Leviticus is transcribed.

The fall of Babylon occurs.

300 B.C.

Sugar cane comes to the Near East from India.

100 B.C.

Bakers become the first professional cooks in Rome.

Jewish forces liberate Jerusalem under Simon Macabee.

Romans use water power for milling grain.

Arab traders introduce pepper.

What They Ate

The Fertile Crescent region was indeed the land of milk and honey, owing its success to the climate and range of terrain, which encouraged a multitude of edible plant species, including many seed-producing annual plants and perennials, fruit trees, beans, and legumes.

Here grew the first strains of wheat (emmer and eikorn), barley, flax, chickpeas, peas, lentils, and bitter vetch, a legume similar to lentils, used extensively as herd feed. Eventually, the land was settled permanently; mankind embraced agriculture and raised crops.

The following list includes foods known to have been grown and consumed throughout the Fertile Crescent during biblical times. The list is far from complete but still extensive. Foods in biblical times provided not only adequate nutrition but also enjoyable flavors and culinary distinction.

Almonds—nut

Anise—an herb whose seed is dried and used as a spice

Apples—tree fruit

Barley—grain

Bay—tree leaf, used as a spice

Beans—fava, garbanzo

Bitter herbs—arugula (rocket), chicory, dandelion, endive, lovage, sorrel, watercress

Bread—cooked paste made from grain paste

Bullock—a castrated bull

Butter—soft cheese or cream—cooking and frying

Cakes—fried or baked flat mass of dough of grain, meal, or flour

Calf—not range fed, but raised in an enclosure; its fatty meat had high value

Camel—not meat, but milk may have been used a little, although the flavor was considered inferior and it quickly soured

Cane—wild sugar cane chewed as sweet

Chamois—hunted wild antelope

Cheese—curds, from the milk of ewes, goats, cows, coagulated with rennin or acid

Chicken—used for eggs, feathers, and meat

Cinnamon—imported into Judea by Phoenicians

Coriander—both seeds and leaves

Corn—not maize, but a term which referred to generic grain

Cucumbers—vegetable

Cumin—an herb whose dried seed is used as a spice

Deer—wild game animal

Eggs—from chicken, geese, wild quail, and wild partridge

Figs—tree fruit

Fish—freshwater from Sea of Galilee and imported fish from Mediterranean, dried or preserved in salt

Fish Sauce—a fermented condiment called Garum

Flour—not to be confused with coarser "meal," flour was ground from only the inner kernels and was consequently finer and more expensive

Fowl—chicken, duck, geese, pigeon, doves, quail, partridge

Garlic—vegetable bulb

Gazelle—wild game animal

Geese—raised in enclosures and prized for their fat

Goat—used for milk and meat, considered inferior to lamb

Gourds—probably opo squashes

Grapes—eaten fresh, dried, crushed into juice, and fermented into wine

Hart—wild male deer

Honey—not only bee honey, but any sweet syrup made from juice

Husks—pods from carob tree eaten in time of famine by the very poor

Hyssop—an herb, the berries of which were pickled in vinegar

Ibex—wild mountain goat

Juniper root—eaten in time of famine and used medicinally

Kid—young goat

Kine—cows

Lamb—young sheep

Leaven—previous day's yeast-fermented dough, mixed with water as first step for baking

Leeks—both wild and cultivated

Lentils—several cultivated varieties

Liquor—strong drink from syrup of the date palm tree

Locust—roasted and eaten in Near East

Mallow—annual succulent plant eaten as a leaf vegetable

Meal—coarsely ground whole cereal grains and legumes, usually made into gruel

Melons—musk melon and watermelon

Milk—sheep, goat, cow; drunk fresh, kept in skin bottles, or made into cheese

Millet—grain

Mint—herb

Mulberry—black and red

Mustard seed—ground for oil and eaten as a condiment

Nuts—almond, pistachios, walnuts

Olive Oil—added to nearly every dish and used as lamp oil, ointment for wounds, sacred ointment, and temple offerings

Olives—tree fruit

Onions—vegetable bulb

Ox—domesticated animal

Palms—date palms

Partridge—wild game bird

Pigeon— bird, both wild and domesticated

Pomegranate—seeds eaten and juice reduced to syrup or fermented into wine

Pulse—edible seed of pod plant

Quail—hunted game bird

Raisin—dried grape

Roebuck—wild male deer

Rue—herb

Saffron—used to enhance the flavor of wine, as a stimulant, and a perfume

Salt—evaporated from sea water or mined near city of Sodom

Sheep—domesticated animal

Spelt—species of wheat

Turtledoves—commonly eaten and used as temple offering

Vinegar—soured wine, used as a condiment, a pickling agent, and diluted with water for a refreshing drink

Wheat—grain

Wine—new (unfermented) or old (fermented)

Although many products were grown, the Bible lists seven specific crops:

"The Lord your God is bringing you into a good land—a land with wheat and barley, vines and fig trees, pomegranates, olive oil and honey;" (Deuteronomy 8:7-8)

These seven species represent the specific agricultural challenges of Israel. The success of these crops depends on delicate timing. During the growing period, the weather shifts from hot southern winds and dry heat to cold northern wind from the northwest, bringing thunderstorms. These seven species flower before other crops of the region, and a bad string of cold, windy, rainy days could ruin a year's crop. Likewise, these crops cannot survive in a year of drought.

Biblical Culture

In addition to commemorating the Exodus and freedom of the Israelites from Egypt, Passover marks the beginning of the barley harvest in ancient Israel. The Torah mandates a seven-week *Counting of the Omer*, from Passover to *Shavuot*. An *omer* is a measure of barley, and this 49-day period marks the barley harvest and ends at the beginning of the wheat harvest, Shavuot. Shavuot also celebrates the day God gave Moses the Torah on Mt. Sinai.

In a time and place where pagan beliefs and multiple deities surrounded the Jews, such a volatile agricultural condition tested one's devotion to God. So while they cultivated other crops, no others were considered sacred.

As a further proclamation of devotion to God, nonanimal offerings brought to the temple in Jerusalem could only be of these seven species. This was to underscore the dependence of mankind on God, the giver of fruit. Because the labor and care taken by the farmer to raise these crops might easily be interpreted as a magnificent feat of the farmer, offerings were made to help keep things in perspective.

Olives

The olive tree is native to the Syrian-Palestine region and has been cultivated from around 4000 B.C. Its oil was used more than its fruit, not only for cooking but also in lamps and for soap. The olive branch is the symbol of peace, and for centuries its wood, with uniquely shaped light and dark grains, has been used in decorative arts. Olive trees are highly valued to this day, and some living, fruiting specimens are upwards of 1000 years old. Olive oil is still a hot commodity, used today as much for its low cholesterol as for its rich flavor. Israeli law prohibits cutting down olive trees that bear fruit.

Black and green olives come from the same tree but are harvested at different stages and processed in different ways. Under-ripe olives are always green. Ripe olives range from deep green to purple-black. Fresh olives must be fermented to remove their natural bitterness. First they are soaked in lye; then they are soaked in brine, or dry-cured, to soften and infuse flavors.

Grapes

Grapes, the world's largest fruit crop, have been cultivated since the Copper Age, beginning around 4500 B.C. The vines originated in Anatolia, the northern peninsula of Western Asia to the north of the Fertile Crescent, encompassing much of modern Turkey. This region includes Mt. Ararat, where Noah's ark landed and where he subsequently sowed grape seed.

"Noah, a man of the soil, proceeded to plant a vineyard." (Genesis 9:20)

Most grapes are grown for wine production. Table grapes and raisins, which were made from dried grapes in the Early Bronze Age, are limited to a few specific varieties.

In addition to fruit and wine, grapes were used for vinegar sugar (reduced to a syrup); even the leaves were used to wrap food for cooking and eating, and the wood of the vine was used to build shelter.

Wheat

In biblical times, as today, bread was a staple element of the diet, and wheat has been a main crop throughout Israel, Egypt, and parts of Mesopotamia for millennia. Two species of wheat, emmer and einkorn, were, along with barley, the first cereals man cultivated. These grains, as well as four legumes and flax, are known as Neolithic founder crops.

At Ohalo II, an archaeological site on the southern shores of the Sea of Galilee, archaeologists have found grains of wild emmer wheat dating to 17000 B.C. Domesticated emmer has been dated to 7700 B.C. from a site south of Damascus, Tel Aswad.

Einkorn is the second strain of wild wheat that ancients domesticated and cultivated. Samples of einkorn found in Southern Turkey date to the pre-pottery Neolithic period, around 9600–8000 B.C.

Today, wheat is cultivated worldwide and is the second largest cereal crop, just behind corn. The wheat seed contains an outer husk, called the bran; a reproductive seed, called the germ; and the protein-rich center, called the endosperm. The raw wheat seed, known as whole wheat, is typically powdered into flour. It is also available with the bran removed as cracked wheat or bulghur. White flour is made by removing the outer bran and the germ and grinding only the endosperm.

Barley

Barley, the first crop to ripen in Israel, signals the start of the spring harvest season that connects Passover and Shavuot. When wheat fell out of popularity around 3300 B.C., barley became the dominant crop. Like wheat, the earliest domesticated barley dates to the pre-pottery Neolithic Age, about 9000 B.C. Cultivated abundantly in ancient Egypt, it was used for both bread and beer.

Today, barley is relatively unimportant in culinary use, sometimes added to soups and stews. As a brewing ingredient, half of the world's barley crop is processed into malt, which is used to make beer, whiskey, and vinegar, by allowing the grain to germinate and then dry quickly. The rest of the world's barley is fed to animals.

Hulled barley has its outer inedible hull intact but maintains the nutritious bran and germ. When the bran and germ are removed, the barley is called polished, or pearled.

Pomegranates

Native from the Mediterranean to India, the pomegranate was eaten as fruit, juiced and made into wine, boiled down to syrup for sugar, and used for dye. Carbonized fruit from the early Bronze Age has been found in tombs at Jericho.

In pagan symbolism, the pomegranate was a sign of fertility because of its abundant seeds. And a common belief held that the pomegranate contained 613 seeds. And

God gave Moses 613 Mitzvah, or commandments. Because of this, the pomegranate is a common motif of religious items and artwork across lines of faith as we can see from this Exodus quote.

"Make pomegranates of blue, purple and scarlet yarn around the hem of the robe, with gold bells between them. The gold bells and the pomegranates are to alternate around the hem of the robe. Aaron must wear it when he ministers." (Exodus 28:33-35)

Pomegranates are a good source of vitamin C, folic acid, and antioxidants. In recent years they have been marketed in the United States for their health benefits, mainly in the form of pomegranate juice.

Figs

Botanically, a fig is not just one fruit. What we think of as seeds are really hundreds of tiny male and female fruits growing together inside a vase-shaped skin, called a syconium. Wild figs rely on the symbiotic fig wasp for pollination. When the wasp crawls up inside the fruit to lay its eggs, it pollinates the fig by crawling around inside. Man figured out how to propagate the fig with cuttings, and consequently, the fig wasp is not present in domesticated figs. Archaeologists who recently unearthed a stash of fossilized figs dating from 9300 B.C. at Gilgal I, a pre-pottery Neolithic archaeological site in the Jordan Valley, noticed an interesting fact. The discovered figs showed no signs of the fig wasp, indicating that man had domesticated the fig several hundred years before wheat, barley, or even rice in China.

The fig is first mentioned in the early chapters of Genesis, when Adam and Eve used its leaves to cover their nakedness. It was well-loved both fresh and dried.

"That fading flower, his glorious beauty, set on the head of a fertile valley, will be like a fig ripe before harvest—as soon as someone sees it and takes it in his hand, he swallows it." (Isaiah 28:4)

The finest figs were dried in the sun individually or strung on long strands and hung out to dry. More commonly, though, they were pressed into cakes, suitable for storage and easy to pack for long journeys. Figs were also used to flavor soups and broths, fermented into wine, and reduced into syrup for sugar. In I Samuel 25:18, Abigail sent a hundred such cakes, among other foods, to David in the wilderness to atone for her husband Nabal's behavior.

Today figs are grown in mild climates all over the world. Introduced to the United States in the 1700s by Spanish missionaries in California, they now enjoy a thriving industry there. The first such tree was planted at Mission San Diego, and a tree was planted in each of the 21 missions that spread north up the West Coast.

Dates (Honey)

Scholars think the kind of honey referred to as one of the Seven Species was date honey. While bees were ever-present and flowers bloomed in abundance, Israel did not have a large enough bee population to make honey in large quantities. What's more, bee honey did not present the worrisome agricultural obstacles of the other six species. The abundant wildflowers, which bloom even in dry years, promise a consistent supply of honey. Date palms, on the other hand, flower late and can easily be thwarted by poor environmental conditions.

Date honey, and honey from other fruits, was made by boiling the fruit in water and scooping up the sugar that rose to the surface. Jam makers are familiar with this phenomenon, as they must constantly skim sweet foam off the top of their boiling jam pots.

Date palms grew throughout the Jordan Valley, and thanks to irrigation, can be found by the Dead Sea and beyond.

So many dates grew in Jericho that it was known as the city of palm trees. Dates are so widespread throughout the Mediterranean region that their exact origin is the subject of much debate. Because of their popularity, many countries throughout the Middle East, Africa, and Southwest Asia claim to be the site of origin. Some folks are even trying to place the first date palms in Texas!

Eaten fresh, not dried, dates are an excellent source of vitamin C. All dates are a good source of iron and potassium and supply modest amounts of vitamin A, folate, and the B vitamins. However, when dried, vitamin C dissipates, and is replaced in prominence by B-complex vitamins. They are also a great source of fiber and complex carbohydrates.

Dried dates are eaten whole, pitted and stuffed, or chopped and added into recipes. Date shoots and date flowers are edible, and the sap is tapped and converted to palm sugar (also known as *jaggery*).

Modern Methods

Americans in general are a very unhealthy bunch of people. Our lifestyle has evolved into a sedentary pattern with virtually no physical activity. Meanwhile, technology has improved, and our markets are packed with cheap, good-tasting, high-caloric foods. No wonder two thirds of us are overweight!

The problem stems from the physiological traits that have allowed us to evolve in the first place. As a species, our bodies were designed to enjoy and consume as much high-caloric food as possible. Extra calories were designed to be stored away until winter or a time of famine. Lucky for us, we rarely have famine in the Western world. Unfortunately, our physiology has not compensated for our technological advances.

The technology of underdeveloped countries is not at our level, but neither is their rate of obesity. When people from underdeveloped parts of the world immigrate to the West, their rate of weight gain quickly catches up to ours.

Nutritional Guidelines

The United States Department of Agriculture (USDA), and similar agencies world-wide, have addressed the nutritional needs of modern man, and provide us with handy guidelines to follow. Unfortunately, we don't. Every American over the age of 7 recognizes the Food Pyramid, but few can fill it in properly, and fewer still live by its guidelines.

The pyramid has evolved over the years. Dietary guidelines were first instituted during World War II when in 1941 a national Food and Nutrition Board convened to investigate the relationship between nutrition and national defense. Later, in the 1960s and 1970s, kids were taught about square meals and the Basic Four food groups. The graphic for this curriculum was a square divided into four equal quadrants. Each space held one of the food groups: meat, bread, fruit and vegetables, and dairy.

There were multiple problems with this model. First, little representation was given to the choices within each group. Therefore, chocolate milk, bacon, and white toast with grape jelly was considered a well-rounded breakfast. The second problem was directly related to the graphic. Regardless of the servings recommended, the four squares suggested that each food group should be eaten in four equal proportions.

In 1980 the USDA revolutionized nutrition with the pyramid. This shape demonstrated, visually, the quantity of each food that should be consumed every day, and which foods should be limited. In 2005 the My Pyramid program was released, with even more detail, and an added exercise component.

The bottom of the pyramid depicts the grain and cereal group, representing the food group we should consume most of every day. This is in line with the way our ancestors ate. Even today, grains make up the largest component of the world's healthiest diets. On average, adults need about 8 ounces of whole grains every day. Products made with refined white flour do not contribute enough fiber or nutrients. Our preference for white flour is one of the biggest contributors to our nation's health crisis.

Vegetables are the next crucial component of the pyramid, but most Americans don't eat enough. Adults should be eating at least 3 cups of brightly colored vegetables every day. (A taco salad with iceberg lettuce, meat, sour cream, cheese, and a fried tortilla bowl does not count here.) Fruit is important, but not nearly as vital as vegetables. In fact, we actually eat too much fruit.

Fruit provides vitamins, minerals, and carbohydrates. Vegetables provide many of the same nutrients without the excess sugar. Between canned fruit, dried fruit, fruit fillings, and fruit juices, Americans overconsume fruit. It has become an especially large contributor to childhood obesity.

Protein is another overconsumed food. To stay healthy, build and maintain muscles, organs, connective tissues, skin, bones, teeth, blood, and our DNA, we need only 5-6 ounces a day. But most Americans eat much more. This category includes meat, fish, poultry, eggs, beans, and nuts. Our biblical ancestors did quite well on legumes with an occasional fatted calf or leg of lamb thrown in for special occasions. Theirs was a lighter diet, with less saturated fat stemming from less consumption of animal products.

Dairy products are an important source of calcium for strong bones and teeth, but dairy need is not nearly as important as we have come to make it in this country. Whole milk products contain large amounts of saturated fat. The recommended amount of milk is only two to three cups a day, but between the milk with meals, milk in recipes, and cheese dripping and melting into everything, we overeat dairy. Calcium is also available in dark green vegetables like broccoli and collard greens, as well as soy products and molasses.

Recommended Daily Diet

The following are the recommended foods and respective quantities that are suggested for healthy American adults. The following lists the recommended foods and the quantities in which they should be enjoyed on a daily basis.

Grains   Grain 6-8 ounces

An ounce is 1 slice of bread, 1 cup of cereal, $\frac{1}{2}$ cup of pasta or cooked grain such as rice or oats. Choose whole grain pasta, whole grain breads, brown rice, and other whole grains (see Chapter 14).

Vegetables   3 cups

Choose vegetables that are dark green and leafy and those that are bright orange, red, and purple. Eat a variety of vegetables throughout the week, so your overall nutrient intake is broad.

Fruit   1½-2 cups

While fruit juice counts, it is much healthier to eat a whole piece of fruit because it contains fiber. Eat peels and skin when possible because many of the nutrients are concentrated in the skin of the fruit. Dried fruits provide nutrients but also higher sugar levels, so beware.

Dairy   2 cups

Choose the lowest-fat dairy products available. Milk, cheese, and plain yogurt are the best choices. Other dairy products contain calcium but also excessive fat and sugar.

Meat and Beans   5-6½ ounces

Beans and nuts are the healthiest choices. Choose lean meats, with skin and fat removed. Look for organic peanut butter with no added sugar.

Oils   limit intake

Choose oils that contain unsaturated fats such as olive and peanut oils. Stay away from margarine and other hydrogenated oils.

Sugars   limit intake

Stay away from refined sugars as much as possible. Eat fresh and dried fruits for your sweet fix. Sweeten baked goods with honey, date sugar, or stevia, a sweetener extracted from an herb (called stevia, sweetleaf, or sugarleaf) that is 300 times sweeter than granulated sugar.

Water

While the traditional recommendation is 8 (8 oz.) glasses of water per day, there is no real evidence showing this to be beneficial. But we do know that dehydration causes fatigue, lack of concentration, mood swings, dry mouth, lightheadedness, and eventually loss of consciousness, so keeping well hydrated is essential. The best advice is to drink water with meals and occasionally throughout the day to maintain good fluid balance and stay mentally alert. Beverages with sugar, caffeine, artificial flavors, colors, and preservatives do not rehydrate you and will generally dehydrate you. Never chug large amounts of water all at once.

Much of the food we eat ends up in the junk-food category, which is where we get into trouble. Fats and oils, refined sugars, and salt are the main culprits.

Our bodies need fat to stay healthy. Fat insulates us and cushions our organs. But we do not need it in the quantities in which we consume it. The naturally occurring fat in grains (such as wheat germ), fruits (olives and nuts), and animal products (fish and yogurt) is adequate when these foods are eaten in the recommended amounts.

Sugar, too, is essential for good nutrition. It gives us energy and helps our body function properly. But we were never meant to eat it in a refined state. Our bodies need the full benefit of the nutrients that come with a piece of fruit, or a bit of honey. These natural foods take time to digest, entering the body slowly, and are put to use where and when they are needed. When these nutrients are stripped away, the straight glucose goes right to work giving us instant energy. It is used up quickly, and our bodies feel the resulting loss of energy in a "crash." The effect continues with unnatural cravings that are not related to fueling the body.

Salt is also a vital mineral, but our bodies need less than a teaspoon a day, which is a fraction of what is consumed in a typical Western diet. Although salt helps regulate body fluids and electrolytes, too much can dehydrate us, and in some persons high sodium intake has been linked to high blood pressure and osteoporosis. We get an overly adequate amount of sodium naturally when we eat the recommended foods in the recommended quantities.

The Consequences

Our bodies suffer when we ignore dietary recommendations. When we eat more than what our body needs, it stores the calories and nutrients for later use. Because they are not called upon to sustain us through lean years, as was the case with our ancestors, we store it in the form of fat.

These excess stores of fat are not only aesthetically troubling, but physically, financially, and socially troubling as well. Overweight people are at higher risk for developing heart disease, high blood pressure, osteoporosis, osteoarthritis, infertility, stroke, diabetes, and numerous forms of cancer. In a 2004 study, the Centers for Disease Control and Prevention (CDC) reported that obesity is quickly approaching tobacco as the leading cause of preventable death. In 1998 Americans spent nearly 80 billion dollars in obesity-related health care. Additionally, we buy weight-loss books, healthcare memberships, magic fat-melting pills, and surgical procedures to suck away our fat.

Instead of concentrating on weight loss, concentrate on eating right. I designed the recipes in this book to help you do just that.

The Least You Need to Know

◆ The Fertile Crescent is a significant spot for human evolution.

◆ The foods that emerged through early agriculture are still significant to the human diet.

◆ Early crops held spiritual significance, in addition to nutritional importance.

◆ Ancient foods contribute a great deal of nutritional value to modern diets.

Part 2

Breakfast and Baking

The old cliché is true. Breakfast is the most important meal of the day. Yet too many of us miss it, and too many kids go off to school without it. Teachers can tell which kids skipped that vital meal. They are the ones with a short attention span, high rate of absenteeism, and lower test scores. Adults who skip this meal have a higher rate of obesity, making up for lack of the morning meal by overeating in the afternoon.

Eating in the morning is important, but not just any meal will do. It should be nutrient rich, and low in sugar. Chapters 3 and 4 look at healthier breakfast and baking options, for entertaining and everyday eating. Focus is on low refined sugar, low saturated fat, and high whole-grain content, all designed to get your day started right.

3

Breakfast

In This Chapter

- ◆ Eggs and grains
- ◆ Basic baking skills
- ◆ Breakfast baked, griddled, and fried

"Why spend money on what is not bread, and your labor on what does not satisfy? Listen, listen to me, and eat what is good, and your soul will delight in the richest of fare." (Isaiah 55:2)

In biblical times, breakfast was certainly an important meal, but it was not eaten as we do today. Seldom would it have been a meal enjoyed by a family together, nor would it consist of as many choices as we enjoy. A simple bite before starting work would have had to sustain a man until an afternoon meal, when the family came together to eat and pray. A bite of bread or a handful of dried fruits washed down with wine would have done the trick.

Eggs

Eggs were eaten in biblical times, though probably not for breakfast. Practicing Hebrews were allowed only eggs from clean birds, and the chicken would have been included in that group. Domesticated early from the Asian Red Jungle Fowl, chickens were eaten in Israel as early as the seventh century B.C. Chickens appear in Greek poetry and art around the fifth century B.C., and the early Romans used chickens as oracles. We know they were present in the first century, as Matthew and Mark recount the story in which Jesus foretells of Peter's triple denial before a rooster crows.

The nutritional value of the egg cannot be denied. Loaded with protein, they are used as a measure for other proteins. What's more, they contain almost every essential vitamin and mineral humans need.

The egg yolk contains a high percentage of cholesterol, so people watching their cholesterol should avoid them. But normal, healthy, active humans can, and should, benefit from the incredible egg.

Recipes that call for eggs are referring to large eggs unless otherwise stated. If you use a smaller egg, the recipe will be a touch drier due to the lack of moisture. Conversely, a larger egg will yield a slightly wetter result.

When possible, look for organic eggs from free-range chickens because they are regulated, to a certain extent, by the USDA. No antibiotics or hormones are allowed, and the animals are provided with access to the outdoors.

Grains

Grains were a vital source of nutrition for the people of the Holy Land. They made up the bulk of their diet, with fruits and vegetables sprinkled in when the seasons allowed, along with meat and dairy for those with livestock.

The first grains were simply eaten, but it soon became apparent that some sort of cooking needed to occur in order for them to be digestible. Simply toasting on a hot rock gave way to grinding.

Pancakes were probably the first form of bread, albeit not in the manner we are used to. To make the ground grains palatable, they were mixed into a paste with water. Someone tried cooking a bit of this paste on a flat rock near the fire, and the rest is IHOP history.

Flour

Today, our grains are highly refined, and our daily grain intake usually comes in the form of flour. The most common flour, all-purpose, has had most of the nutrients removed, leaving behind bleached white starch (see Chapter 14).

The recipes in this chapter are made with whole-wheat flour because the nutritional benefit of whole-grain products is far superior to that of refined grains. In addition to vitamins, minerals, protein, and antioxidants, whole grains have about 4 four times the dietary fiber as refined flour. Consuming adequate fiber reduces the risk of developing digestive disorders, diabetes, obesity, coronary heart disease, and certain forms of cancer. Most Americans do not consume an adequate amount of fiber.

Cakes, muffins, and delicate pastries often need flour with more starch and less protein to keep the crumbs light and tender. Chefs prefer cake or pastry flour for these products. Whole-wheat pastry flour is readily available at most supermarkets and through internet sources (see Appendix B).

Sugar

The main culprit of our national diet is refined sugar. Americans consume nearly 175 pounds of it a year. Unfortunately, refined sugar, or sucrose, has no nutritional value. Although it is derived from plants (sugar cane and beets) it has been depleted of all vitamins and minerals. What remains is pure carbohydrate, a form the human body is not built to utilize efficiently.

So strong is the reaction of our body that we physically feel a rush of energy. Unlike the sugar we get from fruits, milk, or honey, refined sugar is metabolized instantly. And once our body uses it, it craves more, and sends us into withdrawal, when more is not consumed, in the form of the inevitable crash. Our body reacts to what is essentially poison by sending nutrients to help keep us in balance. Vitamins, minerals, and enzymes rush to the rescue, resulting in depletion of these nutrients throughout the body.

In an effort to curb the intake of refined sugars, most recipes here use honey as a sweetener. Twice as sweet as sucrose, honey has a unique flavor that enhances baked goods. It is rich in antioxidants, and long-term use has been shown to provide long-term health benefits, including improved digestion, a stronger immune system, and lower cholesterol.

Date sugar is another ingredient I use in place of table sugar. It is nothing but ground dried dates, but it is equally as sweet as refined sugar and has the added benefit of fiber, which slows down its digestion and absorption by the body. Date sugar is readily available in heath-conscious food stores. See Appendix B for organic and whole food sources.

Baking Powder

In biblical times, the only known leaven was yeast, harvested from a fermenting mash of grain and fruits. Today we have an assortment of leavening agents to choose from, and I use baking powder to leaven pancakes, muffins, and quick breads.

Anything made with baking powder comes out lighter and fluffier if you allow the batter to rest for a few minutes before cooking it. Most baking powder available today is double-acting, which means that the reaction producing carbon dioxide gas, which makes the product rise, occurs twice, once when it is moistened and again when it is heated. Once the batter is wet, give the baking powder a chance to bubble up a bit. You'll be amazed at the result.

The Cut-in Technique

Streusel, scones, and pie dough are all made with the cut-in technique, a method that combines fat and flour together by crumbling. However, the butter and flour do not actually combine because the butter stays in small chunks and floats within the flour. These chunks are the key to flakiness. In the oven, moisture in the fat evaporates into steam and rises, pushing up the dough and leaving a small pocket of air. This pocket of air is read by our mouths as flakiness.

Work to get the butter down to pea-size pieces; they don't have to be round but should be about that size. To do this, keep the ingredients cold. If they warm up, the butter will cream into the flour and produce a paste, which is not at all what you want. Freeze cubes of butter before adding them, and freeze flour, too, if the room temperature is warm.

To break up the butter, use your fingertips, forks, butter knives, or a pastry blender.

Equipment

A nonstick pan is a must in the battery of your culinary arsenal. The nonstick coating makes cooking and cleanup a whole lot easier, but never use metal utensils as they might scrape off the nonstick coating. Instead, use a wooden spoon, or get yourself a heatproof rubber spatula, designed to resist melting in the pan. Similarly, when cleaning, use a brush or sponge, never a scouring pad, to prolong the life of your pan.

Cast iron is the best surface for griddle cooking, because it holds heat well, browns evenly, and if properly seasoned, needs no oil. Seasoning keeps the food from sticking to the cooking surface by filling in and smoothing out the roughness we can't see with the naked eye.

To season your cast iron, coat it evenly with a thin layer of shortening and bake it at 300 degrees for 30 minutes. Pour off any excess liquid fat, and continue baking for two hours. Cool the pan upside down on a stack of newspaper. The first few times you use the pan, use a lot of oil to continue the seasoning process. You can also repeat the seasoning steps a couple more times for a really good seal. Never scrub a seasoned pan as this would remove the oiled coating and expose new crevices for food to stick to. A light wipe with warm water is sufficient cleaning. This gentle cleaning also prolongs the life of the pan.

When cooking on the griddle, adjust the heat accordingly. Cast iron holds heat well, but even over a low flame it will continue to heat up during prolonged cooking. If the food is browning too fast, turn down the heat; wait about five minutes, then resume cooking.

Mushroom and Herb Omelet

The key to a good omelet is a nonstick frying pan. Without it, the only way to achieve success is with an excessive amount of oil, which is no way to wake up in the morning.

Serves 2
Prep time: 10 minutes
Cook time: 10 minutes

4 eggs

½ cup cream

¼ tsp. kosher salt

⅛ tsp. ground black pepper

3 TB. chopped fresh herbs, such as parsley, tarragon, chives, thyme, or basil

3 TB. olive oil

2 cups chopped mushrooms

1. Whisk together eggs, cream, salt, pepper, and herbs. Set aside.

2. Heat a large nonstick sauté pan over high heat. Add butter, let it foam; add mushrooms and sauté until tender, about 5 minutes. Add egg mixture, all at once. With a heatproof spatula, stir eggs and mushrooms together briefly. Gently lift edges of cooked egg, and tilt the pan so that raw egg can slide underneath. Do this around edges until omelet looks firm, about 2 minutes. Carefully flip omelet over, and cook for another minute before serving. Divide omelet into two, and slide it out of the pan and onto each plate.

Suggestions: There is no biblical restriction for eating eggs with cheese, so a gooey cheese omelet is not out of the question. But health-wise, such a cholesterol-laden entrée is not the best choice. If a cheese omelet is on your mind, try a low-fat cheese or one that packs a flavorful punch, like Swiss, where a little goes a long way.

Kitchen Tips

If the prospect of flipping an omelet intimidates you, finish cooking the omelet in the oven. Preheat the broiler before you start the recipe; then place it under the broiler for 1-2 minutes. This method requires an ovenproof pan.

Corned Beef Hash

Sometimes it seems pork is the only choice for breakfast meat, but don't overlook this old-fashioned option. Hash was originally a method of utilizing leftovers but became popular enough to warrant canning it ready-made, which is always an option if you have hunger, but not time.

3 TB. olive oil

1 medium yellow onion, diced

3 stalks celery, diced

2 cloves garlic

2 lb. (about 4 cups) cooked or canned *corned* beef, diced

3 cups boiled potatoes, diced

¼ tsp. kosher salt

¼ tsp. ground black pepper

1 TB. Worcestershire sauce

½ cup cold water

Serves 4	
Prep time: 30 minutes	
Cook time: 30 minutes	

1. Heat oil in a large sauté pan over high heat. Cook onion, celery, and garlic until tender. Add corned beef and cook, stirring, for 5 minutes until hot and crispy on the edges.

2. Add potatoes, salt, pepper, Worcestershire sauce, and water, and continue cooking, stirring, until water is absorbed, about 5 minutes. Serve hot, topped with poached eggs (see following recipe).

Suggestions: Use any meat you have on hand; also use other vegetables, including squash, pumpkin, or sweet potatoes.

def•i•ni•tion

Corned refers to the kernel-size salt traditionally used to cure the meat.

Poached Eggs

When poaching eggs, break each egg into a small dish before cooking. This keeps them together in one mass as they cook and avoids breaking yolks. The swirling motion of the water keeps the egg together as it cooks.

Serves 4
Prep time: 10 minutes
Cook time: 30-40 minutes

3 qt. water **2 tsp. vinegar**

1 tsp. salt **8 eggs**

1. Bring water, salt, and vinegar to a boil. At the boil, reduce the heat and keep it at a bare simmer.

2. Break one egg into a small dish. Stir water into a gentle whirlpool motion, then slide egg from the dish down the side of the pan into swirling, simmering water. Simmer 3-5 minutes until white is firm but yolk is still soft. Carefully remove egg with a slotted spoon and transfer to a bowl of cold water. Repeat with remaining eggs.

3. Hold poached eggs in a bowl of cold water until you're ready to serve them. To reheat, bring water back to a simmer, and drop eggs in briefly just before serving.

Suggestions: Eat eggs on top of buttered toast or English muffins, or use them as a part of another recipe.

Kitchen Tips

Why use the cold water to hold the eggs? The cool temperature stops the egg from cooking, and the water keeps the egg floating in weightless safety until the time comes to eat it. If you hold the delicate poached eggs on a plate, the yolks will likely break.

Three Cheese Strata

You are by no means limited to cheddar, Jack, and Swiss for this recipe. Use your favorite cheese, or stop into a local cheese shop and try something new!

2 TB. olive oil

1 medium onion, diced

2 TB. chopped fresh parsley or 1 tsp. dried

15 slices day-old bread, crusts removed

1 cup each grated sharp cheddar, Jack, and Swiss cheese

6 eggs

3 cups milk

1 tsp. dry mustard

½ tsp. grated nutmeg

1 tsp. salt

½ tsp. pepper

1 cup heavy cream

Serves 6
Prep time: 30 minutes, plus 1 hour cooling time
Cook time: 50 minutes

1. Coat a casserole dish with pan spray. Heat oil in a large sauté pan over medium heat. Cook onion until tender and golden brown. Add parsley and set aside to cool. Dice bread into 1-inch cubes, and layer half on the bottom of the casserole dish. Top with cheese, onions, and remaining bread.

2. Break eggs into a large bowl and whisk to combine. Stir in milk, mustard, nutmeg, salt, and pepper; pour over the casserole, then refrigerate for at least 1 hour or overnight.

3. Preheat oven to 350°F. Just before baking, top strata with cream. Bake 45 minutes, until firm and golden brown. Rest 5 minutes before serving.

Suggestions: This dish is high in fat, so use in moderation. Reserve it for company, topped with a dollop of sour cream and served with a side of fresh, seasonal fruit.

Kitchen Tips

Strata is basically a savory breakfast bread pudding, popular during the Depression Era because it was a great way to use leftovers. It works best with day-old bread because dry bread absorbs more of the yummy custard as it bakes.

Spinach and Onion Quiche

Quiche is a French egg custard tart, filled with any number of ingredients, including vegetables, cheese, or meats. The nutmeg is a classic element of French savory custards and adds a certain *je ne sais quoi.*

Serves 4-6
Prep time: 30 minutes
Cook time: 60 minutes

2 TB. olive oil

1 medium yellow onion, diced

3 cups fresh spinach, chopped, or 1 (10 oz.) package frozen chopped spinach, defrosted and squeezed dry

3 whole eggs

2 cups milk

¼ tsp. kosher salt

¼ tsp. ground black pepper

¼ tsp. ground nutmeg

½ cup Swiss cheese, grated

1 (9-inch) pie shell lined with *Basic Pie Dough*, blind baked (see Chapter 15)

1. Preheat oven to 375°F. Heat oil in a large sauté pan over high heat. Cook onion until tender. Add spinach and cook until wilted and dry. Set aside.

2. Whisk together eggs, milk, salt, pepper, and nutmeg. Layer spinach and cheese in the bottom of pie shell, and pour custard on top. Bake for 30-40 minutes, until golden brown.

Suggestions: Quiche is best at room temperature as the flavors have time to mingle, and the custard cuts cleaner. Make it the night before, chill in the fridge, and bring to room temperature before serving.

Biblical Culture
While the Bible makes no mention of quiche, there are records of tarts in ancient Rome. However, the tart recipes in Apicius have no dough and are formed more like a cake or loaf.

Banana Walnut Pancakes

For a superior banana walnut pancake, use bananas that are nearly over-ripe.

1½ cups whole-wheat flour

2½ tsp. baking powder

½ tsp. kosher salt

1½ cups milk

3 TB. peanut oil

3 TB. honey

2 eggs

1 cup toasted walnuts

2 bananas, sliced

Serves 4	
Prep time: 20 minutes	
Cook time: 30 minutes	

1. In a medium-size bowl, sift together flour, baking powder, and salt. In a separate bowl, combine milk, oil, honey, and eggs. Whisk together thoroughly. Pour egg mixture into sifted dry ingredients, add nuts and bananas, and stir to combine. Be careful not to overmix. A few lumps are okay. Set aside at room temperature for 10 minutes.

2. Heat a griddle over high heat. Test the griddle by sprinkling with a little water. If it sizzles and evaporates, it's ready. If your griddle is not seasoned, oil it lightly with vegetable oil or pan spray. Lower the heat to medium, and ladle on batter. Cook for 1-2 minutes, until bubbles appear. Flip pancake and cook other side, about 1-2 minutes. Adjust the heat of your griddle as necessary. Repeat with remaining batter. Serve immediately or keep warm in a 200°F oven, covered with foil.

Suggestions: To serve up a great breakfast, warm the syrup on the stove or in the microwave.

 Kitchen Tips

Toast your nuts in the oven. The surrounding heat of an oven toasts all edges of the nut evenly. Toasting nuts in a pan on the stove browns only the portion of the nut that touches the pan. They end up spotted, unevenly flavored, and often burnt.

Cinnamon Spice French Toast

French toast is modeled after the French *pain perdu*, which translates to "lost bread." Lost bread is bread that is too stale to eat.

Serves 2
Prep time: 15 minutes
Cook time: 20 minutes

2 eggs

1 cup half-and-half

2 tsp. honey

½ tsp. salt

1 tsp. vanilla extract

1 tsp. ground nutmeg

½ tsp. ground ginger

1 TB. ground cinnamon

Grated zest of 1 lemon

4 slices bread, preferably day-old

4 TB. peanut oil

1. In a large bowl, whisk together eggs and half-and-half. Add honey, salt, vanilla, nutmeg, and lemon zest, and stir to combine.

2. Heat 1-2 tablespoons of oil in a nonstick sauté pan. Dip bread, 1 slice at a time, into egg mixture, then place in the pan, and fry until golden brown, about 2 minutes per side. Repeat with remaining bread. Serve hot.

Suggestions: For an elegant presentation, top your French toast with fresh berries and a dusting of powdered sugar.

Kitchen Tips

Stale bread is the best bread to use for French toast recipes because without its moisture, it has more room to soak up the moisture of the egg custard. Try making it with old sweet rolls, croissants, or egg bread. The richer and thicker the bread, the more luscious the French toast will be.

Homemade Granola

Deliciously healthy is not an oxymoron, and this recipe is proof of that. It's so good, there's no need to restrict it to breakfast duty. Granola makes a great snack, a perfect pre-race carbo-load, and a healthy alternative to a Twinkie.

¼ **cup peanut oil**

¼ **cup honey**

1 tsp. vanilla extract

4 cups rolled oats

½ **cup whole-wheat flour**

½ **cup oat bran**

½ **cup wheat germ**

½ **cup hulled sunflower seeds**

1 cup raisins

1 cup dates

1 cup chopped almonds

Serves 8	
Prep time: 10 minutes	
Cook time: 60 minutes	

1. Preheat oven to 325°F. Coat a baking sheet with pan spray. In a small saucepan, combine oil, honey, and vanilla. Warm over medium heat until mixture begins to simmer.

2. Meanwhile, in a large bowl combine oats, flour, bran, wheat germ, and sunflower seeds. Stir in warm oil mixture and toss together to thoroughly moisten. Spread granola onto the baking sheet in an even, thin layer. Toast in the oven for 1 hour, stirring every 10 minutes to promote even browning.

3. Cool, then mix in raisins, dates, and almonds. Serve with milk, yogurt, or eat it as is for a great snack. Store airtight for up to 1 week at room temperature or in the refrigerator for up to 1 month.

Suggestions: This makes a great trail mix. Stir in a handful of M&M's or chocolate chips for the young and young at heart. Try adding cashews, dried pineapple, and banana chips. Or pump up the antioxidant factor with dried blueberries, cranberries, and cherries.

Biblical Culture

Cereal is an ancient food. Grains were probably the first foods domesticated, and eating them toasted by the handful would have been the easiest way to find nourishment.

Honey Bran Muffins

Bran is 100 percent fiber, and consuming at least 25 grams of fiber a day can help prevent all sorts of health problems, including diabetes, heart disease, and certain types of cancer. Because these muffins contain oil and sugar, they are not exactly health food but are a tasty way to get your fiber.

Makes 1 dozen muffins
Prep time: 20 minutes
Cook time: 30 minutes

2 eggs

⅓ **cup canola oil**

⅓ **cup honey**

⅓ **cup molasses**

1 TB. vanilla extract

1⅓ cup buttermilk

1 cup whole-wheat flour

1 cup wheat germ

2 cups wheat bran

1 cup oat bran

1 tsp. baking powder

2 tsp. baking soda

½ tsp. kosher salt

1 tsp. ground ginger

1 tsp. ground cinnamon

1 tsp. ground nutmeg

Biblical Culture

Bran, which is pure plant fiber, or cellulose, would have been left on biblical grains along with the grain's germ. Flour of that time, lacking in the refinement of our processing methods, was tougher to chew, but more nutritious.

1. Preheat oven to 375°F. Coat muffin pan cups and top surface with pan spray and line with muffin cups. Beat together eggs, oil, honey, molasses, vanilla, and buttermilk, and set aside.

2. In a separate bowl, stir together flour, wheat germ, wheat bran, oat bran, baking powder, baking soda, salt, ginger, cinnamon, and nutmeg. Pour egg mixture into flour mixture, and stir together until just incorporated.

3. Fill muffin cups to the rim with muffin batter. Bake until golden brown, about 20 minutes. A pick inserted into the middle muffin should come out clean. Cool 15 minutes before removing. Store airtight at room temperature for 2 days, or freeze for up to 2 weeks.

Suggestions: Fold in dried fruits, like dates, figs, cranberries, or apricots, for an additional burst of chewy sweetness.

Banana Date Bread

Dates were abundant in the Holy Land. Today they are available in many forms, including whole, pitted, and chopped. If you have the patience, buy them whole and chop them yourself. They will be much juicier. Plump dried-out dates for 30 minutes in warm water or cider before adding them to a recipe.

1¾ cup whole-wheat flour	⅔ cup date sugar
½ tsp. kosher salt	1 tsp. grated orange zest
1 TB. baking powder	2 eggs
1 cup dates, pitted and chopped	1½ cup ripe banana pulp
⅓ cup peanut oil	½ cup shredded coconut

Serves 6-8

Prep time: 30 minutes

Cook time: 60 minutes

1. Preheat oven to 350°F. Coat a loaf pan with pan spray, and line with a strip of parchment or wax paper. Sift together flour, salt, and baking powder. Stir in dates, and set aside.

2. Beat together oil, date sugar, and zest until creamy. Add eggs 1 at a time, and stir in bananas. Slowly stir in dry ingredients until smooth. Fill loaf pan to ¹/₂-inch from the top, and sprinkle with coconut. Bake until risen, firm, and golden brown, about 50 minutes. A pick inserted into the middle should come out clean. Cool for 15 minutes before removing. Store airtight at room temperature for 2 days, or freeze for up to 2 weeks.

Suggestions: Serve toasted with butter or cream cheese, or use for an unforgettable peanut butter sandwich.

Biblical Culture

Bananas were common in India and in the settlements along the Indus River, but were known in the Holy Land only to travelers.

Chapter 4

Breads

In This Chapter

- ◆ Bread-baking techniques
- ◆ Sweet and savory loaves
- ◆ Swirls, crackers, buns, and braids

"Take thou also unto thee wheat, and barley, and beans, and lentils, and millet, and fitches, and put them in one vessel, and make thee bread thereof, according to the number of the days that thou shalt lie upon thy side, three hundred and ninety days shalt thou eat thereof." (Ezekiel 4:9 KJV)

Bread is an ancient food. Archeologists have found loaves and grains in Egyptian tombs, along with drawings of busy bakeries and carvings of people kneading dough. Bakeries have been unearthed in Giza dating to 2600 B.C. As technology improved, bread evolved into a variety of shapes: large loaves baked in pots, small cylindrical cones, flat discs, triangles, representative shapes of animals or people, and common flat bread.

Ancient Bread

The common man living in the Eastern Mediterranean region in biblical times had a diet that consisted mainly of grains. Ancient wheat species, including emmer, einkorn, kamut, and spelt grew in the region. These grains have a higher protein content than modern wheat, making them nutritionally important and perfect for bread production. Barley, rye, and millet were also used, as were legumes. (God gave Ezekiel instructions for a bread utilizing all these foods in Ezekiel 4:9.)

Throughout the Bible both leavened and unleavened breads are mentioned. The long process of making bread with naturally occurring yeast was typically the duty of the wife. But the rich and powerful soon operated bakeries, and the baker as tradesman evolved. In later centuries, bakeries included a central oven in which poorer townspeople could bake their dough.

Flour Choices

Modern white flour is far less nutritious than flour used in biblical times. Grains, cracked to reveal the inner protein, vitamins, and minerals, with the outer bran intact, are a highly nutritious food. But that's not what we do today.

Modern flour production removes and discards the fibrous bran and nutrient-rich germ, leaving only the inner endosperm, which consists of just starch and gluten proteins. This endosperm is then ground fine, enriched with the nutrients just discarded, and bleached with peroxide to whiten it. This flour, found in countless products at our supermarkets, leaves us malnourished and prone to disease.

By far, the best flour to bake and cook with is whole-grain flour. You can use it wherever all-purpose flour appears; however, there is no denying your baked goods will have a different outcome. The effect is not unpleasant, but it is different. If your family is addicted to white flour, it will be a slow process to switch them over. But it is a process worth undertaking, for their overall, lifelong health.

Whole-wheat flours are available in most markets and through the Internet (see Appendix B). For bread making, flour with a high gluten content will stretch and rise more, yielding a lighter loaf. Some recipes in this chapter use a portion of bread flour, in addition to whole-wheat flour, to increase the gluten content necessary for bread making. Again, whole-grain bread flour is available if you know where to look.

Using Flour

Baking bread is an inexact science. The amount of flour a particular recipe will hold depends on several variables, including human error.

In most recipes in this chapter I will give the flour measurement with a range of 1 or 2 cups. Variables include temperature, humidity, measurement accuracy, and type and manufacturer of flour. All these factors contribute to the amount of flour a recipe will hold on any given day. There is only one sure way to know how much is enough, and that is by looking and feeling. The dough should be smooth and soft but not sticky and not so tough that it's hard to knead. Reserve the last cup of flour called for in any bread recipe, adding it slowly, a little at a time, as you knead. Let each addition work in completely before you decide to add more. Sometimes the recipe will require more than what is called for, sometimes less. That's what makes baking so exciting!

Yeast

Yeast is a living organism that occurs naturally in the air all around us. It was first utilized around 3000 B.C. for fermentation of beer and wine and, soon after, harvested to leaven pastes of grain mash.

Yeast feeds on carbohydrates and prefers an environment that is warm and moist. This knowledge led to the development of yeast starters, which was the only way to make bread until the twentieth century. Not until the invention of the microscope in the mid-1800s did man figure out that yeast was responsible for fermentation. Once isolated, commercial production of yeast began and revolutionized baking.

Water Temperature

Most recipes for bread call for warm water. This is because the higher temperatures encourage the yeast to begin feeding on carbohydrates, and thereby releasing carbon dioxide. The ideal temperature is about 100°F. The easiest way to judge this temperature is to feel the water, which should feel barely warm, just above your body temperature. Making bread with cold water works, too, although the rise will take a bit longer. Some think that, if time allows, a longer rise is preferable because more fermentation produces a more flavorful bread.

Fat in Bread

Fat plays an important role in bread dough as it moistens the dough, tenderizes the crumb, and prolongs the shelf life. It also weighs down the dough, preventing large pockets of carbon dioxide from forming during fermentation. The absence of large bubbles of gas results in the absence of large holes in the finished bread. Bread with fat makes the best sandwiches because the peanut butter won't fall through to your hand as you spread it.

Bread recipes that include butter as an ingredient should not be eaten in a meal that includes meat, as butter is a dairy food. Luckily, it is easy to substitute an equal amount of oil into the recipe. If the bread is sweet, use a neutral canola oil. More savory breads can handle flavorful olive oil. You can do the same thing in the other direction. If you are concerned about your cholesterol level, use a monounsaturated oil such as olive, canola, or peanut instead.

Baking

The best breads are baked on hot tiles with a little steam injected into the oven periodically to promote a thin crust. However, few of us have such an oven at our disposal. Your regular oven works just fine, and the results will astound first-time bread bakers.

To judge whether or not a loaf is done, you must look at it and feel it. A loaf should be lighter coming out than it was going in because the moisture should have evaporated. This is the reason it makes a hollow sound when thumped. But if you are unsure, you can always take its temperature. An instant-read thermometer is a handy tool. Just insert it into the thickest part of what you're cooking and it will tell you the internal temperature. Though it's usually used to check the internal temperature of meat, it works on any food, including bread, which should be in the range of 200-210°F when cooked through.

Braided Egg Bread

In the Jewish tradition, this bread, known as *challah*, is traditionally served on the Sabbath. Since the first meals of the Sabbath typically contain meat, the *challah* is made without dairy.

½ cup warm water

2 (.25 oz.) packages active dry yeast

1 TB. honey

2½ cups bread flour, divided (more as needed)

1 tsp. kosher salt

¼ cup plus 1 TB. olive oil

2 eggs

1 egg white (reserve yolk for glaze)

1 TB. water

Serves 6-8
Prep time: 20 minutes, plus 1½ hours to rise
Cook time: 45 minutes

1. In a medium bowl, combine water, yeast, honey, and 1 cup flour, and beat together for 2 minutes. Add salt, oil, eggs, and egg white, and mix thoroughly. Add enough remaining flour to create a firm dough. Turn dough out onto a floured surface and knead, adding flour only when necessary, until dough becomes smooth and elastic, about 8-10 minutes. Return to the bowl, cover with plastic wrap, and set in a warm place to rise until doubled in volume, about 1 hour.

2. Coat baking sheet with pan spray. Divide dough into three equal pieces and roll into ropes. Pinch three ends together and braid, bringing each outside rope over center rope, alternately. At the end of the braid, pinch ends together. Place loaves on prepared pan, dust with flour, cover with plastic, and set aside to rise again for 30 minutes. Preheat oven to 400°F.

3. Combine remaining egg yolk with a tablespoon of water and brush over surface of the braid. Bake them at 350°F until golden brown and firm, about 30-40 minutes. Test for doneness with an instant-read thermometer. Cool completely before slicing. Store bread for 2 days at room temperature wrapped airtight, or freeze for up to 2 weeks.

Suggestions: Decorate your braid by sprinkling on sesame seeds, poppy seeds, or other spices after brushing on the egg. And save day-old egg bread for French toast, strata, or bread pudding.

Biblical Culture

In biblical times a small portion of dough was set aside as an offering to the priesthood. In Hebrew this ritual was called *hafrashat challah*.

Cinnamon Swirl Bread

This is a basic rolling technique that you can use for dozens of cinnamon roll variations.

Makes 2 loaves
Prep time: 2 hours
Cook time: 90 minutes

1½ cup warm water

2 (.25 oz.) packages active dry yeast

½ cup honey, divided

3 eggs, divided

¼ cup canola oil

1 tsp. kosher salt

4-5 cups bread flour

⅓ cup cinnamon

⅔ cup sugar

½ tsp. salt

1 TB. water

Biblical Culture

Cinnamon was well known in the Holy Land, but it didn't grow there. The spice is bark from an Asian evergreen tree. The inner bark is skillfully stripped from the trees when they are moist from annual rains. Spice trade between Egypt and Asia was recorded as early as 2600 B.C., and such foreign delicacies would have been available to those who could afford them.

1. Coat 2 loaf pans with pan spray, and line with a strip of parchment or wax paper. In a medium bowl, stir together warm water, yeast, and ¼ cup honey. Add 2 eggs, oil, and salt, and mix thoroughly.

2. Add enough flour to create a firm dough. Turn dough out onto a floured surface and knead, adding flour only when necessary, until dough becomes smooth and elastic, about 8-10 minutes. Return to the bowl, cover with plastic wrap, and set in a warm place to rise until doubled in volume, about 1 hour.

3. Preheat oven to 350°F. Turn dough out onto a floured surface and, with a rolling pin, roll into an 18"×24" rectangle. Warm remaining honey, brush it over entire surface, and sprinkle with cinnamon. Starting on a long edge, roll dough into a log. Cut the log into two 9-inch loaves. Place each loaf in a pan, seam-side down, dust with flour, cover with plastic wrap, and let rise again for 30 minutes. Combine remaining egg with tablespoon of water and brush over surface of breads. Bake until golden brown and firm, about 50-60 minutes. Cool completely before slicing. Store bread for 2 days at room temperature wrapped airtight, or freeze for up to 2 weeks.

Suggestions: Jazz up this loaf by adding dried fruits or nuts into the swirl. Sprinkle them evenly on top of the cinnamon. Use leftover bread for French toast and bread pudding.

Multi-Grain Bread

This bread is great for sandwiches, or form it into rolls for your table's bread basket. These specialty grains are available at any health food store, and you can order them on line. (See Appendix B.)

2½ cup warm water

¼ cup cracked wheat

2 (.25 oz.) packages active dry yeast

½ cup honey

¼ cup rye flour

¼ cup rolled oats

¼ cup corn meal

1 cup whole-wheat flour

1 tsp. kosher salt

3-4 cups bread flour

1 egg

1 TB. water

Makes 2 loaves
Prep time: 2½ hours
Cook time: 1 hour

1. In a medium bowl, combine water, cracked wheat, yeast, honey, and let stand 30 minutes. Add rye flour, oats, corn meal, wheat flour, and salt, and combine thoroughly. Add enough bread flour to create a firm dough. Turn dough out onto a floured surface and knead, adding flour only when necessary, until it becomes smooth and elastic, about 8-10 minutes. Return to the bowl, cover with plastic wrap, and set in a warm place to rise until doubled in volume, about 1 hour.

2. Coat two loaf pans with pan spray and line with a strip of parchment or wax paper. Turn dough out onto a floured surface and, with a rolling pin, roll into a 18"×24" rectangle. Starting on a long edge, roll dough up into a log. Cut the log into two (9-inch) loaves and place each loaf in a pan, seam-side down. Dust with flour, cover with plastic wrap, and let rise again for 30 minutes.

3. Preheat oven to 350°F. Combine egg with 1 tablespoon water, and brush over surface of breads. Bake until golden brown and firm, about 50-60 minutes. Cool completely before slicing. Store bread for 2 days at room temperature wrapped airtight, or freeze for up to 2 weeks.

Suggestions: Garnish the top of these loaves with a sprinkle of flour, cracked wheat, or sunflower seeds.

Kitchen Tips

Whole grains contain natural oils, which can quickly turn rancid. Store unused grains in the freezer for up to 4 months to ensure freshness.

Whole-Wheat Baguette

Baguette is a long French loaf with a crispy crust. It is light, airy, and fat-free, unless you smear it with butter.

Makes 3 (18-inch) loaves
Prep time: 2 hours
Cook time: 30 minutes

2 cups warm water

2 (.25 oz.) packages active dry yeast

1 TB. honey

2 cups whole-wheat flour

1 TB. kosher salt

3 cups bread flour

¼ cup cornmeal

1. In a medium bowl, combine water, yeast, and honey, and let stand 10 minutes. Add whole-wheat flour and salt, and combine thoroughly. Slowly add enough bread flour to create a firm dough. Turn out onto floured surface and knead, adding flour only as necessary, until dough becomes smooth and elastic, about 8-10 minutes. Return to the bowl, cover with plastic wrap, and set in a warm place to rise until doubled in volume, about 1 hour.

2. Coat a baking sheet with pan spray, and sprinkle with cornmeal. Turn dough out onto a floured surface and divide into three equal portions. Roll each piece into a tight rope, and taper the ends slightly. Place loaves on pan, dust with flour, cover with plastic wrap, and let rise another 30 minutes. Preheat oven to 400°F.

3. Score ¼-inch deep angled cuts in the top of each loaf to allow dough to expand decoratively during baking. Bake until golden brown and firm, about 15-20 minutes. Cool completely before slicing. Store bread for 2 days at room temperature wrapped airtight, or freeze for up to 2 weeks.

Suggestions: Form this dough into any number of shapes, including large round loaves, rolls, and even bread sticks. Brush the surface of the dough with olive oil or egg for a different finished glaze.

Kitchen Tips

Cornmeal sprinkled on a baking sheet helps keep the dough from sticking, but more importantly, it gives the appearance of a hearth-baked loaf. In a brick oven the cornmeal is used to keep the bread from sticking to the hearth and to ease transport between the paddle (called a *peele*) to the hearth and back again.

Crusty Herb Rolls

These rolls make terrific sandwiches and are great on the dinner table, dipped in extra virgin olive oil.

2 cups warm water

2 (.25 oz.) packages active dry yeast

1 TB. honey

½ cup chopped mixed herbs, including basil, rosemary, tarragon, thyme, and parsley

1 cup whole-wheat flour

1 TB. kosher salt

3-4 cups bread flour

¼ cup cornmeal

Makes 12 rolls
Prep time: 2½ hours
Cook time: 30 minutes

1. In a medium bowl, stir together water, yeast, honey, herbs, whole-wheat flour, and let stand 1 hour, until bubbles appear. This is a sponge. Add salt and enough bread flour to the sponge to create a firm dough. Turn out onto a floured surface and knead, adding flour only as necessary, until dough becomes smooth and elastic, about 8-10 minutes. Return to the bowl, cover with plastic wrap, and set in a warm place to rise until doubled in volume, about 1 hour.

2. Coat two baking sheets with pan spray, and sprinkle with cornmeal. Turn dough out onto a floured surface and divide into 12 equal portions. Roll each piece into a tight ball, and place evenly spaced on the baking sheet. Dust with flour, cover with plastic wrap, and let rise again for 30 minutes. Preheat oven to 400°F.

3. Bake until golden brown and firm, about 15-20 minutes. Cool completely before slicing. Store bread for 2 days at room temperature wrapped airtight, or freeze for up to 2 weeks.

Suggestions: This dough can have any number of variations, depending on your choice of herbs. Also replace the herbs with up to 1½ cups chopped olives, walnuts, or sautéed onions.

def•i•ni•tion

A **sponge** is a pre-dough, or thin batter, made from a portion of yeast, liquid, and flour of a particular recipe. The purpose is to give the fermentation a head start. The longer a dough ferments, the more flavorful the finished bread will be. The increased yeast action also creates a lighter loaf and a crispier crust.

Pocket Bread

This bread is called *pita*, or just plain *flat bread*. The key to the pocket is the thickness and the rest period between rolling and baking. This rest allows a skin to form that traps the steam and forces it to build up inside the dough.

Makes 5 pocket breads
Prep time: 2½ hours
Cook time: 20 minutes

1½ cup warm water

2 (.25 oz.) packages active dry yeast

1 TB. honey

1 TB. olive oil

1 TB. kosher salt

½ cup whole-wheat flour

2-3 cups bread flour

Kitchen Tips

Pocket bread must remain pale if it is to be flexible. If it gets too browned, it will be too hard, like a cracker. It's still delicious but no use as pocket bread.

1. In a medium bowl, stir together water, yeast, honey, and set aside for 15 minutes.

2. Stir in oil, salt, whole-wheat flour, and enough bread flour to create a firm dough. Turn dough out onto a floured surface and knead, adding flour only as necessary, until dough becomes smooth and elastic, about 8-10 minutes. Return to the bowl, cover with plastic wrap, and set in a warm place to rise until doubled in volume, about 1½ hours.

3. Preheat oven to 500°F, and preheat a clean, dry baking sheet. Turn dough out onto a floured surface, divide it into five equal portions, and roll each into a tight ball. Using a rolling pin, form each ball into a flat disc, ¼-inch thick. Keep uncovered and rest 20 minutes. One at a time, toss each disc onto the preheated baking sheet in the oven. Bake exactly 3 minutes. Remove carefully with tongs, and repeat with remaining dough. Finished bread will be puffed and very pale. Cool completely before slicing and opening. Store for 2 days at room temperature wrapped airtight, or freeze for up to 2 weeks.

Suggestions: When cool, slice discs in half and carefully spread open the pocket. Fill the inside with your favorite salad or sandwich fixings. Slice it into triangles and use it for pita chips, or serve it with your favorite dips (see Chapter 6).

Biblical Culture
"With the dough they had brought from Egypt, they baked cakes of unleavened bread. The dough was without yeast because they had been driven out of Egypt and did not have time to prepare food for themselves." (Exodus 12:39)

5-Seed Crackers

The seeds in this recipe are just suggestions. You can experiment with others, or keep it simple and pick just one or two.

⅔ **cup warm water**

⅓ **cup olive oil**

½ **tsp. salt**

1 tsp. baking powder

2-3 cups whole-wheat flour

1 egg white

1 TB. each sesame seeds, poppy seeds, flax seeds, dill seeds, and caraway seeds

Makes 12-15 crackers
Prep time: 30 minutes
Cook time: 20 minutes

1. In a large bowl combine water, oil, and salt. Add baking powder and enough flour to create a firm dough. Turn out onto a floured surface and knead, adding flour only as necessary, for 5 minutes. Return to the bowl, dust with flour, cover with plastic wrap, and rest at room temperature for 15 minutes. Preheat oven to 425°F.

2. Coat a baking sheet with pan spray. Turn dough out onto a floured surface and divide it into three equal portions. Roll each portion to ¼-inch thick with a rolling pin, and pierce each piece all over with a fork. Arrange on baking sheet, and bake until edges are brown, about 10-15 minutes. When cool, break crackers into serving-size pieces. Store for 2 days at room temperature wrapped airtight, or freeze for up to 2 weeks.

Suggestions: Cut this dough into decorative shapes with a cookie cutter before baking.

Kitchen Tips

To ease the rolling of this dough, give it plenty of rest. Gluten proteins tighten whenever a wheat-based dough is worked. Roll it as far as it wants to go; then let it rest and move on to the next piece. After 2-3 minutes the gluten in the dough will relax, and you can roll it much thinner.

Spoon Biscuits

This recipe is quick and easy because it requires no rolling pin or cutters. It contains dairy, so avoid using these biscuits in meals with meat.

Makes 6-8 biscuits

Prep time: 20 minutes

Cook time: 20 minutes

1 cup whole-wheat flour

1 cup all-purpose flour

½ tsp. salt

1 TB. baking powder

4 oz. (1 stick) chilled unsalted butter, cut into small dice

1 cup milk

¼ cup heavy cream

¼ cup grated Parmesan cheese

1. Preheat oven to 375°F. Coat baking sheet with pan spray. In a large bowl sift together whole-wheat flour, all-purpose flour, salt, and baking powder. Cut in chilled butter to dry ingredients, breaking into small, pea-size pieces with your fingertips or a pastry blender. Add milk mixture, and stir until just moistened.

2. Drop batter by large spoonfuls, evenly spaced, onto prepared baking sheet. Brush with cream, sprinkle with Parmesan cheese, and bake until golden brown, about 15 minutes. Store cooled at room temperature in an airtight container for 2 days, or freeze for up to 2 weeks.

Suggestions: Embellish biscuits with the addition of fresh herbs, olives, nuts, or cheese. Use dough as the topping for a pot pie, or simmer as dumplings on top of soup or stew.

Italian Rosemary Bread

The finer you chop the rosemary; the better this recipe will be. That's because more rosemary oil will be released into the recipe. A coffee or spice grinder is the perfect tool for this job.

1 cup warm water

2 (.25 oz.) packages active dry yeast

3 TB. finely chopped fresh rosemary

1 TB. honey

1 cup milk

1 TB. kosher salt

2 TB. olive oil

1 cup whole-wheat flour

2-3 cups bread flour

¼ cup cornmeal

Makes 2 loaves	
Prep time: 2 hours	
Cook time: 40 minutes	

1. In a medium bowl, combine water, yeast, rosemary, and honey, and let stand 10 minutes. Add milk, salt, olive oil, whole-wheat flour, and combine thoroughly. Slowly add enough bread flour to create a firm dough. Turn dough out onto a floured surface and knead, adding flour only as necessary, until dough becomes smooth and elastic, about 8-10 minutes. Return to the bowl, dust with flour, cover with plastic wrap, and set in a warm place to rise until doubled in volume, about 1 hour.

2. Coat a baking sheet with pan spray, and sprinkle with cornmeal. Turn dough out onto a floured surface and divide into two equal portions. Roll each piece into a tight football shape, and taper the ends slightly. Place loaves on prepared pan, dust with flour, cover with plastic wrap, and let rise another 30 minutes. Preheat oven to 450°F.

3. Score ¼-inch-deep angled cuts in top of each loaf, to allow dough to expand decoratively during baking. Bake until golden brown and firm, about 30-40 minutes. Cool completely before slicing. Store bread for 2 days at room temperature wrapped airtight, or freeze for up to 2 weeks.

Suggestions: This is a good choice for Savory Italian Toast (see recipe Chapter 5); it makes delicious Strata (see recipe Chapter 3); and croutons or stuffing made from it aren't too shabby either.

> **Biblical Culture**
>
> Rosemary is native to the Mediterranean region. It was known in ancient Greece, where it was thought to improve memory.

Part 3

Snacks and Starters

America loves snacking. We do it everywhere we go and with everything we do. We eat snack foods right from the package, box, or carton. We snack riding in the car, waiting in line, and watching television. We snack when we're not even hungry.

God did not create food as relief from boredom. He meant it to nourish us, both physically and spiritually. The recipes in these chapters are designed to do just that. They are standard fare with a healthy twist. They contain less saturated fat and frying, more fresh vegetables and whole grains. This fine-tuning has created recipes worth sharing with those you love.

Chapter 5

Hors d'oeuvres

In This Chapter

◆ Tasty treats, rolled, stuffed, and toasted

◆ Pockets and skewers

◆ Hot and cold cheese for dipping and spreading

"And Levi made him a great feast in his own house: and there was a great company of publicans and of others that sat down with them." (Luke 5:29 KJV)

Bite-size snacks are an international tradition. In English we call them *appetizers* because they whet our appetite for the meal ahead. The Spaniards call them *tapas;* the Russians call them *zakuski;* and in the Middle East they're called mezze.

Hors d'oeuvre is a French architectural term meaning "outside the main" and originally referred to small buildings set apart from the main house. The word was borrowed by culinarians to mean outside the main meal.

They consist of only one or two bites and are typically passed around, eaten standing up, without a plate or silverware. However, in modern American cuisine, appetizers are typically larger and are eaten on plates while seated at a table.

The Spirit of Snacking

In the United States appetizers are an add-on to the meal, something ordered on special occasions or when one feels particularly hungry. They have also become a big money maker for bars and restaurants, capitalizing on America's voracious habits and love of snacking.

Many cultures eat an assortment of these tiny plates as a meal, serving an array of flavors to be nibbled and savored. This puts the focus on the social aspect of eating and encourages sharing, talking, and fellowship. I give the recipes in this chapter with that spirit in mind as they are meant to be shared. Use them for entertaining, and enjoy them with friends.

Most appetizers and snacks we eat today are fried or laden with cheese, and the recipes in this chapter reflect that trend. But I have lightened these recipes and minimized their fat content. Foods that are traditionally deep-fried are oven-baked or pan-fried in a much smaller amount of monounsaturated olive oil. But as with all eating, moderation is the most important aspect of snacking. These dishes are not meant to fill you up. They are only little nibbles.

The number of servings in each recipe reflects this nibble concept. If you intend for more than one or two bites per person, adjust the recipe accordingly.

Cheese Fondue

Traditionally, fondue is made with Emmentaler, a very mild Swiss cheese, and Gruyère, a very pungent Swiss cheese. A half-and-half mixture is pleasing to most, but feel free to adjust the proportions to your liking. Or substitute your favorite Swiss-style cheese.

2 TB. cornstarch

¼ cup kirsch

1 clove garlic

1½ cup dry white wine

3 cups (12 oz.) Emmentaler cheese, grated

3 cups (12 oz.) Gruyère cheese, grated

¼ tsp. white pepper

¼ tsp. nutmeg

1 loaf crusty French bread, cut into 1-inch cubes

Serves 4-6
Prep time: 15 minutes
Cook time: 20 minutes

1. Combine cornstarch and kirsch and set aside. Slice garlic clove in half and rub over interior surface of large saucepan, then discard. Bring wine to a boil over high heat. Reduce heat to medium, and add cheese slowly, stirring continuously until melted.

2. Add cornstarch mixture, pepper, and nutmeg, and stir until thickened. Transfer to fondue pot or keep warm over low flame.

Suggestions: Use fondue as a dip for French bread, new potatoes, asparagus, broccoli, green beans, zucchini, mushrooms, or any of your favorite vegetables.

Kitchen Tips

Kirsch is cherry brandy, available where most liquor is sold. You can easily omit it, but without it, the recipe loses its authenticity. If you'd prefer to omit alcohol completely, replace the wine with 1 ¼ cup water and ¼ cup white wine vinegar.

Cheese Puffs

These delectable cheesy puffs hail from the Burgundy region of France, where they go by the name *gougere* and typically appear accompanying the region's fabulous wines. They are made with the classic French pastry dough pâte a choux, which is the same dough used to make profiteroles, cream puffs, and éclairs.

Serves 8-10

Prep time: 45 minutes
Cook time: 20 minutes

---

2 cups water

5 oz. (1¼ stick) butter

1 TB. sugar

1 tsp. salt

1⅔ cup all-purpose flour

7 eggs

2 cups grated Gruyère cheese

1 egg yolk

1 TB. cream

Kitchen Tips

This recipe requires strong arm muscles, as the incorporation of the eggs takes some effort. If you lack the muscle, use an electric mixer, but beware. Overmixing this batter will make it soupy. Mix it just enough to incorporate each egg.

1. Preheat oven to 400°F. Coat a baking sheet with pan spray. In a large saucepan combine water, butter, sugar, salt, and bring to a boil. At the boil add flour and stir vigorously with a sturdy spoon for at least 3 minutes, until all flour is absorbed and mixture resembles mashed potatoes. Remove from heat and cool slightly. Add eggs, one at a time, blending each one thoroughly before adding the next. When all eggs are in, add cheese and mix well.

2. Using a small ice cream scoop, or two spoons, drop by tablespoon onto prepared baking sheet, 1 inch apart. Combine egg yolk and cream, and brush lightly on top of each puff. Bake at 400°F until puffed and dark golden brown, about 15 minutes. Serve warm or at room temperature. Make these ahead, store airtight in the freezer, then reheat in the oven just before serving.

Suggestions: Flavor this batter in a number of ways, by stirring in one cup of additional garnish. Try sautéed mushrooms, chopped chives, caramelized onions, or spice it up with curry powder, Italian seasoning, or herbes de Provence.

Spinach Pockets

This is a Greek recipe called *spanakopita*. Filo dough is available fresh in Middle Eastern or Greek markets or frozen in most large supermarkets. If you use frozen, defrost it slowly in the refrigerator overnight. Defrosting at room temperature or in the microwave is a bad idea because it will leave the center portion frozen and the outer layers gummy.

2 lb. fresh chopped spinach, stems removed, or 1 (10 oz.) pkg. frozen spinach, thawed and well-drained

3 TB. olive oil

1 cup green onions, chopped

1 TB. fresh dill, minced

1 tsp. cinnamon

1 cup feta cheese

2 eggs, beaten

½ tsp. kosher salt

½ tsp. black pepper

¼ cup lemon juice

8-10 sheets filo dough

4 oz. (1 stick) unsalted butter, melted

Serves 6-8	
Prep time: 60 minutes	
Cook time: 20 minutes	

1. Heat oil into a large sauté pan over high heat, and sauté spinach, onions, dill, and cinnamon until tender, about 5 minutes. Remove from heat and stir in cheese, eggs, salt, pepper, and lemon juice. Mix thoroughly.

2. Preheat oven to 350°F. Coat a baking sheet with pan spray. Layer three sheets of filo dough with butter brushed between each sheet and on the top layer. Slice in half lengthwise for two long rectangles. Place tablespoon spinach mixture at bottom of rectangle and fold or roll up into an envelope. Place on the prepared pan and repeat with remaining dough.

3. Brush each spinach pocket with butter and bake 10-15 minutes, until golden brown.

Suggestions: If you have trouble finding feta cheese, use any soft cheese. Try ricotta, goat cheese, cottage cheese, or cream cheese instead.

Kitchen Tips

The classic form for spanakopita is a triangle. When forming the pockets, fold the dough up the same way you fold a flag, forming a right triangle with each turn. Form and freeze them up to 3 days in advance. Bake them frozen just before serving.

Chicken Liver Mousse

This is a delectable dish, reminiscent of classic French pâté. It requires a fine purée, best done in a food processor, blender, or food mill.

Serves 6-8
Prep time: 30 minutes
Cook time: 20 minutes, plus 1 hour to chill

Kitchen Tips

To clean chicken livers, rinse under cold water, and remove any visible membranes.

3 TB. olive oil, divided

1 large yellow onion, minced

2 granny smith apples, peeled, cored, and grated

1 tsp. honey

½ cup brandy

1 lb. chicken livers, cleaned

1 tsp. kosher salt

1 tsp. ground black pepper

2 tsp. dry mustard

½ cup raisins

1. Heat 2 tablespoons oil in a large sauté pan over high heat. Cook onion until tender. Add apples, honey, and brandy, and cook until dry. Add chicken livers and cook until tender and pink in the center, about 5 minutes. Remove from heat.

2. In a food processor or blender, combine chicken liver mixture, salt, pepper, and mustard, and purée until smooth. Stir in raisins by hand and transfer to a serving dish. Brush remaining oil on top to seal, and chill completely.

Suggestions: Serve in small dishes, surrounded by slices of toasted Braided Egg Bread or Baguette. (See recipe Chapter 4.)

Stuffed Mushrooms

People get excited when you serve anything stuffed. The assumption is that the host has fussed, but this recipe couldn't be easier.

20 large brown mushrooms

2 TB. olive oil

3 cloves garlic, minced

4 shallots, minced

¼ cup sherry

½ cup Parmesan cheese, divided

1 cup cream cheese, softened

1 cup Monterey Jack cheese, grated

2 TB. chopped chives

Serves 8-10
Prep time: 30 minutes
Cook time: 20 minutes

1. Preheat oven to 350°F. Wash and dry mushrooms, remove and mince stems. Heat oil in a large sauté pan over high heat. Cook garlic, shallots, and stems until golden brown. Deglaze with sherry and remove from heat. Add ¼ cup of Parmesan cheese, cream cheese, Jack cheese, chives, and blend thoroughly.

2. Coat a baking sheet with pan spray. Use a spoon to fill each mushroom cap with cheese mixture. Arrange stuffed caps on pan, top with remaining Parmesan cheese, and bake until golden brown and bubbly, about 15-20 minutes.

Suggestions: Stuff these mushrooms up to a day ahead, and keep refrigerated. Bake them as company arrives for a piping hot presentation.

Biblical Culture

Mushrooms have been gathered for centuries. They are depicted on Neolithic cave painting in Algeria (Tassili n'Ajjer), and it is said that Egyptian pharaohs decreed them reserved for royalty. Despite their popularity, the cultivation of mushrooms was not fully understood until the 1600s.

Deviled Eggs

This easy treat is always a hit.

Serves 8
Prep time: 45 minutes

8 eggs

¼ **cup mayonnaise**

1 TB. Dijon mustard

½ **tsp. powdered onion**

½ **tsp. kosher salt**

½ **tsp. ground black pepper**

Paprika for dusting

1. Place eggs in a small saucepan and cover with water. Boil over high heat for 5 minutes. Turn off heat and let eggs sit in hot water 20 minutes. Transfer to a bowl of ice water and chill for 10 minutes.

2. Peel cooled eggs and slice in half, lengthwise. Carefully remove yolks from whites; set whites on a plate, and place yolks in a large bowl. To yolks, add mayonnaise, mustard, onion powder, and stir well to combine. Season with salt and pepper.

3. Spoon yolk mixture into a piping bag, and pipe decoratively into empty whites. Lightly dust tops with paprika and serve. Store deviled eggs in the refrigerator for up to 24 hours.

Suggestions: Leftover deviled eggs make great egg salad. Just add some chopped celery, onions, and radishes, and mash it up!

Kitchen Tips

Piping bags are easy to find and easy to use. Most large supermarkets carry them, as do craft supply stores. The choice of tip is a matter of preference, but I like to use a star tip for deviled eggs. Be sure the egg yolk mixture is smooth, or it won't flow through the tip. If you have no piping bag, a plastic bag works in a pinch. Just fill the bag with the deviled egg mix, seal the top, cut off one small corner, and squeeze the yolk through the hole. Since the plastic bag has no decorative tip, try adding a small leaf of chervil or flat-leaf parsley on top of each egg to make it pretty.

Chicken Skewers with Peanut Sauce

This is an Indonesian dish called *satay*, popular throughout Southeast Asia. The meats and seasonings change by region, but the basic principle of thin meats skewered and grilled remains constant.

1 tsp. fresh ginger, grated	1 cup peanut butter
3 cloves garlic, minced	¼ cup soy sauce
1 TB. curry powder	2 tsp. Tabasco sauce
2 TB. fresh cilantro, minced	2 TB. honey
1½ lb. chicken breast, cut into ½-inch strips	¼ cup lime juice
	½ cup hot water

Serves 6-8
Prep time: 30 minutes, plus at least 2 hours to marinate
Cook time: 30 minutes

1. In a large zipper bag combine ginger, garlic, curry, cilantro, and chicken. Seal, rub marinade into meat, and refrigerate at least 2 hours or overnight. Soak 20 wooden skewers in water for 30 minutes.

2. Combine peanut butter, soy sauce, Tabasco, honey, and lime juice in a blender. With machine running, drizzle in hot water until sauce is consistency of heavy cream. Set aside.

3. Preheat broiler to 500-550°F. Coat baking sheet with pan spray. Thread chicken onto skewers, working skewer in and out, down middle of piece of meat. Place on prepared baking sheet, and broil until brown and sizzling, about 5 minutes per side. Serve hot with peanut sauce for dipping.

Suggestions: Cook the skewers on a hot grill.

Kitchen Tips

Cilantro is most associated with Mexican cuisine but is a common ingredient throughout Asia. You can sometimes find it marketed under the names Chinese parsley or fresh coriander.

Fresh Vegetables for Dip

This dish is commonly referred to by its French name, *crudités*. Use as many or as few vegetable varieties as you have on hand.

Serves 6-8
Prep time: 45 minutes
Cook time: 5 minutes

1 recipe Creamy Herb or Blue Cheese Dip (see Chapter 7)

8 cups water

1 tsp. kosher salt

4 cups ice water

1 cup green beans

1 cup broccoli florets

1 cup cauliflower florets

1 cup snap peas

1 cup radishes

3 carrots, peeled

3 stalks celery

1 cucumber, peeled

1 red bell pepper

1 yellow bell pepper

1 cup cherry tomatoes

1 cup cilantro leaves

1. Bring water and salt to a boil. At the boil add green beans, broccoli, and cauliflower. Blanch for 30 seconds, then immediately transfer to ice water.

2. Remove radish stems and roots. Cut carrots and celery into $^1/_2$-inch thick sticks. Slice cucumber into $^1/_2$-inch thick wheels. Slice bell peppers in half, remove seeds and white membrane, and slice into strips. Remove stems from tomatoes. Refrigerate vegetables in ice water at least 1 hour to crisp before serving. Arrange on a platter around a bowl of dip. Garnish with leaves of cilantro.

Suggestions: Use a bowl made of purple cabbage leaves as your center dip bowl, or hollow out a large pepper or tomato. It looks beautiful and makes cleanup easy.

Kitchen Tips

You can decoratively cut vegetables several ways for this type of presentation. Peel cucumber skin off lengthwise in strips, or score lengthwise with a fork before slicing. Make a radish look like a rose by slicing half-moon slits up and around its skin like petals. Submerge in ice water to open petals. Slice celery and carrots in angled rounds on the bias, or use a specialized knife with a wavy blade.

Little Rolled Tacos

This recipe, commonly known as *taquitos*, calls for beef, but it is commonly made with chicken, too. Many versions of this dish utilize pre-mixed taco seasoning. If you choose this route, omit the salt. Pre-mixed spice blends are loaded with sodium.

2 TB. olive oil	**1 tsp kosher salt**
1 medium yellow onion, minced	**2 TB. chili powder**
4 cloves garlic, minced	**2 TB. paprika**
1 red bell pepper, diced	**2 TB. ground cumin**
2 lb. ground beef	**½ cup vegetable oil, divided**
	24 medium corn tortillas

Serves 10-12
Prep time: 45 minutes
Cook time: 30 minutes

1. Heat oil in a large sauté pan over high heat. Cook onion, garlic, and peppers until tender, about 5 minutes. Add beef, salt, chili powder, paprika, and cumin, and cook until beef is browned. Remove from heat, drain off excess fat, and cool.

2. Heat 2 tablespoons vegetable oil over high heat, and fry each tortilla until tender and limp, about 10 seconds each. Drain. Place 2 tablespoons beef filling in center of each tortilla. Roll up like a cigar and secure with a toothpick. Fry in 2 tablespoons hot vegetable oil 2-3 minutes, until tortilla holds its shape. Drain and remove picks.

Suggestions: Serve with Guacamole and Salsa Fresca. (See recipes Chapter 6.) Observant households should not garnish with sour cream.

Kitchen Tips

Cut the fat in this Little Rolled Tacos recipe by baking them instead of frying. Soften the tortillas by wrapping them in foil and warming in the oven. Once formed, secure with picks and bake at 400°F until firm and golden.

Biblical Culture

Of course, they never mention tacos in the Bible. But food wrapped in flat bread is an ancient way to eat. Every emerging culture had a flat bread of some sort, which served as an eating utensil until forks or chopsticks were developed.

Savory Italian Toast

Known as *bruschetta* in Italian, this simple recipe is a showcase for wonderful tomatoes and fabulous bread. If your tomatoes aren't ripe or your bread is subpar, consider making something else.

Serves 6-8
Prep time: 60 minutes
Cook time: 10 minutes

¼ **cup olive oil**

2 TB. balsamic vinegar

¼ **cup fresh basil, chopped**

5 medium ripe tomatoes, seeded and diced

½ **tsp. kosher salt**

½ **tsp black pepper**

1 loaf crusty Italian Bread (see recipe Chapter 4)

2 cloves garlic, sliced in half

2 TB. freshly grated Parmesan cheese

1. In a large bowl combine oil, vinegar, basil, tomatoes, salt, and pepper. Toss together and set aside 30-60 minutes to marinate.

2. Slice bread into ½–inch slices. Toast, then rub each with cut side of garlic clove. Top with tomato mixture and a few shaves of Parmesan cheese.

Suggestions: This recipe is best made with good-quality, fresh Parmesan cheese. Buy a hunk and grate it yourself. The primo Parmesan is Parmigiano-Reggiano, from Parma, Italy. Several similar styles of cheese of varying quality are available, but any hunk of aged Parmesan is 100 times better than the powdered cheese in the green can.

Kitchen Tips

Seeding a tomato is easy. Slice it in half through its middle (not stem end to end). This exposes all the seed cavities.

Then squeeze the tomato like you would an orange for juice, releasing all the slimy seeds and juice and leaving only the tender tomato meat.

Pita Chips

These chips are great for dipping but also stand alone as a terrific snack. They are a healthy, and surprisingly popular, alternative to potato chips.

8 pita pocket bread rounds

½ cup olive oil

2 cloves garlic, minced

½ tsp. dried oregano

½ tsp. dried basil

½ tsp. dried rosemary

½ tsp. black pepper

½ cup Parmesan cheese

Serves 6-8

Prep time: 40 minutes

Cook time: 10 minutes

---

1. In a small bowl combine olive oil, garlic, oregano, basil, rosemary, and black pepper. Stir to combine and set aside to infuse flavors, at least 30 minutes or overnight.

2. Preheat oven to 400°F. Coat two or three baking sheets with pan spray. Cut each pita round into 8 triangles; separate halves and spread on baking sheets in one layer. Brush oil mixture lightly onto each pita triangle. Sprinkle with Parmesan cheese and bake 5-7 minutes, until golden brown and crisp.

Suggestions: Adjust the seasoning to your liking, and make variations using spicy Cajun seasoning, curry powders, or even cinnamon sugar. (Omit the oil, and simply sprinkle the sugar on the triangles before baking.)

Kitchen Tips

Watch pita chips carefully when baking. The bread is very thin and can burn easily. Stir a little to ensure even browning.

Chapter 6

Dips and Spreads

In This Chapter

◆ Roasted vegetable purées

◆ Smooth and flavorful spreads

◆ Herbed and spicy cheeses

"Do you not know that your body is a temple of the Holy Spirit … You are not your own; you were bought at a price. Therefore honor God with your body. (1 Corinthians 6:19-20 NIV)

Dips are an easy way to feed a crowd: quick to prepare, easy to serve, and fun to eat. There is a vast array of options, with a dip suited to every cuisine imaginable. What's more, dips are good for more than just dipping. You can use them as sauces and spreads for all types of hot and cold foods.

Purée

Anything can be made into a dip if it's puréed. A purée is a smooth paste created by pulverizing cooked or raw foods.

Traditionally, food was pounded either between rocks or in a mortar. As technology improved, food was pressed through a sieve to break down its particles. Today blenders and food processors make quick work of a once arduous task.

Handheld immersion blenders, basically blenders on a stick, are another option. You insert a little propeller into a pot of food, and it whizzes around and draws the food into the blade. The advantage is that you only need to clean the blade. The downside is that is a little harder to get a really thin, fine purée.

Food mills are an old-fashioned manual option that work really well but take a little extra effort. Regardless of the purée method you choose, always cool cooked food as much as possible before puréeing.

Cheese

Cheese is a common ingredient in dips and spreads, not only because of its flavor and texture but also because it accepts other flavors particularly well. The most common cheese for dips is cream cheese, which is fairly neutral in flavor, with only a slight tang. However, hundreds of other cheeses are out there just waiting to be tried.

Some easy substitutions for cream cheese include Greek *feta* or *manouri* cheese, Italian *stracchino*, German *kochkase*, Middle Eastern *brizna*, California *teleme* and goat cheese, and French *boursault*, Saint Andre, and *explorateur*. These are all categorized as soft cheese, easily spreadable, and very distinct. If you have a cheese purveyor near you, visit for some samples.

> **Biblical Culture**
>
> Bedouins have made cheese similar to feta, called *'afiq*, for centuries. Because curds are compressed, salted, and dried in the sun, this cheese can be stored for weeks and reconstituted when needed.

Remember that cheese always tastes and spreads better at room temperature. If your cheese dip or spread has been chilling, pull it out of the fridge 30-60 minutes before you plan to serve it.

When following biblical dietary law, cheese should not be served at the same time, or within the same meal, as meat.

Dippers

A number of products on the market are designed for dipping. Crackers, chips, and bread all work fine. Just be wary of what you purchase. What a shame it would be to make a fresh and healthy dip, then shovel it into your mouth with something made with hydrogenated fat, corn syrup, excessive sodium, artificial colors, and MSG. But beware: these ingredients show up in nearly every snack cracker and chip on the shelf!

Instead, look for organic, low-fat options (see Appendix B), use vegetables, or make your own bread and crackers (see Chapter 4). If you enjoy cooking, homemade crackers are fun, easy to make, and certainly impressive. Make them a week or two in advance, and store them in the freezer, wrapped airtight, until you need them.

Middle Eastern Chickpea Dip

This recipe, known as hummus, is a staple item in every Middle Eastern household. Recipes vary; some are thick, some thin, and some heavy on the tahini, garlic, or lemon. It is all a matter of taste, so feel free to adjust this recipe according to your taste.

Serves 6-8
Prep time: 20 minutes

2 (15 oz.) cans chickpeas (reserve liquid)

4 cloves garlic

1 medium yellow onion, chopped

¼ cup tahini

¼ cup lemon juice

¼-½ cup olive oil

½ tsp. kosher salt

½ tsp. ground black pepper

chopped parsley

ground paprika

1. Purée chickpeas, garlic, onion, tahini, lemon juice, ¼ cup oil, salt, and pepper together. Add enough reserved chickpea liquid to reach a smooth, yogurt consistency.

2. Transfer mixture to a serving bowl, and swirl top with a spoon. Drizzle on remaining olive oil, and sprinkle liberally with chopped parsley and/or ground paprika.

Suggestions: Serve this dish the traditional way, with soft pita bread ripped into pieces, or turn the bread into pita chips (see Chapter 5).

Biblical Culture
Chickpeas are one of the world's first domesticated crops. They were common throughout the Holy Land, both fresh and dried. Along with other legumes, they were an important source of protein.

Roasted Eggplant Dip

The name of this recipe is *babaganooj*, and like hummus, it is a common sight on the Middle Eastern table.

2 large eggplants

2 heads garlic

¼-½ cup olive oil

1 large yellow onion

¼ cup tahini

¼ cup lemon juice

½ tsp. kosher salt

½ tsp. ground black pepper

2-3 TB. chopped parsley

Serves 6-8
Prep time: 1 hour
Cook time: 15 minutes

1. Preheat oven to 400°F. Coat eggplant and garlic lightly with olive oil, place on a baking sheet, and roast until brown and soft, 30-40 minutes.

2. Purée eggplant, garlic, onion, tahini, lemon juice, salt, and pepper together. Add enough olive oil to reach a smooth, yogurt consistency. Transfer to a serving bowl and swirl top with a spoon. Drizzle on remaining olive oil, and sprinkle liberally with chopped parsley.

Suggestions: Serve in the same manner as hummus, or use it as a spread for sandwiches, a topping for pizzas, or a sauce for grilled meats.

Kitchen Tips

Roast eggplant and garlic ahead of time. In fact, the purée is easier to make if these ingredients have had time to cool.

Butternut Squash Dip

Squash is a traditional autumn crop but are available year-round in most states, and this recipe is a welcome change from traditional summer snacks.

Serves 6-8
Prep time: 1 hour
Cook time: 15 minutes

1 butternut squash, peeled and diced in 2-inch cubes

10 cloves garlic

2 TB. fresh rosemary

¼-½ cup olive oil

1 tsp. kosher salt

2 TB. lemon juice

¼ cup chopped toasted pecans

1. Preheat oven to 450°F. Coat a baking sheet with pan spray. In a large bowl combine squash, garlic, rosemary, ¼ cup oil, and salt. Toss together well, and spread into a single layer on prepared pan. Bake 30-45 minutes, until squash is tender to touch and beginning to brown. Cool to room temperature.

2. Transfer squash mixture to food processor and blend until smooth. Add lemon juice, and check seasoning. Transfer to a serving bowl and swirl top with a spoon. Drizzle on remaining olive oil, and sprinkle liberally with chopped toasted pecans.

Suggestions: Serve this dip with croutons of toasted rosemary bread (see Chapter 4). Try using sweet potatoes or yams for a slightly sweeter variation.

Kitchen Tips

Peeling a butternut squash may seem daunting. Put away the potato peeler and get out a big knife. Slice the squash into 3- to 4-inch lengths. Stand them up flat on your board, and use the knife to trim off the thick skin. The seeds only occur in the rounded bulb area of the squash. To remove them, cut it in half after that section is peeled, and scoop out the seeds. Then dice.

Smoked White Fish Spread

Smoked white fish is available at fish markets and better grocers. It's worth searching out for this fantastic spread.

2 cups (16 oz.) smoked white fish

¼ cup sour cream

½ cup white onion, minced

¼ cup grated fresh horseradish

1 tsp. Old Bay Seasoning

½ tsp. Tabasco sauce

3 TB. lemon juice

½ tsp. black pepper

1 (8 oz.) package cream cheese, softened

¼ cup fresh parsley, minced

Serves 6-8
Prep time: 30 minutes

1. Combine fish, sour cream, onion, horseradish, Old Bay, Tabasco, lemon juice, and pepper in a food processor and blend until smooth. Transfer to a large bowl, and blend by hand with cream cheese until thoroughly combined. Transfer to serving bowl, and keep chilled.

Suggestions: This spread is a traditional bagel spread and makes a great dip for bagel chips, cucumbers, or bread sticks.

Kitchen Tips

The cream cheese in this recipe is added by hand because it can easily be overblended in a machine and become soupy.

Garlic and White Bean Spread

Several varieties of white beans are available both dried and canned, including northern white, cannellini, and navy beans.

Serves 10-12	
Prep time: 15 minutes	
Cook time: 15 minutes	

½ cup olive oil

4 cloves garlic, roughly chopped

1 (15 oz.) can white beans, drained

2 TB. white wine

1 TB. white wine vinegar

½ tsp. kosher salt

2 TB. fresh sage or basil, minced

Biblical Culture

Several legumes, including fava beans, lentils, and chick-peas, were first cultivated in the Fertile Crescent, but the common bean was domesticated first in the Americas.

1. Heat 2 TB. oil in a sauté pan over medium heat. Cook garlic until lightly golden brown. Remove from heat and set aside.

2. In a food processor combine beans, wine, vinegar, and salt. Add sautéed garlic and process until smooth, adding 3-4 tablespoons olive oil in a slow stream until mixture reaches yogurt-like consistency. Transfer to a serving bowl and swirl top with a spoon. Drizzle with remaining olive oil and sprinkle with chopped sage.

Suggestions: Serve with slices of toasted Italian bread or pita chips.

Black Olive Spread

This traditional dish of Provence is called *tapenade* and is best made with *kalamata* olives, available at most supermarkets. You can substitute a can of black olives, but that is not preferred.

2 cups pitted kalamata olives	**1 TB. lemon juice**
1 TB. capers	**2 TB. olive oil**
2 anchovy filets	**½ tsp. black pepper**

> *Serves 6-8*
>
> **Prep time:** 15 minutes

1. Combine olives, capers, and anchovies in a food processor and blend to a coarse paste. Add lemon juice, olive oil, and pepper, and blend until just combined. Transfer to a serving bowl and serve immediately, or allow flavors to mingle in the refrigerator overnight. Bring to room temperature before serving.

Suggestions: This classic dish makes a wonderful dip for crudités (see recipe Chapter 5), a great spread for toast, or a sauce for fresh-grilled fish.

def•i•ni•tion

Greek **kalamata** olives are black olives packed in a salty brine and are completely unlike the common canned black olive. They are plump, juicy, tangy, acidic, and salty. They come with or without pits and can be easily pitted by hand. If you have never tried them, they are worth searching out. The difference is night and day.

Guacamole

There are many variations to guacamole, but this recipe keeps it simple. If you'd like to jazz it up, add chopped onion, tomatoes, chilies, and cilantro.

Serves 4-6
Prep time: 10 minutes

Juice of 1 lime	**½ tsp. pepper**
1 tsp. ground cumin	**2 TB. hot pepper sauce**
½ tsp. salt	**4 ripe avocados**

Biblical Culture

Avocados are a New World crop. They were introduced to Europe in the early 1500s, but didn't make it to the Fertile Crescent until the early 1900s. Today, Israel is a major producer.

1. In a large bowl combine the lime juice, cumin, salt, pepper, and pepper sauce, and mix well. Cut avocados in half by slicing them lengthwise around the pit, then open by twisting. Remove pit by hacking it with a knife and twisting. Scoop out green avocado meat and add it to the bowl. Use a fork to mash it into a fine paste. Store in the refrigerator with plastic wrap pressed directly onto surface of mixture to prevent oxidation. Serve with tortilla chips.

Suggestions: This recipe is best made with the popular Haas (also known as Hass) avocado, which has a dark, thick, wrinkled skin and the fruit inside is rich and creamy when ripe. The Florida variety has a thinner, lighter-green skin, with dense, often fibrous, fruit.

Salsa Fresca

The name means fresh sauce, and nothing is better with tacos, chips, or poured over hot *carne asada* (see recipe Chapter 9).

3 large ripe tomatoes, chopped

3 scallions, chopped

3 cloves garlic, minced

1 bunch cilantro, chopped

2 jalapeño chilies, chopped

Juice of 3 limes

1 TB. ground cumin

1 tsp. Tabasco

1 tsp. kosher salt

Serves 4-6
Prep time: 30 minutes, plus at least 1 hour to marinate

1. In a large bowl, combine tomatoes, scallions, garlic, cilantro, jalapeños, lime juice, cumin, pepper sauce, and salt. Mix well and set aside at room temperature for 1 hour to allow flavors to mingle. Store in refrigerator for 1-2 days.

Suggestions: Add any number of additional ingredients to give your salsa personality. Try cucumbers, radishes, avocados, or jicama.

Biblical Culture
Tomatoes and chilies were nowhere near the Fertile Crescent during biblical times. Discovered in Central America by the Spanish, once introduced to Europe in the early sixteenth century they became popular and quickly spread throughout the Middle East, Asia, and Africa.

7-Layer Bean Dip

You can find this dish on the menu of every Super Bowl party across America. Tortilla chips, beware.

Serves 4
Prep time: 10 minutes
Cook time: 20 minutes

1 (16 oz.) can refried beans

1 TB. ground cumin

1 TB. garlic powder

2 avocados, skin and pit removed

Juice of 1 lime

1 small white onion, grated

2 ripe tomatoes, diced

1 (4 oz.) can diced green chilies

1½ cup sour cream

1 (4.5 oz.) can sliced black olives

1 cup grated cheddar cheese

1. Preheat oven to 350°F. In a large bowl, stir together beans, cumin, and garlic powder; then transfer mixture to a baking dish. Combine avocados, lime, and onion; mash mixture together, and spread on top of beans. Layer tomatoes, chilies, sour cream, olives, and cheese on top of guacamole. Bake until cheese is melted and bubbly, about 20 minutes. Serve immediately.

Suggestions: Add more layers, including green onions, sliced fresh or pickled jalapeños, prepared salsa, black beans, or fresh cilantro.

Blue Cheese Dip

This dip works with any type of blue cheese, but not all blues are equal. Try it several times, using Roquefort, Stilton, Gorgonzola, and Maytag blue for some subtle, delicious variations.

12 oz. (1½ cup) blue cheese, softened

2 cups sour cream

2 TB. tarragon vinegar

½ tsp. dried thyme

½ tsp. black pepper

2-4 TB. milk

½ cup chopped toasted walnuts

½ cup green onions, chopped

Serves 6-8
Prep time: 30 minutes

1. In a large bowl, beat cheese until smooth and soft. Slowly blend in sour cream, vinegar, thyme, and pepper. Add milk until it reaches a sour-cream consistency. Transfer to a serving bowl, and top with chopped walnuts and green onions.

Suggestions: Use this dip for crudités, crackers, French bread, or onion rings. Also thin it out with milk to dress your salad.

 Kitchen Tips

Tarragon vinegar is readily available at better markets. Its subtle licorice essence complements blue cheese nicely. If you have trouble finding it, use white wine vinegar, and add to the recipe a pinch of fresh or dried tarragon, fennel, or anise.

Creamy Herb Dip

This recipe is a natural with vegetables and crackers, but it also makes a great mayonnaise replacement on sandwiches and in salads, like potato, egg, or tuna.

Serves 6-8
Prep time: 20 minutes, plus at least 1 hour cooling time

2 cups cottage cheese

½ cup sour cream

4 green onions, minced

2 TB. fresh chives, minced

2 TB. fresh parsley, minced

1 TB. fresh dill, minced

1 tsp. kosher salt

½ tsp. black pepper

½ tsp. onion powder

1. In a blender, combine cottage cheese and sour cream, and blend until smooth. Transfer to a large bowl and add onions, chives, parsley, dill, salt, pepper, and onion powder. Blend well, cover and chill for at least 1 hour or overnight to mingle flavors.

Suggestions: If you have an abundance of fresh herbs, add them in. This recipe can easily handle up to 1 cup of chopped fresh herbs. Basil, oregano, tarragon, chervil, and thyme are just a few of your options.

Biblical Culture
Fresh herbs were indeed an important element of the biblical diet. Herbs like chicory, mint, lemongrass, and bay were used to flavor foods, aid digestion, and heal ailments.

Curry Dip

Curry is a spice blend that varies throughout the world but is most associated with the cuisine of India. It is available pre-mixed in powder or paste form in most supermarkets. You can also create your own blend. See the Kitchen Tips sidebar for the how-to.

2 cups mayonnaise	**1 TB. Tabasco**
2 cups sour cream	**1 tsp. tomato paste**
3 TB. curry powder or paste	**1 small white onion, minced**
1 TB. lemon juice	**1 TB. grated horseradish**
1 TB. honey	

Serves 6-8
Prep time: 20 minutes, plus at least 1 hour cooling time

1. In a large bowl combine mayonnaise, sour cream, and curry powder, and mix thoroughly. Mix in lemon juice, honey, Tabasco, tomato paste, onion, and horseradish. Cover and chill for at least 1 hour or overnight.

Suggestions: To accentuate the exotic flavors of this dip, top it with a layer of mango chutney, and serve it with flat bread and cucumber slices.

Kitchen Tips

Garam Masala is one of the most popular curries. *Garam* means "warm" or "hot," but this is not a spicy heat. Rather, it makes you feel warm after you've eaten it. Combine 1 cup bay leaves, ½ cup cumin seed, ¼ cup coriander seed, 3 TB. each black peppercorns, cardamom seeds, cloves, and nutmeg. Mix together, then toast in a dry skillet before grinding to a fine powder.

Chapter 7

Soups

In This Chapter

- ◆ Healing broths
- ◆ Hearty purées
- ◆ Chunky chowder and chili

"Beloved, I pray that you may prosper in all things and be in health, just as your soul prospers." (3 John 1:2 NKJV)

Because soup is comforting and warm, it can be a first course, an entire meal, or a restorative tonic. Soup is one of the most basic foods, yet most people are familiar only with the kind that comes in cans. Making soup from scratch is a surefire way to show you care.

The First Soup

We might assume that soup began with the advent of pottery. After all, one needs a vessel to boil water. It appears, however, that soup has been around a bit longer.

Archaeologists working in La-Chapelle-aux-Saints, in Central France, uncovered Neanderthal remains that suggest man cared for the sick and invalid with soup. Remnants of crippled adults and old people without teeth suggest that despite their inability to contribute to society through the hunt, these elders were kept alive on some kind of liquid diet. Being the premilk era, it is thought that soup sustained them.

Exactly how the Neanderthal kitchen operated is a matter of conjecture, but generally we believe they suspended animal skins over a fire, to which water was added and boiled. The skin would not burn but cook with the heat of the water. Such a broth, with remnants of the animal as a part of the cooking vessel, would have been protein-rich.

The Mother Broth

Broth is the essential ingredient of all soups and brings flavor and nutrients to the pot. Making broth at home may seem troublesome at first, but can be quite a satisfying endeavor.

Recipes for broth include bones (for meat broth) and aromatic vegetables. These are readily available, and the frugal cook can save them from everyday cooking. Thrifty chefs commonly add scraps and peelings from vegetables into stockpots. Onion skins, carrot peelings, stems, cores, wilted herbs, and otherwise unusable vegetation still contain vital nutrients and flavor and can enrich a broth. You can keep a container in the freezer and add scraps throughout the week. Then, when the container is full, make a large batch of broth, freeze it for several weeks, and it's ready to use when you need it. You can save bones and meat scraps in this manner, too.

Knowing that vegetables for soups will never be seen whole, many chefs save money buying less-expensive produce that is damaged or past its prime. Look for smaller markets that may offer such bargains.

The Power of Homemade

Making soup at home is simple, yet many people are unwilling to invest the time. Our busy schedules do not always permit a gentle five-hour simmer. But the arguments for doing it yourself are persuasive.

Most canned soup contains saturated fat, very little fiber, and overcooked vegetables, with much of the nutrition leached out. If you make the soup, not only can you monitor the cooking but you can also consume the nutrient-rich liquid the vegetables are cooked in. The same cannot be said for soup in a can.

Canned soup is also loaded with sodium. Most recommendations for daily sodium intake hover around 1500 mg for an average adult. Canned chicken noodle soup has 2290 mg per serving. This excess sodium increases your blood volume, making it harder for the heart to pump blood through blood vessels. This, in turn, leads to cardiovascular and kidney diseases.

Sodium is found in virtually every store-bought product and takes some forethought to avoid. Homemade soup is an easy place to start.

Beef Broth

This is a basic brown stock. The roasted bones and vegetables give it a rich color and flavor.

Makes 4 quarts
Prep time: 1 hour
Cook time: 6 hours

4 lb. beef bones, cut into 1-inch pieces, preferably joints, cartilage, and beef scraps

2 carrots, chopped

4 stalks celery, chopped

1 large yellow onion, chopped

1 (6 oz.) can tomato paste

1 bay leaf

1 tsp. black peppercorn

1 clove

1 sprig fresh parsley

1 sprig fresh thyme

About 4 qt. cold water

 Kitchen Tips

Make a light broth by skipping the browning stage and putting everything directly into the pot. It's a good method to use when you want the other flavors and colors of a recipe to shine.

1. Preheat oven to 500°F. Wash meat and bones and spread onto a roasting pan in one layer. Bake until well browned, about 30 minutes. Add carrots, celery, onion, and tomato paste, and return to oven for 10 more minutes. Remove from oven and place in stockpot.

2. Add, bay leaf, pepper, clove, parsley, and thyme. Cover with cold water, bring to a boil over high heat; then reduce heat and cook at a bare simmer for 4-6 hours. Skim top periodically to remove any residue.

3. Drain broth and cool. If meat is left on bones, cool and pick meat off for use in soups and stews. To degrease, refrigerate overnight, and remove fat that has solidified on top. Good stock will have a jellied consistency when chilled. Store refrigerated for up to four days or frozen for a month.

Suggestions: Many butchers will give away extra beef bones for free. It doesn't hurt to ask.

Chicken Broth

No canned broth can compare to a homemade one.

4 lb. chicken bones, carcass, or wings, with scrap meat

2 carrots, chopped

4 stalks celery, chopped

1 large yellow onion, chopped

1 bay leaf

1 tsp. black peppercorn

1 clove

1 sprig fresh parsley

1 sprig fresh thyme

About 4 qt. cold water

Makes 4 quarts
Prep time: 1 hour
Cook time: 3 hours

1. Preheat oven to 500°F. Spread bones and meat onto a roasting pan in one layer. Bake until well browned, about 30 minutes. Remove from oven and place in stockpot.

2. Add carrots, celery, onion, bay leaf, pepper, clove, parsley, and thyme. Cover with cold water, bring to a boil over high heat, reduce heat, and cook at a bare simmer for 2-3 hours. Skim top periodically to remove any residue.

3. Drain broth and cool. If meat is left on bones, cool, and pick meat off for use in soups and stews. To degrease, refrigerate overnight, and remove solidified fat on top. Good broth will have a jellied consistency when chilled. Store refrigerated for up to four days or frozen for a month.

Suggestions: If you have leftover roasted bird, don't bother roasting it again. Just add it right to the pot.

Kitchen Tips

Use this recipe for other birds, too, like turkey or duck. And if you are cooking another type of bird, make a quickie broth by simmering their gizzards and scraps in chicken broth. It picks up the other bird's flavor nicely and can be used for corresponding sauces, soups, and side dishes.

Fish Broth

This is a quickie. Fish have strong flavors and don't need much coaxing to release into this broth.

Makes 4 quarts
Prep time: 30 minutes
Cook time: 1 hour

3 TB. olive oil

4 lb. fish bones

4 stalks celery, chopped

1 large yellow onion, chopped

2 cups mushroom trimmings

1 bay leaf

1 tsp. black peppercorn

1 tsp. celery seed

1 tsp. allspice berries

1 tsp. mustard seed

1 clove

1 sprig fresh parsley

1 sprig fresh thyme

2 cups white wine

About 4 qt. cold water

Kitchen Tips

Choose lean, white-fleshed fish to make broth. The flavor of salmon or trout is too strong, and the excessive oil really makes for a greasy broth.

1. Heat olive oil in a stockpot over high heat. Add bones and cook, stirring, for 10 minutes until barely brown. Add celery, onion, and mushrooms, and cook another 5 minutes.

2. Add bay leaf, peppercorn, celery seed, allspice, mustard seed, clove, parsley, and thyme. Cover with wine and cold water, and bring to a boil over high heat. Reduce heat, and cook at a bare simmer for 45 minutes. Skim top periodically to remove any residue.

3. Drain broth and cool. To degrease, refrigerate overnight; then remove solidified fat on top. Good broth will have a jellied consistency when chilled. Store refrigerated for up to four days or frozen for a month.

Suggestions: This broth makes an excellent poaching liquid for fish and vegetables. Simmer gently, under the boil, to cook your delicate filets.

Vegetable Broth

If you are a vegetarian or are following biblical dietary guidelines, this is an essential recipe to have. It brings flavor to recipes that would otherwise be made with plain water.

3 TB. olive oil

2 large yellow onions, chopped

2 leeks, chopped

4 cloves garlic, chopped

2 carrots, chopped

4 stalks celery, chopped

2 cups green cabbage, chopped

2 turnips, chopped

4 tomatoes, chopped

1 bay leaf

1 tsp. black peppercorn

2 cloves

1 tsp. fennel seeds

1 sprig fresh parsley

1 sprig fresh thyme

About 4 qt. cold water

Makes 4 quarts
Prep time: 1 hour
Cook time: 6 hours

1. Heat olive oil in stockpot over high heat. Add onions, leeks, garlic, carrots, celery, cabbage, turnips, and tomatoes. Cook, stirring for 10-20 minutes, until they begin to brown. Add bay leaf, peppercorn, cloves, fennel seed, parsley, and thyme, and cook another 5 minutes. Cover with cold water, bring to a boil over high heat, reduce heat, and cook at a bare simmer for 2-3 hours. Skim top periodically to remove any residue.

2. Drain broth and cool. To degrease, refrigerate overnight, and remove solidified oil on top. Store refrigerated for up to four days or frozen for a month.

Suggestions: Vegetable broth is great to have on hand. Use it in place of a meat-based broth or in recipes calling for water, such as rice.

Kitchen Tips

You can add just about any vegetable to vegetable broth, but beware. Bright pigments will color the broth, and strong flavors can overpower. Keep the flavors and colors in balance.

Vegetable Soup

This recipe is a breeze, especially if you have broth on hand.

Serves 4
Prep time: 10 minutes
Cook time: 40 minutes

2 TB. olive oil

1 small yellow onion, chopped

2 stalks celery, chopped

1 carrot, chopped

2 parsnips, chopped

1 tsp. dried thyme

6 cups vegetable broth or water

2 cups fresh or canned tomatoes, chopped

1 cup fresh or frozen peas

1 cup fresh or frozen green beans

1 cup fresh or frozen chopped broccoli

1. Heat olive oil in a large saucepan over high heat. Sauté onion, celery, carrot, parsnips, and thyme until tender. Add broth and tomatoes, and simmer until carrots and parsnips are tender, about 30 minutes.

2. Add peas, beans, and broccoli, and simmer another 5 minutes before serving.

Suggestions: Turn this into vegetable bean or barley soup by adding cooked beans or pearled barley to the sautéing onions.

 Kitchen Tips

Make this recipe season-specific by using baby vegetables in the spring and root vegetables in the fall. You can also adjust the seasoning to reflect a specific cuisine by trying Italian, curry, or Cajun spice blends.

Minestrone

In Italian *minestrone* means "big soup," and that's just what this healthy soup is—big on nutrition.

2 TB. olive oil

1 small yellow onion, chopped

2 stalks celery, chopped

1 carrot, chopped

2 parsnips, chopped

2 TB. dried oregano

6 cups vegetable stock or water

2 cups fresh or canned tomatoes, chopped

1 (15 oz.) can *cannellini* beans

2 cups dried pasta

1 cup zucchini, chopped

1 cup fresh or frozen green beans

1 cup green cabbage, chopped

¼ cup fresh basil, chopped

1 cup Parmesan cheese, grated

Serves 4	
Prep time: 10 minutes	
Cook time: 40 minutes	

1. In a large soup pot sauté onion, celery, carrot, and parsnips in oil until translucent. Add stock and tomatoes, and simmer until carrots and parsnips are tender, about 30 minutes.

2. Add cannellini beans and pasta, and cook until pasta is tender. Add zucchini, green beans, and cabbage, and simmer another 5 minutes before serving, topped with fresh basil and Parmesan cheese.

Suggestions: Use any pasta shape you have on hand; traditionally it is crushed vermicelli.

def•i•ni•tion

Also known as white kidney beans, or fagioli beans, **cannellini** beans are creamy white and have a subtle nutty flavor. They are related to, and can be replaced by, navy and great northern beans.

Navy Bean Soup

This recipe is traditionally based on broth made from ham hocks. To stay in step with a biblical diet, I substitute chicken or vegetable broth.

Serves 6
Prep time: 10 minutes
Cook time: 30 minutes

2 TB. olive oil

1 large yellow onion, diced

3 cloves garlic, minced

1 stalk celery, diced

1 bay leaf

1 lb. dried *navy beans*, soaked overnight

6 cups beef, chicken, or vegetable broth

1 tsp. Worcestershire sauce

½ tsp. kosher salt

½ tsp. black pepper

1. In a large soup pot sauté onion, garlic, celery, and bay leaf in oil until translucent. Add beans and broth, and simmer 2 hours. Skim top of soup, and add water as necessary. Add Worcestershire, salt, and pepper, and simmer another 2 hours, until beans are tender.

Suggestions: This soup improves with age, so make it the day before you want to serve it if you have the time.

def•i•ni•tion

Sometimes called the Boston Bean, or the Yankee bean, the **navy bean** was a staple food of the United States Navy, and Navy bean soup is still a regular item on the Navy's menu rotation. These small white beans are available both canned and dried. Use lima or cannellini beans as a substitute if necessary.

Southwestern Corn Chowder

Here's a spicy twist on an old favorite.

3 TB. olive oil

1 large yellow onion, diced

3 cloves garlic, chopped

1 TB. ground cumin

2 TB. all-purpose flour

2 cups chicken or vegetable broth

4-6 new red potatoes, diced

1 (4 oz.) can diced green chiles

2 red bell peppers, roasted, seeded, and chopped

1 (10 oz.) package frozen corn

2 cups milk

½ cup heavy cream

½ tsp. kosher salt

½ tsp. ground black pepper

Serves 6	
Prep time: 30 minutes	
Cook time: 45 minutes	

1. Heat oil in a large saucepan over high heat. Cook onions and garlic until golden. Add cumin and flour, and stir in until fat is absorbed. Slowly add broth while whisking. Increase heat and bring liquid to a boil, stirring periodically.

2. At the boil, add potatoes and reduce heat. Simmer until tender, about 15-20 minutes. Add chiles, peppers, and corn, and simmer 10 minutes. Add milk, cream, salt, and pepper, and simmer another 5 minutes. Do not return to a boil after milk is added, or it will curdle.

Suggestions: Serve this soup with a garnish of chopped avocado, a dollop of sour cream, a sprinkling of chopped cilantro, and a few tortilla chips on the side.

def•i•ni•tion

Chowder comes from the French word *chaudiere*, which means "cauldron." It is traditionally a fish stew, concocted by fishermen from scraps of the day's catch. In America the all-time favorite is New England clam, and any recipe that resembles it can claim the name *chowder*.

Chicken Soup

Here's the perfect recipe for what ails you.

Serves 6
Prep time: 10 minutes
Cook time: 30 minutes

6 cups chicken stock

1 tsp. dried sage

1 tsp. dried thyme

1 tsp. dried oregano

1 carrot, diced

1 stalk celery, diced

2 cups cooked chicken meat, diced

1 cup fresh or frozen peas

½ tsp. kosher salt

½ tsp. ground black pepper

1. Combine stock, sage, thyme, oregano, carrot, and celery in a saucepan, and simmer until vegetables are tender, about 15 minutes. Add chicken and peas, and cook until they are warmed through, about 5 minutes more. Season with salt and pepper.

Suggestions: Make chicken noodle or chicken with rice soup by adding two cups of cooked pasta or rice with the chicken.

Biblical Culture
The restorative powers of chicken soup are common knowledge in kitchens around the world. Persian writings in the tenth century suggest its use as a cure-all. Korean chicken soup, *sagyetang*, is believed to not only cure illness but also prevent it. University studies suggest that chicken soup acts as an anti-inflammatory, easing the discomfort of symptoms.

Beef and Barley Soup

This classic combination is best when it's made at home.

2 TB. olive oil	6 cups beef broth
1 large yellow onion, diced	1 bay leaf
1 carrot, diced	1 tsp. dried oregano
1 stalk celery, diced	1 cup pearled barley
2 cups cooked shredded beef	½ tsp. kosher salt
3 tomatoes, diced	½ tsp. black pepper

Serves 6
Prep time: 10 minutes
Cook time: 30 minutes

1. Heat oil in a large soup pot over high heat. Brown onion until golden. Add carrot, celery, and beef, and cook 10 minutes, stirring until browned. Add tomatoes, broth, bay leaf, and oregano, and simmer 30 minutes. Add barley, salt, and pepper, and simmer another 30 minutes until tender.

Suggestions: Add another grain, such as brown rice or wild rice. Beans would be another healthful, and hearty, addition. Cook them first or use canned beans.

Kitchen Tips

Use pearled or polished barley in this recipe. If you use hulled barley, you must increase the cooking. Hulled is healthier as it has the bran intact, but it takes up to an hour to cook. Pearled barley has the bran removed and is done in about half the time.

Thai Chicken Soup with Coconut

In Thailand the name of this soup is *Thom Kha Gai*. The flavor combination of lime, coconut, and ginger is heavenly.

Serves 6
Prep time: 20 minutes
Cook time: 60 minutes

1 (5.6 oz.) can coconut milk

4 cups chicken broth

¼ cup fresh ginger, grated

2 TB. grated lemon zest

2 TB. grated lime zest

4 TB. *fish sauce* (*nam pla*) or soy sauce

2 TB. red chili flakes

3 cups cooked chicken, shredded

¼ cup fresh cilantro, chopped

1. In a large soup pot, combine coconut milk, chicken broth, ginger, lemon zest, and lime zest. Bring to a boil, reduce heat, and simmer 30 minutes. Strain and return liquid to the pot.

2. Add sauce, chili, and chicken, and simmer 30 minutes more. Serve hot with lime wedges and cilantro.

Suggestions: Serve Thai iced tea with this soup. Steep together 6 tea bags (standard black tea), 1 (4 oz.) can evaporated milk, ¼ cup honey, 1 TB. each ground cinnamon and ground cardamom. Serve over crushed ice.

def•i•ni•tion

Fish sauce, also called *nam pla* in Thailand, is an ancient condiment, well loved by the Romans and produced throughout the Mediterranean region. They called it *garum*. You can find it wherever Asian groceries are sold.

Fish Soup with Saffron and Rice

Be careful not to overcook this soup. The fish can easily become rubbery.

3 TB. olive oil

1 large yellow onion, diced

4 cloves garlic, minced

8 new potatoes, quartered

3 carrots, diced

1 bay leaf

1 tsp. ground fennel seeds

1 sprig fresh thyme

3 large tomatoes, diced

½ tsp. (a large pinch) saffron threads, infused in ¼ cup hot water

1 cup dry white wine

3 cups fish broth

1 cup brown rice

1 lb. firm fish, such as halibut, cod, or haddock

1 red bell pepper, diced fine

Serves 6
Prep time: 30 minutes
Cook time: 90 minutes

1. Heat oil in a large saucepan over high heat. Brown onion until golden. Add garlic, potatoes, carrots, bay leaf, fennel, and thyme, and cook 10 minutes, stirring until browned. Add tomatoes, saffron water, wine, and broth; reduce heat and simmer 30 minutes.

2. Add rice and simmer another 30 minutes until tender. Add fish and bell pepper, and simmer 10 minutes until firm. Serve immediately.

Suggestions: Serve lots of crusty bread to sop up this luscious broth.

Kitchen Tips

Saffron is expensive because harvesting it is backbreaking. The stigma of its low-growing flowers must be plucked one by one. Luckily, you don't need much. The best way to utilize what you have is to steep it in a little liquid before adding it to a recipe. Alternatively, you can carefully toast saffron threads and crumble them into a pot. Both methods open up the cells of the spice, allowing them to release more oils and pigment into a recipe.

Creamy Potato and Onion Soup

The key to this recipe is the caramelized onions. The slow, steady heat releases all the onions' sugar, making them creamy and sweet. Don't cook them too fast, or they'll become bitter.

Serves 6
Prep time: 15 minutes
Cook time: 45 minutes

3 TB. olive oil

3 large yellow onions, diced

3 cloves garlic

2 stalks celery, chopped

2 TB. whole-wheat flour

4 cups vegetable stock

2 lb. russet potatoes, peeled and chopped

2 cups milk

½ cup heavy cream

½ tsp. kosher salt

½ tsp. black pepper

1. Heat oil in a large soup pot over high heat. Add onions, reduce heat to low, and cook, stirring, until tender and golden, about 30 minutes. Add garlic and celery, and cook until tender. Add flour and cook until fat is absorbed. While whisking, slowly add stock. Increase heat and bring liquid to a boil, stirring periodically. At the boil, add potatoes and reduce heat. Simmer until potatoes are tender, about 15-20 minutes.

2. Allow soup to cool for 15-20 minutes, then purée. Return to the heat, add milk, cream, salt, and pepper, and simmer another 5 minutes before serving. Do not return to a boil after milk is added, or it will curdle.

Suggestions: Make this delectable soup with leftover mashed potatoes or with other roasted roots, like butternut squash or celery root.

 Kitchen Tips

Potato soup is really just a flavorful, thinned-down version of mashed potatoes. With that in mind, choose the same potato you would for any good mash. Avoid the waxy new potatoes, and stick with the bakers: russet, Burbank, and Idaho.

Split Pea Soup

Split peas are *legumes*, edible seeds inside a seed pod. The most common ones are beans and peanuts. When the seeds are dried, they are called *pulses*.

2 cups split peas, soaked in 8 cups water overnight, then rinsed

3 TB. olive oil

1 large yellow onion, chopped

2 stalks celery, chopped

1 carrot, chopped

3 cloves garlic, chopped

1 bay leaf

1 tsp. dried thyme

Water to cover

½ tsp. kosher salt

½ tsp. black pepper

Serves 4	
Prep time: 24 hours	
Cook time: 2 hours	

1. Heat oil in a large saucepan over high heat. Cook onion, celery, carrot, and garlic until tender and light brown. Add bay leaf, thyme, and peas; cover with cold water, and bring to a boil. Reduce heat and simmer 1-2 hours, until peas are tender. Season with salt and pepper.

Suggestions: Serve with a big dollop of plain yogurt or sour cream and a hearty hunk of brown bread.

Kitchen Tips

I love cooking dried beans, but I often forget the overnight presoak. Fortunately, I have a quickish method; bring the dried beans to a boil for 5 minutes; then cover and set aside off the heat for an hour. Cut a bean in half to see if it is fully soaked. If it is, it will have an even color throughout. If not, there will be a dry core.

Chapter 8

Salads

In This Chapter

- ◆ Salads for meals and starters
- ◆ Great greens and crisp veggies
- ◆ Bright and aromatic dressings

"Better is a dinner of herbs where love is, than a stalled ox and hatred therewith." (Proverbs 15:17 KJV)

Salads are a refreshing way to get your recommended three cups of vegetables every day. They can accompany lunch or dinner, help curb hunger in the middle of the afternoon, and even serve as the entire meal.

Choose Green

There are dozens of varieties of lettuce on the market, but most salad bowls contain iceberg. This lettuce, pale, bland, and devoid of much nutritional value, is synonymous with salad to most Americans.

In fact, iceberg lettuce has the least nutrition of any lettuce. Dark green vegetables are the ones that keep us healthy. Spinach, romaine, bib lettuce, watercress, chicory, arugula, parsley, basil, and cilantro are all dark, which is an indication of their nutritional value. Eating dark greens, full of iron, antioxidants, vitamin C, beta carotene, calcium, and folic acid, and low in calories (1 cup has about 10 calories) is much better for you than taking a multivitamin. Each leaf contains an enormous amount of vital fiber. What's more, the green pigment, chlorophyll, is a natural breath freshener. So eat your greens!

Washing

Before you add any of the several kinds of greens called for in this chapter to a recipe, washing and thoroughly drying them is imperative. The best method of washing greens is to submerge them in cold water for a couple minutes, then pull them out of the water, allowing dirt and sand to sink to the bottom. Dry the greens in a salad spinner, or let them drain in a colander before patting them dry with paper towels. If you don't dry them, your wet greens will water down the salad dressing.

Many salad greens are now available prewashed, trimmed, and ready to pour into the salad bowl. This is super-convenient, but beware. Once the bag is opened, these lettuces deteriorate much quicker than lettuce still attached to a head.

Onions

Regardless of the cuisine, onions are an important element of cooking. Unfortunately, when eaten raw, they tend to linger on the palate. Luckily, I have a trick to help combat this side effect. Soak onions in cold water before adding them to a recipe. The harsh oils that offend the breath will leach out, but the flavor stays in. The longer the soak, the better. Potent onions can soak overnight, but change the water frequently.

Oils

Oil is an essential part of a salad. Without oil, the dressing would slip off the lettuce and pool at the bottom of the bowl. Oil transfers flavor throughout a recipe like no other ingredient can. But while we need it, we don't need very much.

The oils included in these recipes, mainly olive and peanut oil, contain mostly mono- and polyunsaturated fats, a.k.a. the heart-healthy fats. They help to raise the body's level of high-density lipoprotein (HDL, the good cholesterol). These oils have fairly distinctive flavors and can easily overpower a dish, so use a light hand. If a neutral oil is called for, canola is a good heart-healthy choice.

Also, many of these recipes include mayonnaise. If you are watching your cholesterol, choose one of the fat-free products available or make a substitution. Nonfat plain yogurt is a tangy option, as is light sour cream. You can also purée nonfat cottage cheese or silken tofu in the blender. The texture is a little looser, but the overall effect is the same.

Mixed Green Salad with Lemon Vinaigrette

In most markets, mixed salad greens are available premixed, precut, prewashed, and sealed in bags. Remember these bagged greens spoil quickly once opened, so buy only what you need, and if you can, buy loose mixed greens.

Serves 4
Prep time: 30 minutes

Juice and zest of 1 lemon (about 2 TB.)

½ tsp. kosher salt

½ tsp. ground black pepper

1 TB. Dijon mustard

½ cup olive oil

4 cups mixed greens

1. In a large bowl, whisk together lemon juice and zest, salt, pepper, and mustard. Slowly drizzle in oil while whisking. Add greens, toss to coat, and serve immediately.

Suggestions: Mix your own greens, and choose from a variety of colors, textures, and flavors. Use mild butter or romaine, spicy arugula, mustard, or dandelion, bitter curly or Belgian endive, and colorful radicchio or nasturtium petals.

Biblical Culture

Lettuce was known in biblical times but was bitter in flavor and considered more of a medicine than a luncheon. The wild lettuce that grew in the Fertile Crescent contained a narcotic similar to opium and was used as a sleep aid by the Greeks. The Romans considered it a source of male virility.

5-Bean Salad

This recipe is a great choice for pool parties because it has no mayonnaise and can sit out in the sun all day. It actually tastes better when it's at room (or patio) temperature. It's also a big hit with kids, probably because it's loaded with honey.

½ cup honey

⅓ cup canola oil

½ cup tarragon vinegar

½ cup white wine vinegar

½ tsp. kosher salt

½ tsp. ground black pepper

1 red bell pepper, chopped

1 (15 oz.) can kidney beans

1 (15 oz.) can yellow wax beans

1 (15 oz.) can green string beans

1 (15 oz.) can garbanzo beans

1 (15 oz.) can navy beans

1 small purple onion, chopped and soaked in cold water for 15-20 minutes

2 scallions, chopped

Serves 4
Prep time: 10 minutes, plus at least 2 hours cooling time

1. In a large bowl, combine honey, oil, tarragon and wine vinegars, salt, and pepper, and mix well. Add bell pepper, kidney beans, wax beans, string beans, garbanzo beans, navy beans, and onion. Toss well to coat, cover with plastic wrap, and refrigerate for two hours or overnight.

Suggestions: For a Southwestern version of this salad, add 1 (4 oz.) can of chopped green chilies, 1 cup chopped cilantro, 1 tablespoon ground cumin, 1 teaspoon chili powder; and replace the tarragon vinegar with fresh lime juice. Then, in addition to the original five beans, add 1 can of rinsed black beans and 1 can of corn. Garnish with a dollop of sour cream and crispy fried corn tortilla strips.

Biblical Culture

Legumes were a well-used source of protein in biblical times. However, their choices were more limited, with only lentils, garbanzos, and fava beans.

Tomato, Mozzarella, and Basil Salad

The name of this salad is *Insalata Caprese*, which means salad in the style of Capri. Capri is an island in the Bay of Naples, in the region of Campania. The colors of this salad are said to represent the colors of the Italian flag.

Serves 4
Prep time: 30 minutes

2 ripe tomatoes, thinly sliced

8 oz. buffalo Mozzarella, thinly sliced

1 cup large fresh basil leaves

¼ cup extra virgin olive oil

½ tsp. sea salt

½ tsp. freshly cracked black pepper

1. On each serving plate arrange alternately slices of tomato, mozzarella, and basil leaves. Drizzle with olive oil, sprinkle with salt and pepper, and serve.

Suggestions: If your tomatoes are not ripe, your mozzarella is not buffalo, or your basil leaves are not fresh, consider making another salad.

Kitchen Tips

Mozzarella di Bufala Campana is fresh (not aged) cheese made from the milk of water buffalos. It is exported to the United States and copied by several cheese manufacturers. Fresh mozzarella is sold floating in mild brine and should be consumed within two days of purchase.

Chinese Chicken Salad

This popular salad is a meal in itself.

2 TB. peanut oil

1 TB. sesame oil

1 tsp. grated lemon zest

3 TB. lemon juice

2 TB. honey

¼ cup soy sauce

2 cups cooked chicken, diced or shredded

2 cups romaine lettuce, shredded

2 cups Napa cabbage, shredded

2 medium carrots, sliced thin on an angle

2 scallions, sliced thin on an angle

1 (8 oz.) can sliced water chestnuts

2 cups *rice noodles*, fried

¼ cup cashews, chopped

Serves 4
Prep time: 60 minutes, plus 30-60 minutes cooling time

1. In a large bowl, whisk together peanut and sesame oil, lemon zest and juice, honey, and soy sauce. Add chicken, lettuce, cabbage, carrots, scallions, and water chestnuts. Toss thoroughly to coat all ingredients with dressing. Chill for 30-60 minutes.

2. Just before serving, toss in rice noodles and cashews.

Suggestions: Intimidated by rice noodles? Try crispy chow mien noodles or fried wontons.

def•i•ni•tion

Rice noodles (a.k.a. rice stick noodles or cellophane noodles) look like thin threads of plastic or fishing line. When fried, they puff up into airy, crunchy noodles. Fry small chunks of rice noodles in 1 inch of peanut oil heated to 375°F. When they hit the hot oil, they puff up quickly, so be prepared. Drain on paper towels.

Caesar Salad

This salad, first created in the 1920s by Tijuana restaurateur Caesar Cardini, is very popular but seldom made at home. Don't be alarmed by the appearance of a raw egg yolk. Yolks are necessary to create an emulsified dressing. If your eggs are chilled and you, your equipment, and your kitchen are clean, there is no danger. For your information, the majority of salmonella cases are caused by unwashed fruit (usually melons), not raw eggs or meat. According to the Center for Science in the Public Interest (CSPI), from 1990 to 2001 poultry accounted for 121 salmonella outbreaks and produce accounted for 80. But in 2002-2003, produce accounted for 31 salmonella outbreaks and poultry accounted for 29.

Serves 4
Prep time: 20 minutes

1 egg yolk

1 clove garlic, minced

4 anchovy filets, minced

3 TB. lemon juice

¼ cup olive oil

Salt and pepper to taste

1 head romaine lettuce, washed, dried, and chopped

½ cup freshly grated Parmesan cheese

1 cup garlic croutons

12 anchovy filets

Kitchen Tips

Buy croutons at any supermarket, or easily make your own. Dice bread, and toss with olive oil, garlic, and herbs. Spread onto a cookie sheet and bake until toasted, about 5 minutes at 400°F.

1. In a large bowl, whisk together egg yolk, garlic, anchovies, and lemon juice. Slowly drizzle in olive oil while whisking, taking 3-4 minutes to add oil. Season with salt and pepper, then set aside.

2. Add romaine, Parmesan, and croutons. Toss well to coat; then divide between four plates. Top each salad with three anchovy filets and serve.

Suggestions: This salad was traditionally made tableside, assembled by skilled waiters. You can do this for your guests, too. Get a nice big wooden bowl, and build the salad from the dressing up. (Practice at least once before you go in front of an audience.)

Waldorf Salad

Created in the 1890s by the maitre d' of the Waldorf Astoria Hotel in New York City, the original version used only apples, celery, and mayonnaise. Nuts and grapes appeared in recipes starting in the 1920s.

2 red apples, diced, skin on

4 stalks celery, diced

1 cup walnuts, toasted and chopped

1 cup green or red grapes, halved

1 cup mayonnaise

Serves 4
Prep time: 20 minutes

1. In a large bowl combine apples, celery, walnuts, and grapes. Toss with mayonnaise to coat, and serve chilled.

Suggestions: Lighten this salad by replacing mayonnaise with nonfat plain yogurt.

Kitchen Tips

Use any apple you like in this recipe. It should be one that you enjoy eating out of hand. The Fuji is my personal favorite. This salad is also quite good when made with pears.

Cucumber Yogurt Salad

This salad is known as *raita* throughout India, and its cooling effect is a welcome relief during a spicy meal of curries.

Serves 4
Prep time: 20 minutes, plus at least 1 hour cooling time

1 cup nonfat plain yogurt

1 tsp. ground cumin

2 TB. chopped fresh mint

½ tsp. kosher salt

2 cucumbers, peeled, seeded, and sliced

1 medium purple onion, sliced and soaked in cold water for 15-20 minutes

1. In a large bowl, mix together yogurt, cumin, mint, and salt. Add cucumbers and onion. Wrap and refrigerate for one to two hours to allow flavors to mingle. Serve chilled.

Suggestions: Turn this into Greek *tzatziki* by adding dill, oregano, and parsley.

 Kitchen Tips

To seed a cucumber, peel it, slice it in half lengthwise, and remove the seeds by scraping down the center core with a spoon. If you have the opportunity to buy English cucumbers, do so. They have fewer seeds and cause less burps.

Potato Salad

This all-American favorite is practically a requirement at backyard barbecues, block parties, and picnics. Serve it well chilled. The mayonnaise contains protein that, when warm, provides a haven for bacteria.

2 lb. new red potatoes	**½ tsp. kosher salt**
4 cups ice water	**½ tsp. ground black pepper**
1½ cups mayonnaise	**1 cup celery, chopped**
2 TB. Dijon mustard	**1 cup yellow onion, chopped and soaked in cold water for 15-30 minutes**
¼ cup cider vinegar	
½ tsp. grated nutmeg	

Serves 4
Prep time: 40 minutes, plus 1 hour cooling time

1. Cover potatoes with cold water and bring to a boil over high heat. At the boil, turn the heat down to medium and simmer until tender, about 20 minutes. Drain potatoes, and submerge in a bowl of ice water until cool. Cut cooled potatoes into quarters.

2. In a large bowl, combine mayonnaise, mustard, vinegar, nutmeg, salt, and pepper, and mix thoroughly. Add potatoes, celery, and onion, and toss to coat vegetables evenly with dressing. Chill potato salad for one hour before serving. Store refrigerated for two days.

Suggestions: Enjoy a hint of tangy pickles? Add ¼ cup pickle relish to mayonnaise. Also try adding capers or dill.

Kitchen Tips

The most important ingredient in a potato salad is, of course, the potato. The salad should have firm chunks of potato, not a mealy mash. Choose a potato with low starch, also known as waxy potatoes. Waxy potatoes include the new potato, round red, yellow, round white, and purple-skinned potatoes, as well as the heirloom-variety called fingerlings. Baker, russet, Idaho, and Burbank potatoes are all mealy and more suited to baked potatoes and french fries than potato salad.

Curried Chicken Salad

This exotic-sounding salad shows up in all kinds of places. It makes a terrific lunch, a nice summer entrée, and a swanky passed hors d'oeuvre.

Serves 4
Prep time: 30 minutes

½ cup mayonnaise

2 TB. *curry powder*

2 TB. lemon juice

1 tsp. salt

½ tsp. pepper

3 cups cooked chicken

½ cup celery, chopped

1 cup green apple, chopped

½ cup raisins

½ cup sliced almonds, toasted

1. In a large bowl combine mayonnaise, curry powder, lemon juice, salt, and pepper, and mix well. Add chicken, celery, apple, and raisins, and toss to coat. Before serving, top with almonds.

Suggestions: To turn this salad into an hors d'oeuvre, perch it on tiny lettuce leaves, spread it onto apple and cucumber slices, dip into it with crackers, or stuff it into cream puff shells.

def•i•ni•tion

Curry powder is a blend of spices used in various Asian cuisines, most notably Indian. The mix varies from region to region, using specific herbs, seeds, and spices. The best curry powder is ground fresh, but you can also purchase it ready-made in any major supermarket. The most common spices found in a store-bought curry include turmeric, cumin, cinnamon, fennel, cardamom, clove, and pepper. Spice blends vary in degree of heat, color, and potency. Curry pastes are also available, which you can use interchangeably in this recipe.

Orange, Fennel, and Onion Salad

This salad blends three flavors and textures in a most refreshing way.

Juice and zest of 1 lime (about 1 TB. juice)

½ tsp. honey

¼ tsp. kosher salt

¼ tsp. ground black pepper

¼ tsp. cayenne pepper

¼ cup chopped fresh mint

½ cup olive oil

3 sweet oranges, peeled, sectioned, and diced

1 bulb fennel, shaved thin

1 medium purple onion, chopped and soaked in cold water for 15-30 minutes

Serves 4
Prep time: 30 minutes, plus at least 1 hour cooling time

1. In a large bowl, mix together lime zest and juice, honey, salt, black pepper, cayenne, and mint. Drizzle in olive oil while whisking. Add oranges, fennel, and onion, and toss to coat. Cover and refrigerate at least one hour to allow flavors to mingle.

Suggestions: Use this salad as an accompaniment to grilled chicken or fish.

Biblical Culture

Citrus fruits were known in the Holy Land. Although no mention is made of them in the Bible, there is some evidence that the Hebrews would have known citrus while in exile in Babylon. Wall paintings in an Egyptian temple in Karnak depict a citrus-like fruit, which would put them in the region as early as 1400 B.C. Alexander the Great brought citrus back from India and began cultivation of it by the fourth century B.C. Tiles at Pompeii show they were in wide use by the first century A.D.

Roasted Beet Salad

You may have only seen beets pickled at your local salad bar. But if you have never had a plain, roasted beet, you are in for a treat. Beets are sweet, juicy, and loaded with folic acid, potassium, calcium, and antioxidants. They come in different colors, too. Look for golden, pink, and striped varieties.

Serves 4-6
Prep time: 1 hour, plus 1 hour cooling time

5 large beets, scrubbed

¼ cup olive oil, divided

2 TB. raspberry vinegar

1 TB. fresh thyme, chopped

1 TB. fresh oregano, chopped

2 TB. fresh grated or prepared horseradish

2 cloves garlic, minced

¼ cup raspberries

¼ cup olive oil

1 medium purple onion, chopped and soaked in cold water for 15-30 minutes

4 cups fresh spinach leaves, shredded

¼ cup dried cranberries

¼ cup sliced almonds

1. Preheat oven to 450°F. Coat beets lightly in 1 tablespoon olive oil, and wrap together in one large piece of foil. Bake until tender to the touch, about one hour. Cool completely, then peel and slice thinly.

2. In a large bowl, whisk together vinegar, thyme, oregano, horseradish, garlic, and raspberries. Drizzle in remaining oil while whisking. Add beets, onion, spinach, and toss to coat. Cover and refrigerate one hour to allow flavors to mingle. Top with cranberries and almonds just before serving.

Suggestions: Add more crunch with chopped radishes, bell peppers, celery, or jicama.

Kitchen Tips

The lovely fuchsia color of beets looks great on your plate but not on your hands. As soon as you unwrap the cooked beets, you will understand why beets were prized for centuries as a textile dye. Consider wearing gloves for peeling and slicing your beets. You may also want an apron.

Parsley Wheat Salad

The salad goes by the name *tabouleh* (tabbouleh or tabouli) and is a standard item on every Middle Eastern menu. Originally from Syria and Lebanon, it has become popular in South America, thanks to Middle Eastern immigrants.

1 cup bulgur wheat

2 cups water

Juice of 1 lemon

½ tsp. kosher salt

½ tsp. ground black pepper

¼ cup olive oil

1 cup Italian parsley

1 small white onion, chopped and soaked in cold water for 15-30 minutes

1 large tomato, diced

Serves 4-6
Prep time: 30 minutes

1. Combine bulgur and water and soak for 30 minutes, until tender. Drain thoroughly.

2. In a large bowl whisk together lemon juice, salt, pepper, and olive oil. Add parsley, onion, tomato, and bulgur. Toss to coat.

Suggestions: Serve with lemon wedges and spears of romaine lettuce.

Kitchen Tips

Bulgur is wheat that has been dehulled and parboiled. It requires no cooking but must be soaked in water to soften. Cracked wheat has not been parboiled and must be cooked. To use it in this recipe, boil 2 cups water, reduce heat, add cracked wheat, cover, and simmer 15 minutes, until tender.

Part 4

Main Dishes

The family table provides unity and balance in our otherwise hectic world. Coming together for a family meal creates stability and has been shown to improve performance in kids and adults. Kids who eat at a regular time with the entire family are shown to be less depressed, are less likely to use drugs, and show high motivation and achievement. Adults exhibit less stress and stronger relationships overall.

The recipes in these chapters provide a number of options for everyday eating. Classic meals have been adjusted to meet biblical dietary guidelines and modern health concerns. But most importantly, they are delicious.

Chapter 9

Red Meats

In This Chapter

- ◆ The perfect cut of meat
- ◆ Ground beef, grilled, stuffed, and baked
- ◆ Marinades, sauces, and gravies

"For the kingdom of God is not meat and drink; but righteousness, and peace, and joy in the Holy Ghost." (Romans 14:17 KJV)

Today, a well-raised, juicy flavorful steak is the epitome of fine dining. Connoisseurs pay top dollar for Japanese Kobe beef, the black-haired Wagyu cattle that are selectively bred, pampered on a diet of sake and beer mash, and massaged daily. The belief is that a relaxed cow is a delicious cow. Our ancient forbearers held this animal in similar esteem.

Ancient Cows

The modern cow is a descendant of the now-extinct aurochs. From Paleolithic cave paintings and archaeological finds, scholars believe that man tamed this massive, aggressive beast in several places simultaneously.

Archaeological discoveries of stone altars from sixth century B.C. Mesopotamia, Africa, and India include nearby piles of aurochs' bone fragments. Included are numerous skulls with frontal damage, indicating that these beasts were captured and kept for sacrificial use.

To capture such beasts, man probably lured them with salt licks, captured young animals, and raised them in enclosures. Hand-fed and prevented from exercise, the animals would have developed fatty meat. Over time, they were bred, becoming gentle and dependant on their captors for food.

Cattle's Role in Ancient Culture

Cattle and cows are referenced frequently in the Bible but more often in terms of rituals, sacrifices, and paganism than in terms of food. Meat, in general, was reserved for the wealthy or for special feasts. But even in those circumstances, lambs were the preferred meat with goats running a close second.

Cows were large and far more valuable for their draft power. Plowing fields, crushing grains, and pulling carts were their main vocations, and their dung was a vital fuel source. Even when an animal was consumed, the logistics of slaughtering it would have been daunting. Preservation methods revolved around salting, which was not very sophisticated. Unless there was a real crowd to feed, a lamb was more suitable.

Choosing Beef

We no longer harness cattle power, but its meat, milk, and hide easily make the cow our most important domesticated animal.

Today, beef and veal are readily available in modern supermarkets, and for the most part, quality is high. The United States Department of Agriculture (USDA) grades meat for consumption based on muscle-to-bone and fat-to-muscle ratios. Grading is voluntary, and the producer must pay for it. Beef grades, from best to worst, are Prime, Choice, and Select. Lesser grades, used mainly for processed meat products, include Standard, Commercial, and Utility. Grades are stamped in purple on the outer carcass of the animal and are usually prominently advertised by retailers, especially when the grade is high.

Determine the meat you choose by the cooking method you intend to use. Fast, dry-heat cooking, such as grilling and roasting, is best done with lean and tender cuts of meat. Reserve slow, moist cooking for tougher cuts.

Cooking Methods

Meat is muscle, and tough meat is tough because it is a muscle that gets a lot of movement. The lower body parts, such as the legs, shanks, briskets, and round cuts, are full of tough connective tissues. In biblical times, the meat of work animals would have been much tougher than our cattle today. The loin, which runs down the animal's back, sees very little motion and is therefore tender and lean.

If the connective tissue, laced throughout lower cuts of meat, is cooked too hot or too fast, it will toughen. But gentle, moist heat slowly melts those tough fibers away. This explains the prevalence of stewed and braised meat dishes in ancient cuisines.

Braising and stewing are simple techniques and can be done either on the stove top or in the oven. Both methods need a tight-fitting lid or well-placed foil to keep the steam inside the pot. On the stove, keep the flame very low, and check the water level periodically.

Another method of tenderizing meat is the marinade. Acid breaks down protein tissue, so ingredients like vinegar and wine are used, often in conjunction with slow, moist cooking, to soften tough cuts.

Reserve sautéing and grilling for more tender meats. Always preheat the pan or grill so that the meat is seared when it goes on. This quick heat keeps the meat tender and prevents it from sticking. You can heat a grill with anything, including gas flame, charcoal, or wood. Heat wood or briquettes white-hot before starting. If you are grill-less, make the same recipes under the broiler.

For the Love of Beef

Fat that is marbled throughout a piece of meat melts with heat, and its flavor then penetrates the muscle. More fat means more flavor. In today's world we appreciate, and even expect, this level of flavor in our meat, despite full knowledge that saturated fat contributes to elevated cholesterol levels and eventually coronary artery disease.

This appetite for fatty beef has drastically changed the landscape of modern agriculture. Today's farmers breed and raise cattle to provide the most meat with the least cost. According to the USDA, the average American consumes 67 pounds of beef every year.

In biblical times these animals fed on fiber-rich plant life unsuitable for human consumption. Cows today compete with humans for food, consuming grain grown on valuable fertile soil. In the United States, half of the water and 80 percent of harvested grain goes to our livestock.

Pasturing cows had a noticeable environmental impact during the time of Jesus. Much of the land was cultivated, and pasturing was forbidden, except in the wild, because of the damage it did to the land. Today, our herds are still a burden on our ecosystems. Waste seeps into groundwater and contaminates nearby crops. Grazing results in defoliation and erosion. And today, the United Nations recognizes livestock as one of the largest contributors of greenhouse gases.

The damage we do to ourselves and our environment through the consumption of red meat is undeniable. Meat was a rarity in biblical times, and the fatted animals were reserved for special feasts. The key for us is moderation. We would do well to remember that a leaner diet is healthier overall and save the fatted calf for truly worthy occasions.

The Hamburger

The origin of the hamburger sandwich is hotly disputed, with Connecticut, Texas, Wisconsin, the St Louis World's Fair, and, of course, Hamburg, Germany, all taking a claim. Regardless of its beginning, it is a true American original.

2 lb. (85-90 percent lean) ground beef

½ tsp. kosher salt

½ tsp. black pepper

4 large hamburger buns, toasted

1 medium purple onion, sliced and soaked in cold water for 15-30 minutes

1 ripe beefsteak tomato, sliced

6-8 large lettuce leaves, washed and dried

Assorted pickles

Ketchup

Mustard

Mayonnaise

Thousand Island dressing

Serves 6
Prep time: 30 minutes
Cook time: 15 minutes

1. Divide hamburger into six equal portions. Work meat in your hand, patting out air and compacting meat. Form portions into ½-inch thick discs and make hole in very center of each with your finger.

2. Preheat the grill on high heat. Place burgers over direct heat, and cook 2-3 minutes with the lid closed. Open the lid, flip burgers, and cook another 2-3 minutes, or to desired doneness. If burgers do not come off the grill easily for the first flip, close the lid and cook another minute. Serve on buns, and let your guests doctor them up any way they like.

Suggestions: Homemade Thousand Island dressing is much better than the bottled stuff. The standard method mixes 1 cup mayonnaise, ½ cup ketchup, and 2 teaspoons lemon juice. If you'd like a healthier version, mix 1 cup plain nonfat yogurt, 2 tablespoons tomato paste, 2 tablespoons lemon juice, 1 tsp. Dijon mustard, 2 tablespoons grated onion, salt, and pepper.

Kitchen Tips

This recipe calls for poking a hole in the center of each patty, which keeps it from puffing up into a ball on the grill. Another trick for juicy burgers is to resist pressing the burger onto the grill with your spatula. It pushes all the yummy burger juice out.

Shish Kebab

The name means "skewer of roasted meat," and similar dishes are found throughout Eastern Europe, the Middle East, and Asia. Both metal and wooden skewers work fine, but always soak wooden ones in warm water for at least 30 minutes so they won't ignite.

Serves 4
Prep time: 1 hour to overnight
Cook time: 30 minutes

2 lb. beef top round, top sirloin, or lamb shoulder, cut into 2-inch cubes

1 bottle red wine

2 TB. olive oil

1 TB. Worcestershire sauce

1 TB. red wine vinegar

1 TB. dried thyme

1 tsp. kosher salt

1 pint cherry tomatoes

8 oz. small button mushrooms

2 small zucchini, sliced into 2-inch wheels

2 small Chinese eggplant, sliced into 2-inch wheels

1 large yellow onion, quartered

½ cup olive oil

> **Biblical Culture**
>
> Turkish soldiers roasting meat on their swords are said to have originated this dish. But likely the concept began much earlier. The method allows very little food to be cooked over a very small amount of fire.

1. Mix together wine, olive oil, Worcestershire, vinegar, thyme, and salt. Combine with cubed meat in a large zipper bag. Zip tight and massage marinade into beef. Refrigerate for at least one hour or overnight.

2. Preheat grill on high heat. Skewer meat and vegetables separately to ensure even cooking. Brush vegetables with olive oil. Grill meat kebabs over direct high heat for 5-10 minutes, turning frequently to brown evenly. Grill vegetables off direct heat, turning frequently until they are golden brown, about 10 minutes. Remove meat and vegetables from skewers onto platters.

Suggestions: Serve kebabs with a big platter of rice pilaf (Chapter 14) or couscous.

Pot Roast

Pot roast is a cooking method designed to soften tougher, less expensive cuts of meat. The long, low heat breaks down the connective tissue and melts the fatty marbling, adding flavor and moisture to the meat itself. The best cuts for such a dish include chuck and round roasts

3 TB. olive oil	1 (6 oz.) can tomato paste
1 cup whole-wheat flour	4 carrots, diced
1 (3-4 lb.) beef chuck roast	4 new potatoes, quartered
1 large onion, chopped	3 parsnips, diced
1 bay leaf	2 turnips, diced
¼ cup chopped parsley	½ tsp. kosher salt
2 cups red wine	½ tsp. black pepper
2 cups water	

Serves 4-6
Prep time: 30 minutes
Cook time: 3 hours

1. Coat roast evenly with flour and shake off excess. Heat oil in a large pot. Add meat and brown on all sides. Add onion, bay leaf, and parsley, and cook over high heat, stirring, until tender.

2. Add wine and water, and bring to a boil. Reduce the heat to low, cover, and cook at a bare simmer for three hours. During the last 30 minutes of cooking, add carrots, potatoes, parsnips, and turnips, and continue cooking until tender. Remove meat and vegetables, and reduce the cooking liquid to gravy consistency. Season with salt and pepper. Slice meat, arrange on serving plate with vegetables, and top with sauce.

Suggestions: All this dish needs is some crusty French bread to sop up the sauce.

Kitchen Tips

This dish cooks for a long time, and quite a bit of the liquid reduces. For this reason, never add salt until the end. If it were added in the beginning, it would concentrate over time and likely become too salty to eat. Salt also toughens meat, which would defeat the purpose of this slow-cooking method.

Beef Brisket

Brisket is a cut of beef from around the rib cage, which is very thin and full of connective tissue. That makes it terrible for grilling, but perfect for long, slow, moist cooking.

Serves 4-6

Prep time: 30 minutes

Cook time: 3 hours

1 (2-3 lb.) beef brisket

2 large yellow onions, sliced into rings

4 cloves garlic, chopped

¼ cup olive oil

2 cups chopped fresh or canned tomatoes

1 (6 oz.) can tomato paste

2 cups beef broth

½ cup honey

1 can dark beer

1 TB. Worcestershire sauce

1 TB. Tabasco

1 TB. chili powder

1 tsp. dried thyme

1 tsp. black pepper

1. Preheat oven to 300°F. Place brisket at the bottom of a large baking dish, and cover with onion rings. In a separate bowl stir together garlic, oil, tomatoes, tomato paste, broth, honey, beer, Worcestershire, Tabasco, chili powder, thyme, and pepper. Pour mixture over brisket, cover, and bake two hours.

2. After two hours, turn brisket over, stir sauce, and baste meat. Cover and continue cooking another hour until meat easily falls apart.

3. To serve, remove meat from sauce, thinly slice against the grain, arrange on a platter, and cover with pan sauce.

Kitchen Tips

You can buy chili powder ready-made, but if you have the time, freshly ground spices are always better. As soon as a spice is ground, it begins to lose its flavor. Buying spices whole and grinding them yourself is economical and more flavorful. Mix all these ingredients together, then grind to a coarse powder: ½ cup each paprika, dried red New Mexico chilies, cumin, ¼ cup each garlic powder, onion powder, dried oregano, dried thyme, 2 tablespoons each sesame seeds, allspice berries, kosher salt, and 3 cinnamon sticks.

Corned Beef and Cabbage

This dish is associated with the Irish but is not nearly as common in Ireland as it is in the United States. Most corned beef made in Ireland is made for tourists. Pork was the typical meat the Irish preserved with salt and spices, not beef. But when Irish immigrants came to the United States, they used their cooking traditions on the products available here.

1 (3-4 lb.) corned beef brisket

3 large yellow onions, chopped

1 sprig fresh thyme

2 carrots, peeled and chopped into 2-inch pieces

8 new potatoes, scrubbed and left whole

1 green cabbage, washed and cut into quarters

Serves 4-6	
Prep time: 10 minutes	
Cook time: 2½ hours	

1. Place corned beef in a large pot with onions and thyme. Cover with cold water, and bring to a boil over high heat. Reduce the heat and cook at a bare simmer for two hours. Skim residue as necessary.

2. Add carrots, potatoes, and cabbage, and cook another 30 minutes until vegetables are tender.

Suggestions: Slice meat against the grain and arrange on a platter with vegetables. Serve with grainy mustard and horseradish sauce.

def•i•ni•tion

Horseradish is a hot and spicy member of the radish family. (Other members include mustard, brussels sprouts, cauliflower, and kale.) The fresh horseradish looks like a big, dirty, white carrot and can be found in most major supermarkets. Grated fresh, it is commonly mixed with freshly whipped cream. It is also available in prepared form, mixed with vinegar and spices.

Beef Stew

You can easily increase the vegetable content of this recipe to your liking, or add some hearty grains, like barley or brown rice.

Serves 4-6	
Prep time: 30 minutes	
Cook time: 1½ hours	

1 TB. olive oil	1 bay leaf
2 lbs. stew beef cut into 1-inch cubes	6 cups beef stock
2 cups whole-wheat flour	2 large russet potatoes, peeled and diced
2 cloves garlic	2 carrots, diced
1 onion chopped	½ tsp. kosher salt
2 TB. tomato paste	½ tsp. black pepper
1 TB. dried thyme	2 TB. fresh parsley, chopped

Kitchen Tips

Flour is used in this recipe to brown and thicken the sauce. Make a clear sauce by omitting the flour entirely and thickening the sauce by reduction.

1. Coat beef evenly with flour, and shake off excess. Heat oil in a large pot over high heat. Brown meat on all sides. Work in batches if necessary so as not to crowd beef in the pan.

2. Add garlic and onion to beef, and sauté 5 minutes. Add tomato paste, thyme, bay leaf, and stock. Bring to a boil, reduce heat to low, cover, and cook at a bare simmer for an hour. Add potatoes and carrots, cover, and continue cooking another 30 minutes until vegetables are tender. Season with salt and pepper before serving with a sprinkle of fresh parsley on top.

Suggestions: Make Irish stew by using 1 cup dark beer (preferably Guinness Stout). Goulash is also similar but has no potatoes or carrots and includes ¼ cup white vinegar, ¼ cup Hungarian paprika, the zest of 1 lemon, and 1 teaspoon oregano.

Beef Braised in Red Wine

This is known as *Boeuf Bourguignon* in French, beef cooked in the style of Burgundy, the region known for its robust red wines. Any hearty red table wine will work nicely in this dish.

2 lbs. stew beef cut into 1-inch cubes	1 TB. dried thyme
2 cups whole-wheat flour	1 bay leaf
4 shallots, chopped	6 cups red wine
2 cups pearl onions, peeled	¼ cup *cognac* or brandy
8 oz. small button mushrooms	½ tsp. kosher salt
	½ tsp. black pepper

Serves 4-6
Prep time: 30 minutes
Cook time: 2½ hours

1. Heat oil in a large stew pot over high heat. Brown shallots, onions, and mushrooms until tender. Toss beef in flour to coat evenly, and shake off excess. Add to the pot, and brown on all sides. Work in batches if necessary and do not crowd meat in the pan.

2. Add thyme, bay leaf, and wine; bring to a boil, then reduce heat to low. Cover and cook at a bare simmer for two hours until meat is tender. Just before serving, add cognac and simmer for 10 minutes. Season with salt and pepper.

Suggestions: Spoon this stew over buttered noodles, rice, or polenta (Chapter 14).

def•i•ni•tion

> **Cognac** is a city in western France known for its superior aged brandy, distilled from the champagne grapes grown in the region. Substitute any brandy, or omit it completely.

Grilled Rib Eye with Herb Rub

You can use these same instructions for other steaks, too. To get it just the way you want, use an instant-read thermometer to test internal temperatures. Cook the meat to 140°F for rare, 145°F for medium rare, and 150°F for medium.

Serves 2
Prep time: 10 minutes, plus at least 1 hour cooling time
Cook time: 20 minutes

2 TB. dried thyme

2 TB. dried oregano

2 TB. dried parsley

2 TB. granulated garlic

2 TB. onion powder

2 TB. dill seed

½ tsp. kosher salt

½ tsp. black pepper

2 rib eye steaks

1. In a small bowl stir together thyme, oregano, parsley, garlic, onion powder, dill, salt, and pepper. Rub mixture into steaks, coating generously. Cover and refrigerate for at least one hour or overnight.

2. Remove steaks from refrigeration one hour before grilling. Preheat grill on high heat. Grill over direct high heat for 5 minutes. Flip meat over and cook for another 3 minutes for rare, 5 minutes for medium. Remove meat from grill, cover with foil, and rest 5 minutes.

Suggestions: Serve with a green salad and Herb Roasted New Potatoes (Chapter 14).

Kitchen Tips

The rib eye steak, also known as the Delmonico steak, comes from the small end of the rib roast. It has more marbling than other cuts, making it one of the most tender and flavorful steaks available. If your butcher sells the rib eye with the bone in, buy it! The extra fat and moisture from the bone adds flavor and tenderness.

Grilled Marinated Southwestern Flank Steak

In Mexico the name of this dish is *carne asada*, which means "roasted meat." It refers to lime-marinated steak, grilled over an open fire. While Mexican *carne asada* traditionally uses tougher cuts of flank or skirt steak, the dish works great with well-marbled chuck and round steaks as well.

1 bunch cilantro, chopped

5 cloves garlic, chopped

1 bunch green onions, chopped

1-3 jalapeño chilies, chopped

1 TB. ground cumin

1 tsp. black pepper

¼ cup white wine vinegar

2 cups olive oil

Zest and juice of 6 limes

Zest and juice of 1 orange

1 can beer

2-3 lb. beef skirt, flank, or chuck steaks

Serves 4-6
Prep time: 15 minutes, plus 4-12 hour cooling time
Cook time: 30 minutes

1. In a large bowl stir together cilantro, garlic, onions, jalapeños, cumin, and pepper. Add vinegar, oil, lime and orange juice and zest, and beer. Submerge steaks in marinade, cover, and refrigerate for four hours or overnight.

2. Preheat grill on high. Grill over direct high heat for 5 minutes with the lid down. Reduce heat to low, flip meat over, and move off direct heat. Close cover and cook for 10 minutes. Turn and cook to desired doneness with lid open, 5-10 minutes. Remove from grill. Cover with foil and rest 5 minutes.

Suggestions: Slice thin strips against the grain and serve with warm tortillas, Salsa Fresca, and Guacamole (see Chapter 6).

Kitchen Tips

Flank steak is cut from the belly muscle of the cow and is tougher than steaks from the loin or rib, so it must be cooked in a manner designed to tenderize it. Meat can be tenderized by pounding or by soaking in the acid found in wine, citrus juice, or vinegar. Slow, moist cooking also tenderizes. Finally, serve tough cuts like flank in thin slices.

Meatloaf

Meat has been mixed with grains and vegetables for centuries as a means of stretching and economizing. This traditional peasant dish has become an American favorite.

Serves 4-6
Prep time: 15 minutes
Cook time: 55 minutes

2 slices sandwich bread or 1 cup bread scraps or crumbs

½ cup milk

1 egg

¼ tsp. garlic powder

¼ tsp. onion powder

½ tsp. dried oregano

½ tsp. dried basil

½ tsp. chili powder

1½ lb. ground beef

1 cup barbecue sauce (see following recipe)

1. Preheat oven to 350°F. Place bread in a large bowl, and pour milk on top of it. Set aside to soften for 15 minutes. Stir in egg, garlic powder, onion powder, oregano, basil, and chili powder to form paste. Add meat and mix well.

2. Pack meat into the loaf pan, rounding top like a loaf of bread. Bake until brown and bubbly, about 45 minutes. Top with barbecue sauce, and bake an additional 10 minutes to brown.

Suggestions: Lighten this dish with the use of lean ground turkey or chicken. And you can easily leave off the barbecue sauce.

Kitchen Tips

Some cooks prefer their own spice mix to the powdered soup mix. To customize your loaf, try any combination of the following dried spices: garlic, onion, oregano, basil, sage, parsley, rosemary, cumin, chili powder, or cayenne pepper. You can even add pulverized dried mushrooms or sun-dried tomatoes. Grind them yourself in a coffee grinder.

Homemade Barbecue Sauce

This is just one of thousands of barbecue sauce recipes. Make it once, and you'll want to keep playing around with it until you create your own signature blend.

1½ cup tomato sauce

1½ cup coffee

1 cup red wine vinegar

½ cup honey

½ cup molasses

1 TB. Worcestershire sauce

1 TB. chili powder (see recipe under Beef Brisket)

1 TB. black pepper

1 TB. garlic salt

Makes 5 cups of sauce
Prep time: 10 minutes
Cook time: 30 minutes

1. Combine tomato sauce, coffee, vinegar, honey, molasses, Worcestershire, chili powder, pepper, and garlic salt in a medium saucepan, and bring to a boil over high heat. Reduce and simmer for 30 minutes on low, stirring. Cool and store in the refrigerator.

Suggestions: For a smoky sauce, add 2-3 teaspoons of liquid smoke. Spice it up by stirring in 1-4 tablespoons Tabasco and 1 tablespoon cayenne pepper. Make it honey-mustard with ½ cup mustard and additional honey in place of molasses.

Biblical Culture

Ancient peoples did not know barbecue sauce, but they had a popular sauce that appeared as early as eighth century B.C. It was called *garum* and was the ancient precursor to modern fish sauce popular today in the cuisines of Southeast Asia. Made from fish parts that were salted and fermented for months, it was so popular that its production spread throughout the Roman Empire. Ruins of a second century B.C. Roman garum factory can still be seen in Southern Spain, at the site of Baelo Claudia, an ancient fishing metropolis along the Straits of Gibraltar.

Roasted Leg of Lamb

To test the internal temperature of a large lamb roast, insert an instant-read thermometer into the thickest part of the meat away from any bones. For medium rare, cook about 15 minutes per pound, to 140°F. For medium, cook for 20 minutes per pound, to 155°F. For well-done, cook 25 minutes per pound, to an internal temperature of 165°F.

Serves 4-6
Prep time: 30 minutes
Cook time: 2 hours

1 (5-6 lb.) leg of lamb

4 cloves garlic, sliced

½ tsp. kosher salt

½ tsp. black pepper

1 cup whole-wheat flour

1 bunch fresh rosemary

1. Preheat oven to 450°F. Wash and dry lamb, make several short incisions randomly across surface of meat, and insert a slice of garlic into each. Sprinkle salt and pepper over meat, and coat generously with flour. Place leg in roasting pan on a bed of rosemary. Add 2 cups water to the pan, and roast 1½-2 hours to desired doneness. Rest leg at room temperature 15 minutes before carving.

Suggestions: Serve lamb with spicy mustard, or make a traditional mint sauce. Combine 3 cups of mint leaves with ½ tsp. kosher salt and mince. Stir together with 1 tablespoon sugar and ¼ cup hot water, and set aside to cool. Stir in ¼ cup white wine vinegar just before serving.

Biblical Culture

Lamb was a favorite meal throughout the Bible and takes center stage at the Passover Seder. It is a popular meat around the world, except here in the United States, where it is slowly gaining in popularity. There are countless references to sheep throughout Christianity, including Christ as the Good Shepherd (John 10:14).

Chapter 10

Poultry

In This Chapter

◆ Buying smart and carving right

◆ Chicken, turkey, and duck

◆ Roasted, fried, and grilled

"Everything that lives and moves will be food for you. Just as I gave you the green plants, I now give you everything." (Genesis 9:3 NIV)

The only restriction the Bible gives us for birds is a list of those forbidden, which are mainly birds of prey. Domesticated birds and certain foraging wild birds were perfectly acceptable and became part of the ancient diet. Birds of prey do not include birds that hunt worms. The prohibition refers only to birds that hold their prey down with their talons and rip it apart.

But as the world expanded and people began to settle in new and uncharted territories, observant Jews encountered strange new species. And because rabbis knew that not everyone could identify the species listed in the Bible, they simplified the list to four rules. Every bird that is a predator is not kosher; every bird that has a crop (a pouch at the bottom of a chicken's neck used for food storage) is kosher; every bird that has an extra toe is kosher; and every bird that has a gizzard that can be peeled is kosher. These rules were a relief to immigrants encountering turkey for the first time. Today, Israel is the leader in consumption of turkey meat per capita.

Buying Your Bird

You can buy a wide variety of birds at the market. So which one should you pick? Whole chickens are always less expensive than cut-up parts, but unless you possess good butchering skills, it's worth paying a little more for the pre-cut parts. You can make most of the recipes in this chapter with any of the prefabricated chicken pieces in your supermarket.

Whenever possible, buy free-range, organic poultry, and stay away from common chickens. Producers of common chickens raise with profit, not health, in mind as they pack two chickens into a one-foot square pen. These cramped quarters are no doubt stressful, and stress makes chickens weak. Consequently, they are fed antibiotics to fend off disease and are also given growth hormones. This, coupled with lack of exercise, makes them so fat they cannot move, so they live their lives sitting in manure. In addition, they are fed food grown with artificial fertilizers and chemical pesticides. Even if you are indifferent to the chicken's quality of life, you should be concerned about the toxins that you eat.

Several organic options are available in most stores, including organic, free range, and natural birds. Free-range chickens have more flavor because they are allowed to exercise. Natural birds contain nothing synthetic, no preservatives or artificial flavoring or colorings, but standards permit antibiotic and hormone use. Organic birds are fed grains free from chemicals and pesticides. They receive no antibiotics or drugs and must be allowed to go outside and play.

Kosher chickens are organic, free-range, and processed under strict supervision of a rabbi. They are also soaked in salty brine, which gives them a unique flavor.

Cooking Methods

For roasting whole birds, a good-size roasting pan with a rack is ideal, but by no means necessary. I have used cookie sheets and brownie pans. Have no rack? No problem. Use anything to elevate the bird off the base of the pan. A bed of new potatoes or a couple russets cut in half and laid flat-side down work great, and you have the added bonus of yummy potatoes. Carrots, celery, garlic, apples, oranges, and lemons all work, too. I have even resorted to wads of tin foil.

Cast iron is the pan of choice when frying chicken. The heat distributes slowly and evenly, better than any other type of cookware. These skillets are cheap and easy to find at flea markets and garage sales. (Read about seasoning cast iron in Chapter 3). A heavy aluminum pan is the next best choice, and even a countertop deep fryer works.

Marinating

Marinating meat is an ancient form of tenderizing. Wine and vinegar softened tough meat, and spices helped disguise less-than-agreeable flavors that were common in the days before refrigeration.

The best marinated meats soak with as much of the meat submerged for as long as possible. Use a bowl or a pan, or for really good results, try large plastic zipper bags. The plastic helps the marinade cling to the meat.

Law-Abiding Chicken

The biblical dietary law regarding the mixing of dairy and meat includes poultry, so you will find no dairy products in this chapter.

Roast Chicken with Garlic and Lemon

This technique of roasting at high temperatures is a boon to busy cooks. The result is crispy on the outside, juicy on the inside. Plus, it's done in an hour. Set the table!

Serves 4	
Prep time: 10 minutes	
Cook time: 70 minutes	

1 (3-5 lb.) whole chicken, roaster or fryer

1 small yellow onion, chopped

2 lemons, quartered

1 carrot, chopped

5-10 cloves garlic, peeled

1 stalk celery, chopped

1 tsp. salt

4 cups water

½ tsp. pepper

2 TB. whole-wheat flour

1-2 cups water

1 tsp. dried sage

Kitchen Tips

The water at the bottom of the pan keeps your kitchen smoke-free. Roasting at high temperatures causes animal fat to drip into the pan and burn. But the water quickly cools and dilutes the fat.

1. Preheat oven to 500°F. Rinse chicken, remove giblets, and reserve. Bend wings backwards and tuck wing tips behind chicken's back (like he's being cuffed). Place a roasting rack inside a roasting pan, and set bird on the rack, breast facing up. Squeeze lemons over bird; then place lemons and garlic into bird's cavity. Sprinkle with salt and pepper. Fill the bottom of the pan with 1 inch water. Roast for one hour.

2. Meanwhile, put giblets into a small saucepan with onion, carrot, and celery. Cover with water and bring to a boil. Reduce heat, and simmer until roasting chicken is done. Strain out giblets and vegetables, and reserve broth.

3. Remove cooked bird from the oven and let it rest, covered in foil, for 10 minutes. Using tongs, transfer bird to a cutting board. Remove the rack from the pan, and place the roasting pan on a burner over high heat. Take lemon and garlic out of bird and add it to the roasting pan. Over high heat, reduce most water away, then add flour, whisking until all drippings are absorbed. Slowly add broth until gravy reaches desired consistency. Add sage, salt, and pepper, and strain into serving dish.

Suggestions: To serve, use tongs and a sharp knife to cut away the breasts, leg/thigh, and wings portions. Separate the leg from the thigh if you like. Arrange on a serving platter with gravy on the side.

Jerk Chicken

Jerk is a seasoning blend that originated in Jamaica. Recipes vary but always contain chilies, thyme, and allspice.

¼ **cup soy sauce**

¼ **cup sesame oil**

½ **cup rice vinegar**

¼ **cup orange juice**

¼ **cup lime juice**

2 **scallions, chopped**

3 **cloves garlic, chopped**

1 TB. **honey**

1 TB. **ground allspice**

1 TB. **dried thyme**

1 TB. **cayenne pepper**

1 TB. **ground black pepper**

1 tsp. **dried sage**

1 tsp. **ground nutmeg**

1 tsp. **ground cinnamon**

1 tsp. **ground cumin**

1 **scotch bonnet chili, minced**

1 (3-4 lb.) **chicken, cut into serving pieces**

Serves 4-6
Prep time: 20 minutes, plus at least 3 hours cooling time
Cook time: 45 minutes

1. In a large bowl combine soy sauce, oil, vinegar, orange and lime juice, scallions, garlic, honey, allspice, thyme, cayenne, black pepper, sage, nutmeg, cinnamon, cumin, and chili. Mix well. Add chicken, and coat well. Submerge chicken in marinade. Refrigerate at least three hours or overnight.

2. Preheat oven to 400°F. Coat a baking sheet with pan spray. Drain chicken from marinade, spread out onto the baking sheet, and roast 30-45 minutes, until skin is crispy and meat is cooked through.

Suggestions: If you want to grill this chicken, heat the grill on high, then reduce it to low when you add chicken. Cook chicken slowly, with the lid down if possible, to be sure it's cooked through but doesn't burn. Serve with steamed rice.

Kitchen Tips

The scotch bonnet chili is the hottest there is and is, of course, optional. Leave it out entirely, or reduce the heat index by substituting a humble jalapeño.

Chicken and Saffron Rice

In Spanish this dish is called *arroz con pollo* and is an international favorite. This recipe includes saffron, the stigma of a low-growing crocus. It was used as a fabric dye before it was coveted by culinarians. Because the red threads of the stigma must be harvested by hand, it fetches an exorbitant price. The good news is that a little goes a long way.

Serves 4-6
Prep time: 30 minutes
Cook time: 30 minutes

1 (3-4 lb.) chicken, cut into serving pieces

2 TB. olive oil

1 large yellow onion, chopped

1 Anaheim chili pepper, chopped

1 red bell pepper, chopped

1 (4 oz.) can diced green chilies

3 cloves garlic, chopped

3 threads saffron

1 tsp. cumin

1 cup rice

2 cups ripe chopped tomatoes

2 cups chicken stock

1. Heat oil in a large skillet over high heat. Brown chicken on all sides, and remove from the pan. Add onion, chili and red peppers, canned chilies, garlic, saffron, cumin, and rice. Stir well to coat, and cook until tender.

2. Stir in tomatoes and stock, bring to a boil, then reduce the heat to a bare simmer. Return chicken to pan, cover, and simmer 20 minutes, until rice is tender and chicken is cooked through.

Suggestions: Add more vegetables to increase the nutritional value; try carrots, celery, peas, zucchini, diced potatoes, or yams.

Biblical Culture

This dish originated in Spain but took root in every Latin American country. You can guess its origin by the use of saffron, which is common in another Spanish rice dish, *paella*. Many recipes substitute other spices to dye the rice yellow, including annatto and turmeric. If your saffron supply is running low, substitute 1 tablespoon annatto oil or 2 teaspoons turmeric.

Chinese Chicken Stir Fry

The key to this recipe is cooking over very high heat. Woks are designed to hold the heat and transfer it evenly throughout the pan. If you are wok-less, a good sauté pan will do. Remember to keep the stir fry stirring as it cooks.

4 boneless, skinless chicken breasts, cut in strips

2 TB. cornstarch

2 TB. fresh grated ginger

1 tsp. cayenne pepper

¼ cup soy sauce

2 TB. sesame oil

¼ cup sherry

2 TB. honey

¼ cup rice vinegar

3 TB. peanut oil

2 stalks celery, slices

8 oz. mushrooms, sliced

1 cup snow peas

½ cup cashews, chopped

½ cup green onions

Serves 4-6
Prep time: 30 minutes, plus at least 1 hour cooling time
Cook time: 20 minutes

1. In a large bowl combine chicken, cornstarch, ginger, cayenne, soy sauce, oil, sherry, honey, and vinegar. Mix well and marinate at least one hour or overnight.

2. In a wok or sauté pan over high heat, cook chicken in peanut oil, stirring, until done, about 3-4 minutes. Remove chicken from pan and set aside. Continue cooking celery, mushrooms, peas, and cashews in oil until browned. Return chicken to pan, add marinade, and bring to boil. Cook until thick, about 5 minutes. Serve with steamed white rice.

Suggestions: Add as many vegetables as your wok will hold. Try bean sprouts, bamboo shoots, bok choy, baby corn, and water chestnuts.

 Kitchen Tips

Fresh ginger root is available in most supermarkets. Grate it, using the finest holes on your grater, until you reach the fibrous center. Substitute half the amount of ground ginger in this recipe.

Japanese Glazed Chicken Skewers

The name of this dish is *teriyaki* and it is classic Japanese. *Yaki* means "grill," *teri* means "glaze" or "gloss," and the traditional sauce did just that with three ingredients: soy sauce, sake, and mirin, both rice wines. You can prepare any type of meat or fish in this type of marinade before baking, grilling, barbecuing, or frying.

Serves 4-6

Prep time: 15 minutes, plus at least 1 hour cooling time

Cook time: 15 minutes

4 boneless, skinless chicken breasts, cut into strips

2 cups soy sauce

¼ cup sherry

3 cloves garlic, chopped

2 green onions, chopped

2 TB. toasted sesame seeds

1. In a large bowl, combine chicken, soy sauce, sherry, and garlic. Mix well and refrigerate at least one hour or overnight.

2. Soak 20 wooden skewers in hot water for 30 minutes. Heat grill on high. Drain chicken from marinade, and thread onto prepared skewers, weaving in and out of meat. Grill over direct heat for 2-3 minutes per side. Reduce heat and cook until done, about 5 minutes. Transfer to platter and sprinkle with green onions and sesame seeds. Serve with steamed rice.

Suggestions: Sake in the marinade adds a hint of sweet authenticity to this dish. Use it instead of sherry.

Biblical Culture
Small pieces of meat cooked on a skewer is an ancient and international meal. In Persia it is known as *shish kebab*. In French it is a *brochette*. In Portugal they call it *espetada*. Throughout Southeast Asia it is a *satay*. The Russians call it *shashlik*. In Greece, it is *souvlaki*. They are all made slightly differently, but in every language it's yum!

Turkey Mushroom Fricassee

A fricassee is a stew, usually of chicken, veal, or rabbit. What shows up in the fricassee is a matter of preference and, in most cases, includes whatever is on hand. What distinguishes it is that the meat is browned before being stewed.

1 (3-4 lb.) turkey breast, cut into serving pieces

2-4 TB. olive oil

1 large yellow onion, diced

8 oz. mushrooms, sliced

1 tsp. dried thyme

2 TB. whole-wheat flour

2 cups chicken stock

2 cups white wine

½ tsp. kosher salt

½ tsp. ground black pepper

Serves 4-6	
Prep time: 30 minutes	
Cook time: 45 minutes	

1. Heat oil in a large skillet over high heat. Brown turkey, transfer to a platter, and keep warm. Add onion, mushrooms, and thyme. Reduce heat, and cook until tender and golden brown, about 30 minutes.

2. Add flour and cook for 2 minutes, stirring, until oil is absorbed. Slowly add wine and stock while whisking. Increase heat and bring to a boil. Return turkey to pan, reduce heat, and cover. Simmer 10-15 minutes until turkey is cooked through. Remove from heat, and season with salt and pepper.

Suggestions: Add more vegetables, such as peppers, green beans, or squash. Cook them with onions until tender. Serve fricassee with buttered noodles or rice.

Biblical Culture

Turkeys are native to North America and were not known in the Holy Land during biblical times. Wild birds, including quail, pigeon, partridge, and goose, were hunted, and the chicken was domesticated. Turkeys, domesticated by the Aztecs, were introduced to Europe by Spanish explorers.

Turkey Loaf

This is not a dry version of meatloaf, but a deliciously moist recipe in its own right.

Serves 4-6
Prep time: 30 minutes
Cook time: 55 Minutes

3 TB. olive oil

1 small yellow onion, minced

2 stalks celery, minced

2 cloves garlic, minced

2 lb. ground turkey

3 eggs

1 TB. Worcestershire sauce

2 TB. lemon juice

1 tsp. dried sage

1 tsp. dried thyme

1 ½ cup bread crumbs

½ tsp. kosher salt

½ tsp. ground black pepper

1. Heat oil in a large sauté pan over high heat. Add onion, celery, and garlic, and cook until tender and golden. Remove from heat and set aside to cool.

2. Preheat oven to 350°F. In a large bowl, combine turkey, eggs, Worcestershire, lemon juice, sage, thyme, bread crumbs, salt, and pepper. Add cooled onion mixture, and mix together thoroughly. Transfer to loaf pan and pat in place. Bake until cooked through, about 45 minutes. Remove from oven and rest 10 minutes, covered, before serving.

Suggestions: Serve with Glazed Carrots (Chapter 13) and Oven Fries (Chapter 14).

Kitchen Tips

The best way to mix a meatloaf is with your hands. Kneading it like bread ensures that all the ingredients are well distributed. Wash hands well when finished, especially under your nails. Meat protein, even in tiny amounts, will attract bacteria.

Herb Marinated Cornish Game Hens

Games hens make an elegant statement on a plate. But be sure to provide your guests with good sharp knives and plenty of napkins.

4 (1-2 lb.) game hens	2 tsp. dried thyme
¼ cup olive oil	2 tsp. dried rosemary
Zest and juice of 1 lemon	2 tsp. dried tarragon
1 tsp. kosher salt	4 scallions, chopped
½ tsp. black pepper	4 cloves garlic, chopped
½ tsp. paprika	¼-½ cup olive oil, as needed

Serves 4
Prep time: 60 minutes to overnight
Cook time: 60 minutes

1. Rub hens with oil. In a small bowl combine lemon zest and juice, salt, pepper, paprika, thyme, rosemary, tarragon, scallions, and garlic. Place hens in a large zipper bag, and add marinade. Zip tight and massage marinade into birds. Refrigerate at least one hour or overnight.

2. Preheat oven to 450°F. Place marinated birds in a roasting pan and roast 30-45 minutes, basting with reserved marinade every 10 minutes as needed. When cooked, the internal temperature will be 165°F, joints will move freely, and juice will run clear. Let birds rest out of the oven for 5 minutes before serving.

Suggestions: Cook these birds on the grill. Cut out the bird's backbone and open it up flat. Then follow grilling instructions for Barbecued Chicken.

Kitchen Tips

The Cornish game hen is the Cornish variety of a miniature chicken. Despite the name, it is not a game bird, but was domesticated specifically to provide an all white-meat bird of a single serving size. A rock Cornish game hen is a Cornish chicken crossbred with a rock chicken. Any small bird under two pounds will suffice for this recipe. It also works with plain-old chicken, cut into serving-size pieces.

Roasted Duck in Orange Sauce

This classic, also known as Duck a l'Orange, is synonymous with fancy. Luckily, it's also very simple.

Serves 4
Prep time: 15 minutes
Cook time: 90 Minutes

1 (4-5) lb. duck

½ tsp. kosher salt

½ tsp. ground black pepper

3 TB. olive oil

1 yellow onion, chopped

2 carrots, diced

1 TB. dried thyme

1 bay leaf

1 TB. whole-wheat flour

Zest and juice of 3 oranges

1 cup chicken broth

1 cup red wine

½ cup honey

½ cup white wine vinegar

½ cup Grand Marnier

Kitchen Tips

Ducks are the fattiest birds, so prick the skin before roasting and periodically throughout the roasting time to help render the fat. Also, keep plenty of water at the bottom of the roasting pan, or the kitchen will get smoky.

1. Preheat oven to 500°F. Rinse duck and pat dry. Place a roasting rack inside a roasting pan, and set bird on the rack, breast facing up. Prick skin all over, sprinkle with salt and pepper, then roast for 1 hour at 500°F.

2. Heat oil in a large sauté pan over high heat. Add onion, carrots, thyme, and bay leaf, and cook until golden brown. Add flour and cook, stirring, until oil is absorbed. Stir in orange juice and zest. Slowly add broth and wine, whisking until smooth. Reduce heat and simmer 30 minutes. Add honey, vinegar, and Grand Marnier, simmer 5 more minutes, and season with salt and pepper.

3. Remove cooked bird from the oven and let it rest, covered in foil, for 10 minutes. (Internal temperature should be at least 165°F.) Using tongs, transfer bird to a cutting board, and carve into serving pieces, arrange on a platter, and strain sauce over the top. Garnish with orange segments.

Suggestions: Grand Marnier is an orange brandy. Use others, including Cointreau and Triple Sec. Omit the alcohol, and use frozen concentrated orange juice.

Chapter 11

Fish

In This Chapter

- ◆ Seafood stuffed and sautéed
- ◆ Steaks, filets, and whole fish
- ◆ Marinades for grilling

"Come, follow me," Jesus said, "and I will make you fishers of men." (Matthew 4:19 NIV)

As was the case in many coastal societies, fishing played an important role in the history of the Holy Land because it bordered the Mediterranean Sea and included the Sea of Galilee, which is Israel's largest freshwater lake. These waters have hosted thriving fishing industries since the second century B.C. Fish inhabit the Jordan River, which flows from the foothills of Mount Hermon through the Sea of Galilee, full of fish, to the Dead Sea. The port of Acre (modern Akko), which lies north of Jerusalem, was an important trading site as early as 1500 B.C. Mosaics of that era depict fish, including some foreign to Holy Land waters. This indicates either imported fish, or more likely, imported artisans.

The ancient walls of Jerusalem included many gates, including one known as the Fish Gate, often recorded to be so named for its proximity to the ancient fish market. However, the only fish likely to have been eaten in

Jerusalem during biblical times would have been preserved in salt. The closest fishing industry was the Mediterranean Sea, 30 miles away. While their standards of freshness were undoubtedly less picky than our own, the amount of fish consumed may not have been adequate to sustain an entire marketplace of fish.

Godly Fish

Fish was an important player in ancient cuisine and appears throughout the Bible in tales of miracles and sustenance. But not all fish was considered good enough for the people of God.

As stated earlier, strict rules designated clean and unclean fish. For this reason no recipes in this chapter include shellfish or bottom feeders. Also, these species are laden with contaminants that don't benefit your overall health.

Similarly, we have very little frying in this chapter. Though fried fish is most popular, it generally takes place in an excessive amount of saturated or hydrogenated fat. What frying we do have takes place in a much smaller amount of peanut or olive oil, which are primarily comprised of mono- and polyunsaturated fats, which raise the high-density lipoprotein (HDL, the good cholesterol) levels in our bodies ("heart-healthy fat"). Peanut oil is a good choice for crispy frying because it can tolerate a higher temperature than olive oil. The objective here is to cook as healthfully, and flavorfully, as possible.

Buying Fish

If you live near the sea, you likely have an abundance of fish available. Further inland, your fish selection may be more limited. Luckily, frozen fish today are of very high quality, usually flash-frozen onboard the ship that caught them. Thanks to modern technology and a heightened interest in good food, more and more varieties are being made available. Species formerly available in limited sections of the globe can now be had in every corner of it.

When buying frozen fish, be sure it is free of ice and has no signs of having been defrosted and refrozen. Pieces should be in a natural shape, with only a light coating of frost. Look for an expiration date on the packaging as well. Defrost frozen fish slowly, in the refrigerator, for 24-36 hours. Place defrosting fish in a colander or perforated pan to separate run-off juices. Cook smaller pieces directly out of the freezer.

When buying fresh fish, test it for a fresh, oceany smell. If it is off-putting, leave it. When you get fish home, store it in the fridge loosely covered in paper, preferably in a perforated pan to allow any accumulated juices to drain away. If you must store the fish longer than two or three days, wrap it in paper and an airtight bag for storage in the freezer.

10 Minutes per Inch

Cooking fish is simple. Heat penetrates at a relatively even rate, regardless of species, and there is an easy rule of thumb regarding cooking time. For moist, tender filets or steaks, use 10 minutes of moderate heat (350°F) for every inch of thickness. Of course, doneness is a matter of taste, but for the most part, people opt for moist and tender over dry and rubbery. So remember 10 minutes per inch, and you'll get along swimmingly!

Cooking with Wine

Wine is a favorite ingredient in seafood dishes. It works well because the acidity helps cut through natural fish oils. Dry wines do this best. When choosing wine for these recipes or to drink as an accompaniment, any good red or white table wine will do. If you are interested in varietals, look for hearty reds like cabernet or pinot noir. Sauvignon blanc or pinot grigio are good dry white choices. If you prefer to leave the alcohol out of your recipe, substitute each cup of wine with ¼ cup of corresponding wine vinegar and ¾ cup water or broth.

Biblical Culture
In biblical times, fish were commonly worshipped as symbols of fertility and renewal, which led to their inclusion by Moses on the list of symbols the people of Israel should not worship. (Deuteronomy 4:16-18)

Braised Haddock with Wine and Whole Spices

Haddock is similar to cod in flavor, with firm meat that holds up well to prolonged cooking. This dish cooks a little longer, so that the spices have a chance to infuse their flavors.

Serves 4
Prep time: 10 minutes
Cook time: 40 minutes

2 medium yellow onions, chopped

5 cloves garlic, whole

3 cinnamon sticks, crushed

2 TB. allspice berries, crushed

2 TB. star anise pods, crushed

¼ cup fresh ginger, grated

¼ cup pink peppercorns, crushed

4 cups dry white wine

4 (3-4 oz.) haddock filets

½ tsp. kosher salt

½ tsp. white pepper

½ cup sour cream

Kitchen Tips

Nothing compares to the flavor of whole spices. Because they retain their fragrant oils much longer than their ground equivalent, crush them just before adding them to the recipe to release all their flavors.

1. Preheat the oven to 400°F. In a large baking dish, combine onions, garlic, cinnamon, allspice, star anise, ginger, peppercorns, and wine. Stir to combine, add filets, salt, and pepper. Cover with foil and bake 30 minutes, until fish is firm and cooked through.

2. Remove filets from pan, cover with foil, and keep warm. Strain pan juices into a medium saucepan, bring to a boil over high heat, and reduce by half. Lower heat, return fish to sauce, and warm through.

Suggestions: Serve with a dollop of sour cream and a few slices of pumpernickel bread (Chapter 4).

Stuffed Red Snapper

Snapper has a sweet, mild flavor, with lean, moist meat. It stands up well to assertive flavors but doesn't overpower delicate ones. It's the perfect fish.

4 TB. olive oil, divided

1 yellow onion, chopped and divided

3 cloves garlic, minced

2 TB. fresh dill, minced

¼ cup fresh parsley, minced

3 cups dried bread crumbs

1 (3-4 lb.) red snapper, cleaned and gutted, with head and tail intact

1 leek, chopped

2 cups dry white wine

½ tsp. kosher salt

½ tsp. black pepper

Serves 4
Prep time: 15 minutes
Cook time: 40 minutes

1. Preheat the oven to 400°F. Heat 2 tablespoons oil in sauté pan over high heat. Add onion and sauté until tender. Add garlic, dill, and parsley, and reduce heat to low. Add bread crumbs and mix until well toasted. Remove from heat and cool.

2. Rinse and dry snapper inside and out. Reserve ½ cup bread crumb mixture and fill cavity with the rest. Press opening closed, and place fish in a baking dish coated with olive oil. Brush fish with oil, and surround with leek and wine. Sprinkle with salt and pepper, and spread top evenly with reserved crumbs. Drizzle with remaining oil and bake for 30-40 minutes, until firm and cooked through.

Suggestions: Serve the fish hot from the oven with a light, fluffy pilaf (see Chapter 14).

Kitchen Tips

Buying snapper can be tricky because many grocers label any fish with red skin "snapper." On the West Coast red snapper is often rockfish, which has a much different taste and texture. Real snapper has deep red skin along its back fading to pink-red on its belly.

Filet of Sole Roulade

If you are feeling adventurous, use goat cheese for this recipe instead of ricotta. The tangy flavor complements the fish and is more biblically authentic. This recipe will work equally well with farmer's cheese, cottage cheese, or cream cheese.

Serves 4
Prep time: 10 minutes
Cook time: 30 minutes

Kitchen Tips

Sole is a tender white flat fish that has several common names, including Dover sole, petrale sole, flounder, fluke, and dab. The smaller the sole, the better the flavor, so look for those under one pound.

2 TB. olive oil, divided

2 shallots, minced

¼ cup chives, minced

¼ cup fresh flat-leaf parsley, minced

2 TB. fresh dill, minced

12 oz. ricotta cheese

½ tsp. kosher salt

8 (3 oz.) sole filets

2 TB. lemon juice

1. Preheat the oven to 350°F. Heat oil in a medium sauté pan over high heat. Sauté shallots until tender. Add chives, parsley, and dill, and warm through. Remove from heat, and stir in cheese.

2. Coat a baking sheet with pan spray. Lay filets out flat, divide cheese evenly between them, and spread it evenly across filets. Starting from widest end, roll each filet up, and arrange it evenly on the baking sheet, placing each seam-side down to prevent unrolling during baking. Secure with a toothpick if necessary. Brush with lemon juice, remaining olive oil, and bake 10 minutes for every inch of thickness. Meat should be tender, white, and flaky. Serve immediately.

Suggestions: This dish has a delicate flavor but is fairly rich. Serve it with a simple mixed green salad (Chapter 8).

Grilled Sea Bass

Sea bass is a great fish to grill whole because its bone structure is simple and easy to eat around. Cooking fish whole retains maximum flavor and moisture. The skin becomes crispy and light, and the meat is tender and juicy. If you don't have a grill, make this dish in an oven set at 400°F or under the broiler.

4 whole sea bass, cleaned and gutted

¼ cup olive oil

¼ cup capers

3 cloves garlic, minced

1 cup red wine vinegar

¼ cup fresh rosemary, minced

1 cup dry red wine

Serves 4
Prep time: 5 minutes, plus 1-4 hours cooling time
Cook time: 30 minutes

1. In a large plastic zipper bag combine fish, oil, capers, garlic, vinegar, and rosemary. Seal and refrigerate for one to four hours to marinate.

2. Preheat grill on high heat. Remove fish from bag and reserve marinade. Grill fish over direct heat for 5 minutes. Turn fish and grill other side for an additional 5 minutes. Move off direct heat, and grill until firm and cooked through, for a total cooking time of 10 minutes per inch of fish. Remove from grill, cover with foil, and set aside.

3. Combine marinade with red wine in a large sauté pan. Place over high heat and bring to a boil. Reduce liquid by half. Place fish on serving platter, strain pan sauce over top, and serve.

Suggestions: A fresh tomato salad pairs nicely with this dish. The cool temperature and acidic fruit nicely counters the rich meat of this fish. Simply toss a variety of tomato slices with kosher salt, pepper, and an equal amount of olive oil and red wine vinegar.

Kitchen Tips

Fish is eaten whole all around the globe, but here in the United States we are averse to seeing eyes on a plate. You can remove the head just behind the gills, although the resulting dish will be much less moist.

Fish 'n' Chips

In England a chip is a french-fried potato. What we call a potato chip, they call a potato crisp. To make matters more confusing, french fries aren't even French. They're from Belgium!

<table>
<tr><td align="center">Serves 4</td></tr>
<tr><td>Prep time: 30 minutes</td></tr>
<tr><td>Cook time: 30 minutes</td></tr>
</table>

2 cups cracker crumbs

1 tsp. kosher salt

1 tsp. black pepper

1 TB. Old Bay seasoning

2 egg whites, beaten

1½ lbs. cod, pollack, or haddock filet, sliced into strips

1. Preheat the oven to 375°F. Coat a nonstick baking sheet with pan spray. In a large bowl, combine cracker crumbs, salt, pepper, and seasoning. In a separate bowl, beat egg whites to loosen. Dip fish first in egg whites, then in seasoned crumbs until well coated. Place on prepared pan, and rest 10 minutes before baking. Bake for 15-20 minutes, until meat is firm and cooked through. Serve with Oven Fries (Chapter 14).

Suggestion: Serve with malt vinegar, available in most supermarkets. Also popular is tartar sauce and simple lemon wedges.

Kitchen Tips

Cod is a great choice for Fish 'n' Chips because it's the classic white-meat, all-purpose fish. It has a delicate, mild flavor, firm flesh when raw, but tender when cooked. You may know cod by its Spanish name, *bacalao*. Haddock and pollack are closely related and can be used interchangeably. Scrod is a young, smaller cod, haddock, or pollack.

Halibut Baked in Sour Cream

Because halibut is thick and meaty, it holds up well to freezing and retains its flaky, tender texture once defrosted. But once defrosted, it can dry out easily if overcooked, so watch the cooking time carefully.

4 (3 oz.) halibut filets	**2 TB. fresh chives, minced**
2 TB. olive oil	**2 TB. fresh dill, minced**
½ tsp. kosher salt	**2 TB. butter**
½ tsp. black pepper	**1 cup sour cream**
2 shallots, minced	

Serves 4

Prep time: 10 minutes
Cook time: 40 minutes

1. Preheat the oven to 375°F. Coat a baking dish with pan spray. Add filets, brush with oil, and season with salt and pepper. Top with shallots, chives, and dill, and cover with sour cream. Cover and bake for 30-40 minutes until fish is firm and flakes easily with a fork. Bake a final 5 minutes uncovered to brown. Serve immediately.

Suggestions: Try this with a simple baked potato (Chapter 14). With dill and sour cream, it's a match made in heaven.

Biblical Culture

While dairy products should not be consumed with meat, no restriction is placed on dairy and fish.

Pan-Fried Trout Amandine

Amandine is the French culinary term for a dish made with almonds. Almondine is the more common misspelling seen in America.

Serves 4
Prep time: 60 minutes
Cook time: 20 minutes

½ cup white wine vinegar

1 ½ cup water

4 whole trout, gutted, with heads

3 cups whole-wheat flour

1 tsp. salt

1 tsp. pepper

¼ cup *clarified* butter

1 yellow onion, chopped

1 cup sliced almonds

½ cup white wine

4 TB. butter

½ tsp. kosher salt

½ tsp. ground black pepper

1 TB. chopped fresh parsley

1. Combine vinegar and water, and soak trout for 30-60 minutes. Drain and discard liquid. In a medium bowl combine flour, salt, and pepper. Dredge fish in flour, and shake off excess. Set aside at room temperature for 10 minutes.

2. Heat a skillet, add butter, and fry fish until very dark, about 5 minutes per side. Transfer to a serving dish and cover with foil to keep warm. Return pan to heat, add onion and almonds, and sauté until golden brown. Add wine, stirring to scrape up crusty bits from the bottom of the pan. Reduce liquid to 1 tablespoon and remove from heat. Add butter, salt, pepper, and parsley. Pour sauce over fish, and serve immediately.

Suggestions: To increase the tang of this dish, add 2 TB. capers and the juice and zest of 1 lemon. To spice it up, add 1 TB. Cajun seasoning to the flour dredge.

def•i•ni•tion

Clarified butter is pure butter fat minus the salts and solids that burn easily at high temperatures. You can buy it in gourmet markets, but it's just as easy to make. Simmer butter gently until melted. Never stir it. Gentle bubbles force the solids to the surface, where you can easily skim them off. Pour the pure fat off gently for use in recipes. In the bottom of the pan you'll discover more solids that you should also discard. Clarified butter will keep for weeks in the fridge or freezer.

Tuna with Black Olives and Capers

The flavorful topping of this dish gets a lot of salt from the olives and capers. Because of this, use a light hand when salting the fish. It's easier to add more salt at the table than it is to fix it once over-salted.

2 cups kalamata olives, pitted and halved

1 yellow onion, minced

¼ cup *capers*

2 tomatoes, chopped

¼ cup fresh parsley, chopped

½ cup olive oil

½ cup red wine vinegar

4 (3 oz.) tuna steaks

½ cup lemon juice

⅛ tsp. kosher salt

½ tsp. black pepper

Serves 4
Prep time: 10 minutes
Cook time: 20 minutes

1. Preheat grill on high heat. In a large bowl combine olives, onion, capers, tomatoes, parsley, oil, and vinegar. Toss together, and set aside at room temperature.

2. Coat tuna steaks with lemon juice, salt, and pepper and grill. Cook 5-10 minutes per side, until meat is firm and cooked through. Serve immediately topped with olive mixture.

Suggestions: Prepare the topping for this dish up to a day in advance. The added time will intensify the flavors.

def•i•ni•tion

Native to the Mediterranean, **capers** are green buds from a small evergreen bush that are dried and pickled in vinegar brine or packed in salt. Their flavor is tangy and salty, and they work nicely in acidic dishes like this one. Look for them in the same grocery store aisle as pickles and olives. If you buy the salted version, rinse the salt off before you use them.

Tilapia with Cucumber and Dill

Tilapia's pseudonym is Saint Peter's fish, in reference to Matthew's story in which Peter catches a fish that carries a coin in its mouth (Matthew 17:24-27). Tilapia is still plentiful in the Sea of Galilee. Its dark skin spots are said to be Peter's fingerprints.

Serves 4
Prep time: 15 minutes
Cook time: 55 minutes

3 TB. olive oil

1 large yellow onion, sliced ½-inch thick

2 cups orange juice

4 (5 oz.) tilapia filets

3 cucumbers, peeled, seeded, and sliced

1 TB. honey

1 TB. mustard

¼ cup fresh dill, minced

½ tsp. kosher salt

½ tsp. black pepper

½ cup plain yogurt

1. Heat oil in a large sauté pan over high heat. Sauté onion until tender. Add orange juice, and bring to a boil. Reduce heat, add tilapia, cover, and simmer until fish is firm and cooked through, about 10 minutes.

2. In a large bowl combine cucumbers, honey, mustard, dill, salt, and pepper. Toss thoroughly. Serve fish on bed of cucumbers, topped with a dollop of yogurt.

Suggestion: Purchase English cucumbers if you can. They have fewer seeds than common cucumbers. For instructions on seeding cucumbers, see Chapter 8.

Biblical Culture

Matthew's story describes Peter angling, which is fishing with rod, line, and angle or hook. For this reason, some believe the fish with the coin could not have been tilapia, which is a fish that swims deep and must be caught with nets.

Fish Tacos

Fish tacos are a regional specialty of Baja California and can be found throughout the Southwest. This fish is typically deep-fried, but here we cut the fat by simply pan-frying. The peanut oil can take more heat than olive oil and has a more complementary flavor here.

2 eggs

1 cup whole-wheat flour

1 tsp. salt

$1/2$ tsp. black pepper

12 corn tortillas

2-4 TB. peanut oil

1-2 lb. firm white fish sliced into 1-inch strips

Juice of 2 limes

Shredded cabbage

1 recipe Salsa Fresca (Chapter 6)

1 recipe Guacamole (Chapter 6)

1 cup sour cream

Serves 4
Prep time: 35 minutes
Cook time: 20 minutes

1. In medium bowl whisk eggs, flour, salt, and pepper until smooth. Refrigerate 20 minutes. Wrap tortillas in tin foil, and warm in a 200°F oven.

2. In a heavy skillet heat 2 tablespoons peanut oil. Toss fish with lime juice, add to egg batter, stir to coat, then drop piece by piece into hot oil. Fry 2-3 minutes per side, until golden brown. Drain on a paper towel, and sprinkle with salt. To serve, fill tortillas with shredded cabbage, fried fish, salsa, guacamole, and a dollop of sour cream.

Suggestions: This kind of meal is fun to serve buffet style. Line everything up, and let your guests walk through and create their own.

Biblical Culture

There was no corn in the Holy Land, but there was certainly flat bread, which would have been a common accompaniment to fish.

Baked Salmon with Spring Vegetables

Much of the salmon available in markets today is farmed or aquacultured. While salmon is high in the heart-healthy omega-3 fatty acids, recent studies indicate that toxin levels in *aquacultured* salmon are 10 times higher than in wild salmon. Toxins are thought to originate in the feed, which is made from fish caught in polluted waters. So look for wild salmon, and limit your intake of farmed salmon to once or twice a month.

Serves 4
Prep time: 15 minutes
Cook time: 1 hour, 15 minutes

4 (3 oz.) salmon filets

3 TB. olive oil

½ tsp. kosher salt

½ tsp. black pepper

1 cup green onions, chopped

1 cup baby carrots, sliced

1 bunch asparagus, sliced 1 inch wide

1 cup yellow squash, sliced

1 cup zucchini, sliced

1 cup fresh or frozen baby peas

2 TB. fresh dill, minced

1 cup dry white wine

1. Preheat the oven to 400°F. Place salmon in a large baking dish. Brush fish with oil, sprinkle with salt and pepper, and cover with layers of onions, carrots, asparagus, squash, zucchini, peas, and dill. Add wine, cover, and bake for 20-30 minutes until fish is firm and cooked through.

Suggestions: Make a similar version of this dish using fall and winter vegetables. Cut small dice of potatoes, butternut squash, parsnips, artichokes, and string beans, and cook in the same manner.

Kitchen Tips

While most spring vegetables are available to us year-round, the term refers to the young and tender versions that appear in the markets or gardens each spring. Baby versions of carrots, beets, zucchini, and summer squash, thin asparagus, new potatoes, and fresh new peas and beans are what to look for.

Fish Cakes

Use any mild white fish with success in this recipe. Try cod, pollack, or orange roughy.

5 TB. olive oil, divided

2 scallions, chopped

2 cloves garlic, minced

1 (4 oz.) can chopped pimentos, drained

1 tsp. dry dill

1 TB. Dijon mustard

¼ cup buttermilk

1 egg

1 cup bread crumbs, divided

½ tsp. kosher salt

½ tsp. black pepper

1 lb. cooked white fish, flaked

½ cup Parmesan cheese

lemon wedges

sour cream

Serves 4	
Prep time: 1-2 hours	
Cook time: 10 minutes	

1. Heat oil in a large sauté pan over high heat. Sauté scallions and garlic until golden brown. Remove from heat, and add pimentos, dill, and mustard. Combine buttermilk, egg, and add to mixture. Add ½ cup bread crumbs, salt, pepper, and fish, and thoroughly combine.

2. Form mixture into patties 2-3 inches in diameter. Combine remaining bread crumbs and Parmesan. Coat cakes in crumbs, and chill for one to two hours.

3. Heat remaining oil in sauté pan over high heat, and fry cakes until golden brown, about 3-5 minutes per side. Serve immediately with lemon wedges and a dollop of sour cream.

Suggestions: Alter the flavor of these cakes to suit your meal by simply adjusting the seasoning. Try adding Italian, Cajun, or curry spices for a change of pace.

Biblical Culture

You can make an ancient version of this recipe by using salt cod. Soak the dried fish in cold water for two or three days, changing the water frequently. It will plump up to original size and cook up moist and tender.

12

Casseroles

In This Chapter

- ◆ International flavors
- ◆ Savory pies
- ◆ Cheesy classics

"Come, eat my food
  and drink the wine I have mixed.
Leave your simple ways and you will live;
  walk in the way of understanding." (Proverbs 9:5-6 NIV)

The word *casserole* is French and means "stew pan." The word has been a part of the English language for 400 years, and refers to a dish of meat, vegetables, and broth cooked slowly in a covered dish. This method preserves and mingles the flavors and nutrients of the ingredients in a way that no quick-cooking method can.

Casseroles are common all over the world. Their popularity stems from their ability to make cheap, tough cuts of meat and poultry tender and flavorful as well as their ability to disguise leftovers. Throughout history's hard times, these recipes provided an economical way to feed the family by stretching and making palatable what was on hand.

The Importance of Pots

After domestication of animals and wild edible plants, the advent of pottery was mankind's most important culinary advancement.

Someone discovered that baskets, used for storage and transportation, could hold liquid if covered with clay. This led to the firing of clay, first in open fires, which produced fragile pots. When fires were enclosed, the higher temperatures produced more durable pottery, suitable for everyday use. So food that was previously cooked over, or in, an open flame could be boiled, stewed, or braised with liquids. Add an assortment of grains and dried legumes, and you have the world's first casseroles.

Bakeware

The casserole, as we know it today, came to life in the United States in the 1950s. Women's magazines popularized them as a way to free up time, stretch a dollar, and make use of newfangled ovenproof baking materials, such as Corning Ware and Pyrex.

These recipes call for the use of a baking dish. The size and shape is not at all important, other than a general $1\frac{1}{2}$-2 quart capacity. If it's bigger or smaller, simply fill the dish accordingly. Whatever size and shape casserole dish you have will be fine. If you have no casserole dish, any ovenproof container will do, covered with foil if necessary. To ease serving and cleanup, coat the dish lightly with a nonstick spray before filling it.

Plan Ahead

If you think ahead as you plan and cook your meals, casseroles stay true to their heritage and become a frugal dinner option. Save remnants of that roast chicken, and make a pot pie. Grill up an extra steak, and turn it into beef noodle casserole. Save leftover rice pilaf, and use it for Tuna and Rice. If you're reluctant to eat the same thing two nights in a row, freeze the leftovers, and use them later in the week.

You can also use casseroles as a place to use up the odd vegetable. Stir half an onion, broccoli stems, and an extra ear of corn into a casserole for added nutrition, color, and flavor.

To Cheese or Not to Cheese

While much of the allure of the casserole culture revolves around the melty goodness of cheese, you'll find it conspicuously absent from these recipes when meat is present as the combination of dairy and meat is prohibited. This does not mean you cannot enjoy a good casserole. On the contrary, I think you'll find these recipes mouthwatering.

Making a choice to follow rules set thousands of years ago may be harder when cooking a casserole for that next potluck. But by doing so, you are offering both obedience to God and a lifetime of health for your family. Doesn't that sound better than Cheeseburger Macaroni?

Eggplant Parmesan

This dish is essentially lasagna with eggplant instead of noodles. The key is in the salting. Salt draws moisture out of the eggplant. Without this step, your Eggplant Parmesan would be a watery mess.

Serves 4-6

Prep time: 2-3 hours
Cook time: 30 minutes

2 large eggplants

2-3 TB. kosher salt

¼ cup olive oil, divided

1 small yellow onion, chopped

3 cloves garlic, minced

1 (28 oz.) can diced tomatoes

1 tsp. dried oregano

1 tsp. ground fennel seed

4 eggs

½ cup whole-wheat flour

½ cup bread crumbs

1½ lb mozzarella cheese

1 cup grated Parmesan cheese

1 cup fresh basil leaves, chopped

Biblical Culture

The eggplant is native to India and was domesticated around 2000 B.C. Arab traders introduced it to North Africa, where it thrived in the hot Mediterranean climate and gained popularity. The fruit itself is botanically a berry, about an inch in diameter when wild but bred much larger by man.

1. Slice eggplant into ½-inch wheels. Line colander with slices layered with salt, weigh down with a heavy plate, and set aside to drain for two or three hours. Meanwhile, heat 1 tablespoon oil in a large sauté pan over high heat. Cook onion and garlic until tender. Add tomatoes, oregano, and fennel, and cook to warm through about 5 minutes. Set aside to cool.

2. Press drained eggplant, and blot with paper towel to remove excess moisture. Place eggs in a small bowl and whisk. In a separate bowl combine flour and bread crumbs. Dredge eggplant in egg and then in crumbs. In a large sauté pan over high heat, fry eggplant in olive oil until brown on both sides. Work in batches, being careful not to crowd. Drain on paper towels.

3. Preheat oven to 350°F. In a baking dish arrange alternate layers of tomato sauce, eggplant slices, mozzarella, Parmesan, and basil. Bake 30 minutes until brown and bubbly.

Suggestions: Add an additional layer of sliced hard-boiled egg, which adds good, complete protein.

Vegetable Lasagna

This dish is traditionally made with a meat sauce, but to avoid the combination of meat and dairy, try this rich and hearty vegetarian version. You'll never miss the meat.

2-4 TB. olive oil

1 large yellow onion, diced

6 large cloves of garlic, minced

3 TB. dried oregano

2 TB. dried basil

1 TB. dried crushed fennel seed

1 TB. dried sage

8 oz. chopped mushrooms

1 large zucchini, grated

1 (15 oz) can artichokes, chopped

1 (29 oz.) can tomato sauce

1 (1 oz.) package lasagna noodles

1 lb. mozzarella cheese, grated, divided into 4 portions

4 cups fresh spinach leaves

1 (15 oz.) package ricotta cheese (optional)

½ cup Parmesan cheese, grated

Serves 8
Prep time: 45 minutes
Cook time: 60 minutes

1. Preheat the oven to 350°F. In a large saucepan, sauté onion and garlic in olive oil until tender. Add oregano, basil, fennel, sage, mushrooms, and zucchini, and continue to cook until tender and dry. Add artichokes and tomato sauce, reduce heat, and simmer for 10-15 minutes to warm through.

2. Cover the bottom of the lasagna pan with a thin layer of sauce to prevent noodles from burning. Lay three lasagna noodles in the pan, being careful not to overlap too much. Break them into pieces if necessary to cover the bottom of the pan. Add ¼-inch of sauce, a generous handful of mozzarella, a layer of spinach, and 4-5 dollops of ricotta. Cover with another layer of noodles, and repeat layering. Finish layering with sauce, mozzarella, and Parmesan.

3. Cover and bake until sauce is bubbly and cheese is melted, about 30 minutes. Uncover the dish and cook another 10 minutes to brown top. Serve hot.

Suggestions: Serve with a fresh green salad and some crusty Italian bread (see Chapter 4).

 Kitchen Tips

To boil or not to boil; that is the question. After the introduction of no-boil lasagna noodles, some cutting-edge chefs wondered what would happen if we didn't boil traditional noodles. The result? Fantastic! The moisture and heat in the center of the lasagna is enough to cook the noodles in the oven. Try it! You'll be hooked!

Tuna and Rice

There are hundreds of tuna casserole variations. You can use different soups, different vegetables, or different crunchy elements on top, like potato chips, cornflakes, or bread crumbs.

Serves 4
Prep time: 20 minutes
Cook time: 30 minutes

2½ cups water

½ tsp. salt

1 cup brown rice

2 TB. olive oil

1 small yellow onion, chopped

8 oz. mushrooms, sliced

1 (12 oz.) can of tuna fish, undrained

1 cup sour cream

1 cup milk

2 cups frozen peas

1 cup grated cheddar cheese

1 cup crushed saltine crackers

¼ cup grated Parmesan cheese

1. Preheat oven to 350°F. Bring water and salt to a boil over high heat. Add rice, stir, reduce heat to low, cover, and cook 30 minutes until moisture is absorbed and rice is tender. Remove from heat and set aside.

2. Heat oil in a large sauté pan over high heat. Cook onion and mushrooms until tender. Combine in a casserole dish with tuna, sour cream, milk, peas, cheese, and rice. Stir to combine, cover with crackers and Parmesan. Bake until bubbly and golden brown, about 30 minutes.

Suggestions: Make this with a number of other grains, including whole-wheat pasta.

Kitchen Tips

The traditional method for making tuna casserole is to use a can of cream of mushroom soup. But even the name-brand soups are not guaranteed to be organic. If you can find a certified organic version of that classic ingredient, use it to replace the sour cream, onions, and mushrooms.

Shepherd's Pie

This is British peasant food, designed to utilize tough, old mutton. Technically, this casserole can only be called shepherd's pie if it is made from mutton. But in the United States, we prefer to make it with ground beef. If you'd like to make the authentic version, simply replace the beef with an equal amount of ground lamb.

5 large potatoes, peeled and quartered

7 TB. olive oil, divided

4 cloves garlic, minced

2 large eggs

1 large yellow onion, diced

1 stalk celery, chopped

2 large carrots, chopped

1 lb. ground lamb

1 tsp. Worcestershire sauce

1 cup frozen peas

1 (14.5 oz.) can diced tomatoes, drained

½ tsp. kosher salt

½ tsp. black pepper

Serves 6-8	
Prep time: 45 minutes	
Cook time: 30 minutes	

1. Preheat the oven to 350°F. Boil potatoes in a large saucepan until tender. Drain and spread out on a cookie sheet to dry and cool. Meanwhile, sauté garlic in 4 tablespoon olive oil until tender. Set aside. Mash potatoes, and combine with garlic, oil, and eggs. Mix well and set aside.

2. Heat 2 tablespoons oil over high heat. Sauté onion, celery, and carrots until tender. Add meat and brown. Remove from heat, drain off excess fat, and add Worcestershire, peas, tomatoes, salt, and pepper.

3. Spread meat mixture evenly in a baking dish. Top with mashed potatoes, and brush with remaining olive oil. Bake until brown and bubbly, about 30 minutes.

Suggestions: Decorate dish by piping the potatoes through a pastry bag fitted with a star tip. Or drag the tines of a fork across the top to make a pretty pattern. For a more interesting flavor, add some roasted garlic, boiled parsnip, roasted sweet potato, or puréed celery root to your spuds.

Kitchen Tips

Mashing potatoes is not hard, but it can be done wrong. The potato is full of starch, and the more you beat it, the more starch you release. When this happens, the mash becomes gluey. The best method is to force them through a ricer or sieve first, then gently stir in the butter and cream. A hand masher, or fork, is the next best tool. Anything electric, especially a food processor, is much too rough.

Pot Pie

Like all good casseroles, this one began as a way to utilize leftovers. I like it best made with leftover roast turkey or chicken. For special occasions, try cooking your pot pies in individual dishes. They cook faster, more evenly, and make your guests feel special!

Serves 6
Prep time: 30 minutes
Cook time: 30 minutes

4 TB. olive oil

1 medium yellow onion, diced

2 stalks celery, chopped

1 large carrot, chopped

1 tsp. dried thyme

1 tsp. dried sage

1 tsp. dried oregano

4 TB. whole-wheat flour

2-4 cups chicken broth

2 cups cooked chicken meat, chopped or shredded

1 large baking potato, peeled and diced

1 cup green peas, fresh or frozen

1 cup corn, fresh or frozen

½ tsp. kosher salt

½ tsp. ground black pepper

1 recipe pie or biscuit dough

1 egg yolk

1 TB. water

Kitchen Tips

The amount of liquid a roux will hold varies tremendously, especially if vegetables are added. The moisture in the vegetables varies with the size they are chopped, the degree they are cooked, and the water that is retained after washing. The flour plays a role, too. So use your eye, and don't be afraid to add more or less liquid than a recipe calls for.

1. Preheat the oven to 375°F. Heat oil in a large sauté pan over medium heat, and sauté onion, celery, carrot, thyme, sage, and oregano until tender, about 5 minutes. Add flour and stir until it absorbs oil and begins to brown. (This is a roux.) Slowly add broth, ¹/₄ cup at a time, stirring constantly. As roux absorbs each addition, add more broth until a thick-soup consistency is reached.

2. Remove from the heat, and stir in chicken, potato, peas, corn, salt, and pepper. Transfer to a baking dish, and top with pastry dough. Mix yolk with water and brush lightly on top of dough. Bake until brown and bubbly, about 30 minutes.

Suggestions: The crust in a pot pie is a matter of preference. Use the spoon biscuit recipe in Chapter 4, or try the pie dough in Chapter 15. Use a prepared biscuit dough, biscuit mix, or frozen pie dough. Or try an elegant variation using puff pastry.

Baked Beans

Baked beans have a long history. While the protein content was not known, the health and vitality of those who ate beans was surely noticed.

2 TB. olive oil	**3 TB. honey**
1 large yellow onion, diced	**1 (15 oz.) can tomato sauce**
2 (15 oz.) cans great northern beans	**1 cup barbecue sauce (see recipe Chapter 10)**
2 (15 oz.) cans pinto beans	

Serves 8
Prep time: 15 minutes
Cook time: 45 minutes

1. Preheat the oven to 350°F. Heat oil in a medium sauté pan over medium heat, and sauté onion until tender. Remove from heat and stir in great northern and pinto beans, honey, tomato sauce, and barbecue sauce. Transfer to a baking dish and bake for 45 minutes. Remove the lid for the last 10 minutes to brown top.

Suggestions: Adjust the seasonings to suit your preference. Mustard, molasses, brown sugar, beer, broth, and even liquid smoke are all common additions. Just include at least two cups of total liquid.

Kitchen Tips

If you'd like to use dried beans for this recipe, soak 3 cups in cold water overnight, then cook them at a bare simmer, in plenty of water, for 2-3 hours until tender. Then proceed with the recipe as written.

Chicken Madras

Madras is the former name of the fourth largest city in India, now called Chennai, on the country's Southeastern coast. The name Madras, thought to be of Portuguese origin, was favored by the British, but was officially dropped in the 1990s.

Serves 4-6
Prep time: 20 minutes
Cook time: 35 minutes

2 TB. olive oil

1 large yellow onion, diced

4 boneless, skinless chicken breasts, cut into 1-inch dice

3 TB. *madras* or curry powder

Juice of 1 lemon (about 2 TB.)

½ tsp. kosher salt

2 large ripe tomatoes, diced

1 cup unsweetened shredded coconut

¼ cup fresh cilantro, minced

1. In a large sauté pan over high heat, sauté onion in oil until tender. Mix together chicken, curry, lemon juice, and salt. Add to sauté pan and brown, 3-5 minutes. Add tomatoes and coconut, reduce heat, cover, and simmer 20 minutes. Just before serving, stir in cilantro.

Suggestions: Serve with brown rice and cucumber yogurt salad (Chapter 8).

Kitchen Tips

If you buy traditional **madras** sauce or powder, you'll find it red and full of spicy chilies. Yellow curry, or *garam masala*, is generally milder.

Texas Bean Bake

This dish is the perfect accompaniment to anything from the grill. Or serve it over rice for a flavorful vegetarian meal.

2 TB. olive oil

1 large yellow onion

3 cloves garlic, minced

1 lb. lean ground beef

1 TB. brown mustard

2 TB. honey

1 (4 oz.) can diced green chilies

1 (2 oz.) can tomato paste

1 (15 oz.) can kidney beans

1 (15 oz.) can pinto beans

1 (15 oz.) can black beans

Serves 8-10
Prep time: 25 minutes
Cook time: 60 minutes

1. Preheat the oven to 350°F. Heat oil in a large sauté pan over high heat. Cook onion and garlic until tender. Add beef and brown. Remove from heat, pour off fat, and stir in mustard, honey, chilies, tomato paste, and kidney, pinto, and black beans. Transfer to a baking dish, cover, and bake 1 hour, until bubbly and brown.

Suggestions: Make this recipe a day ahead, and let the flavors mingle and intensify in the fridge overnight.

Kitchen Tips

If time allows, replace the canned green chilies with fresh roasted ones. Buy a poblano or pasilla chili, and set it directly on top of a gas burner. (You can use a broiler for this, too). Cook it until it's charred, then, using tongs, turn and continue cooking until all sides are charred. Place it directly into a plastic bag, seal, and cool. The steam it generates will cause the skin to loosen. Wipe off the skin, remove the seeds and stem, and then dice fine.

Macaroni and Cheese

This is a classic kid's favorite. But just because it is most often seen made from elbow macaroni doesn't mean it has to be that way. Try using pasta shells (*conchiglie*), bow-ties (*farfalle*), curly q's (*fusilli*), or tubes (*rigatoni*, *penne*, or *ziti*). Many traditional pasta shapes are now available made from whole wheat.

Serves 4
Prep time: 30 minutes
Cook time: 30 minutes

2 qt. water	2 cups grated cheddar cheese
1 tsp. salt	½ tsp. grated nutmeg
1 lb. whole-wheat pasta	1 tsp. salt
4 TB. olive oil	½ tsp. pepper
½ small yellow onion, diced	1 cup bread or cracker crumbs
2 TB. whole-wheat flour	½ cup grated Parmesan cheese
1½ cups milk	

Kitchen Tips

If noodles are not going to be eaten directly after boiling, a cold water rinse stops the cooking immediately, which keeps them from getting mushy.

1. Preheat the oven to 350°F. Bring water and salt to a full rolling boil. Add pasta, stir, and cook until half done, about 10 minutes. Drain and rinse with cold water. Add 2 tablespoons olive oil, stir to coat, and set aside.

2. Heat remaining oil in a medium saucepan over high heat. Cook onion until tender. Add flour and stir until all fat is absorbed. Slowly add milk while whisking. Remove from heat, add cheddar cheese, and stir until melted. Mix in nutmeg and pasta. Transfer to a baking dish, top with bread crumbs, and sprinkle with Parmesan. Bake until golden brown and bubbly, about 30 minutes.

Suggestions: Round this dish into a meal by adding 2 cups chopped fresh broccoli. Or spice it up with 1 chopped tomato and 1 roasted green chili.

Cheese Enchilada Bake

This is a quick and easy way to satisfy your enchilada fans. The key is the sauce. There are some good organic choices, or make your own. The recipe appears with Tamale Pie.

6-8 corn tortillas, ripped into quarters

1 (15 oz.) can refried beans

1 (4 oz.) can diced green chilies

1 cups cheddar cheese, grated

1 cup Jack cheese, grated

2 cups enchilada sauce

Serves 4
Prep time: 10 minutes
Cook time: 30 minutes

1. Preheat oven to 350°F. In a baking dish, arrange alternating layers of tortilla, beans, chilies, cheddar, and Jack cheese. Reserve a handful of cheese. Pour enchilada sauce over all, top with remaining cheese, cover, and bake for 30 minutes until brown and bubbly.

Suggestions: Serve with a dollop of sour cream and chopped black olives.

Kitchen Tips

Enchilar means to add chili to, and enchilada sauce is a chili-based sauce, usually made from dried red chilies that are roasted, softened, puréed, and seasoned. The enchilada takes on a variety of forms, depending on where you are. Sometimes a filling is rolled in the tortillas, and sometimes it is layered, as in this recipe. In parts of the Southwest you may even find your enchilada topped off with a fried egg.

Part 5

Accompaniments

Man cannot live by meat alone, and these chapters round out the menu. Using the same criteria of low saturated fat and high fiber, these recipes are worthy accompaniments to the most divinely inspired entrée. They are an easy and tasty way to complete the everyday meal.

Chapter 13

Vegetables

In This Chapter

◆ Vibrant vitamins

◆ Greens and beans

◆ Stuffed, wrapped, grilled, baked, and fried

"And out of the ground made the LORD God to grow every tree that is pleasant to the sight, and good for food; the tree of life also in the midst of the garden, and the tree of knowledge of good and evil." (Genesis 2:9 KJV)

There is no better, cheaper, tastier way to get your vitamins than from veggies. They are nutritional powerhouses.

Eat a Rainbow

Color is an indication of the vitamins found within. The more nutrients a plant has, the darker/brighter it will be.

Bright-colored veggies carry more vitamins and minerals than pale ones, and each color is a clue to the goodness inside. Orange and yellow veggies, which include carrots, sweet potatoes, pumpkins, and related squash, contain beta-carotene, a precursor to vitamin A, which, among other things, is good for your eyesight. Its powerful antioxidant helps prevent heart disease and some cancers. It assists in bone growth, tissue repair, and helps the body fight infection.

Vegetables with the red and purple pigment anthocyanine are also high in antioxidants, which can block some cancer-causing chemicals, suppress tumor growth, and improve wound healing. Choose purple cabbage, radicchio, beets, red chard, and red peppers. Red and purple fruits count, too, including pomegranates and berries. Blue pigments, such as those found in cabbage and blueberries, are thought to help slow aging.

Chlorophyll, the green pigment, is a major source of iron and is used to prevent and treat liver, skin, and colon cancers.

It is also a natural breath freshener. So include spinach, chard, broccoli, and fresh herbs in your diet. The cabbage family is thought to fight against breast and prostate cancers.

Cooking Veggies

The nutrients in most vegetables are concentrated near or in the skin, which means that peeling a vegetable reduces its nutritional value. So whenever possible, eat the skin; just be sure to wash it thoroughly. There's no need for fancy food washes; simple water and a gentle scrub is all you need.

The longer a vegetable is subjected to heat, the more nutrients it loses, and this fact is generating the recent boom in raw cuisine. But with careful attention, you can maintain nutrients, even after cooking. Once again, color is the key. If the color is maintained throughout cooking, so will be the bulk of the nutrients. Like pasta, the goal is an *al dente* texture, not crunchy and not soggy but somewhere in between.

Succotash

Succotash comes from the Algonquin word *msickquatash*, meaning "boiled corn" or kernels. The colonists received a similar dish from the Narragansett Indians, but it probably didn't include lima beans until much later when trade routes brought lima beans from Central America.

2 TB. olive oil	**2 cups lima beans, fresh shelled, canned, or frozen**
1 small yellow onion, chopped	**½ tsp. kosher salt**
2 cups corn, fresh off the cob, canned, or frozen	**2 TB. chopped fresh parsley**

Serves 4
Prep time: 10 minutes
Cook time: 20 minutes

1. Heat oil in a large sauté pan over high heat. Add onion, and cook until tender. Add corn, beans, and salt, and cook to warm through. Remove from heat, stir in parsley, and serve.

Suggestions: Add more color and nutrition with diced red bell pepper, carrots, peas, and additional beans, such as fava or garbanzo.

Biblical Culture

Corn and lima beans were not known in the Holy Land until recently. But biblical folk did mix legumes, vegetables, and grains with great frequency. They didn't know it then, but these mixtures provided them with all nine essential amino acids needed for good nutrition.

Glazed Carrots

Glazed carrots are known in France as *carrot à la Vichy*, carrots in the style of Vichy. Vichy is a city in central France where a well-known sparkling mineral water is bottled, and to be authentic, Vichy carrots must be made with Vichy water.

Serves 4
Prep time: 10 minutes
Cook time: 20 minutes

4 cups carrots, peeled and thinly sliced

2 TB. olive oil

1½ TB. honey

½ tsp. kosher salt

1 TB. white wine vinegar

1 cup water

1. In a large sauté pan, combine carrots, oil, honey, salt, vinegar, and water. Set over medium heat, cover tightly, and simmer 10-15 minutes until carrots are tender. Remove lid and cook until liquid is evaporated.

Suggestions: Try carrots in other colors, including purple, if you can find them. Also add some other roots to this dish, such as the sweet parsnip or the vivid beet.

Biblical Culture

Apiaceae (carrot family) pollen has been found dating from the Eocene period, 55 million years ago. People of Afghanistan consumed carrots around 3000 B.C. Egyptian art from 2000 B.C. depicts carrots, and instructions for cultivation were found in a pharaoh's tomb. These carrots were not orange but purple and white. Arab traders spread purple carrots throughout Persia, Asia, and Africa. Varieties in yellow, green, and black sprang up, but the orange carrot didn't appear until the 1400s when Dutch scientists cultivated a mutant orange seed for the Dutch royal family, the House of Orange.

Creamed Spinach

You can certainly make this recipe with fresh spinach, but cook it first. Leafy greens have a lot of water that needs to be reduced. If you don't cook it, the result will be a watery, soupy side dish.

3 TB. olive oil

1 small yellow onion, chopped

2 TB. whole-wheat flour

1 cup vegetable broth

1½ tsp. fresh grated nutmeg

1 tsp. honey

1 (10 oz.) package frozen spinach, thawed and drained

½ tsp. kosher salt

½ tsp. ground black pepper

Serves 4
Prep time: 10 minutes
Cook time: 15 minutes

1. Heat oil in a large sauté pan over medium heat. Add onion and cook until golden brown. Add flour and cook, stirring, until fat is absorbed. Add broth slowly while whisking. Add nutmeg and honey, and stir to combine. Add spinach and stir to coat evenly. Season with salt and pepper.

Suggestions: Make this recipe with Swiss chard, beet greens, pearl onions, or corn.

Kitchen Tips

Creamed spinach classically includes cream among its ingredients, but it also classically accompanies red meat. So to stay true to the Bible's dietary laws, this version has been de-dairied. The name creamed refers to its texture. If you plan to eat this dish with fish or other vegetables, replace the broth with cream.

Roasted Root Vegetables

The more color you have on your plate, the more nutrients you have in your diet. Choose a variety of colorful root vegetables for this dish. Dozens of varieties are available, especially in the fall.

Serves 8
Prep time: 15 minutes
Cook time: 60 minutes

1 small butternut squash, peeled and diced

3 parsnips, peeled and diced

1 turnip, peeled and diced

2 beets, peeled and diced

2 fennel bulbs, sliced

8 new potatoes, halved

4 carrots, peeled and diced

2 large yellow onions, sliced

8 cloves garlic, peeled and left whole

1 cup olive oil

¼ cup fresh rosemary needles, minced

½ tsp. salt

½ tsp. pepper

1. Preheat oven to 400°F. In a large bowl, combine squash, parsnips, turnip, beets, fennel, potatoes, carrots, onions, and garlic. Add oil, rosemary, salt, and pepper, and toss well to thoroughly coat all vegetables. Spread vegetables out onto a cookie sheet in one single layer. Bake, stirring occasionally, until tender and golden brown, about 1 hour.

Suggestions: If you don't have all these roots, use what you have. The same recipe with one or two roots is still good.

Biblical Culture
Roots have been consumed throughout human history. It is thought that early man began walking upright in response to long treks in search of tubers.

Sautéed Mixed Greens

Wilted greens are meant to be just that, not cooked and soggy and not fresh and crisp, but just slightly limp. Watch the cooking time carefully, and don't overdo it.

2 TB. olive oil

3 cloves garlic, minced

1 cup green onions, chopped

2 cups spinach, cleaned and chopped

2 cups Swiss chard, cleaned and chopped

2 cups beet greens, cleaned and chopped

2 cups Napa cabbage, cleaned and chopped

Zest and juice of 1 lemon (about 2 TB. juice)

½ tsp. kosher salt

½ cup pecans, chopped

Serves 8	
Prep time: 30 minutes	
Cook time: 90 minutes	

1. Heat oil in a large sauté pan over high heat. Add garlic and onions and cook until tender. Add spinach, chard, beet greens, and cabbage, stir, and cover for 1-2 minutes until wilted but still bright green. Add lemon, salt, and pecans, and stir to coat evenly.

Suggestions: If serving this with fish or other vegetables, sprinkle the top with crumbled goat or feta cheese. The tangy, creamy cheese is a nice complement to these savory greens.

Kitchen Tips

Fresh garden greens need careful cleaning. Many grow in sandy soil and are reluctant to part with it. Soak them in a sink full of cold water several times, draining and rinsing thoroughly.

Baked Broccoli and Cheese

This dish contains both milk and cheese. Observant homes should reserve it for fish night.

Serves 4
Prep time: 5 minutes
Cook time: 10 minutes

2 lb. broccoli florets and trimmed stems

3 qt. water

2 TB. olive oil

2 TB. whole-wheat flour

1 cup milk

1 TB. Dijon mustard

½ tsp. kosher salt

1 tsp. fresh grated nutmeg

1 cup cheddar cheese

1 cup cracker crumbs

½ cup Parmesan cheese

1. Cook broccoli in boiling water until barely tender, about 5 minutes. Drain and set aside.

2. Preheat oven to 350°F. Heat oil in a large sauté pan over high heat. Add flour, stirring until fat is absorbed. Slowly add milk, and stir until thick. Add mustard, salt, nutmeg, and cheese, and stir to melt. Add broccoli and mix well to coat. Transfer to baking dish, top with crumbs and Parmesan, and bake for 20 minutes until bubbly and brown.

Suggestions: Make this same dish with cauliflower.

Kitchen Tips

Cheddar cheese comes from the village of Cheddar in Somerset, England. There they created the technique of cheddaring, in which the whey is drained from cooked curds. The curds are then stacked, turned, formed, and aged. The orange color comes from the addition of annatto seed and is meant as a means of identification. Excellent cheddars are made all over the world, including some white and yellow varieties. Hundreds of other cheeses will also work in this recipe, but stay away from stringy cheeses like mozzarella, which make the dish hard to eat.

French-Style Squash, Tomato, Peppers, and Eggplant

The name of this dish is ratatouille, and it is a favorite recipe for entertaining. Easy to make, it keeps well for several days and improves with age.

3 cups diced eggplant

3 TB. kosher salt

½ cup olive oil

1 large onion, diced

4 cloves garlic, minced

¼ cup fresh oregano, minced

2 cups red bell peppers, seeded and diced

3 cups zucchini, diced

2 cups Roma tomatoes, peeled, seeded and diced

2 TB. fresh basil, minced

Salt and pepper to taste

Serves 4
Prep time: 30 minutes
Cook time: 60 minutes

1. Combine eggplant and salt in a large colander, mix to coat well, and set aside to drain for 30 minutes.

2. Heat oil in a large sauté pan over medium heat. Add onion and garlic, and cook until tender. Add oregano and cook until golden. Rinse eggplant and add, along with peppers, zucchini, and tomatoes. Cover and simmer 30 minutes. Remove lid and cook to reduce liquid. Add basil, salt, and pepper.

Suggestions: Serve this dish hot or cold. It makes a great side dish, cold salad, or a sauce for grilled fish or chicken and holds well in the refrigerator for up to three days.

Kitchen Tips

To peel and seed a tomato, cut an X in the end, drop it in boiling water for 30 seconds, then transfer directly to ice water. The temperature shock loosens the skin, and it peels right off. To remove the seeds and juice, cut the peeled tomato in half, not from end to end, but through the middle. Squeeze out the seeds and juice as if it were an orange you were juicing. Then dice it up. Voilà! The French term for this technique is *tomato concassé!*

Fava Beans with Artichokes and Garlic

If you don't have fresh beans, use frozen. Canned beans are too soft for this crisp, fresh sauté.

Serves 4
Prep time: 15 minutes
Cook time: 10 minutes

2 TB. olive oil

4 cloves garlic, sliced

1 cup green onions, chopped

4 cups fresh fava beans

1 (15 oz.) can artichoke hearts (not marinated), quartered

2 ripe tomatoes, diced

1 cup dry white wine

1 tsp. dried thyme

½ tsp. kosher salt

½ tsp. ground black pepper

1. Heat oil in a large sauté pan over high heat. Add garlic and onions, and cook until tender. Add beans and artichokes, and cook, stirring, for 3-5 minutes until lightly browned. Add tomatoes, wine, and thyme, and simmer another 2-3 minutes. Season with salt and pepper and serve.

Suggestions: Great hot or cold, this dish is a lovely accompaniment to both red meat and seafood.

White Beans with Tomatoes and Herbs

Kalamata olives, which give this recipe a salty tang, are available in most supermarkets, but if you have trouble finding them, plain black olives will do.

4 TB. olive oil, divided	2 (15 oz.) cans navy or white northern beans
2 shallots, minced	1 cup kalamata olives, chopped
3 large tomatoes, diced	1½ cup bread crumbs
1 TB. fresh oregano	2 cloves garlic, minced
1 TB. fresh sage	¼ cup fresh parsley, minced
1 TB. fresh thyme	

Serves 4
Prep time: 20 minutes
Cook time: 40 minutes

1. Preheat oven to 350°F. In a large sauté pan over high heat, cook shallots in 2 tablespoons olive oil until tender. Add tomatoes, oregano, sage, thyme, navy and northern beans, and olives. Reduce heat and simmer 5 minutes, then transfer to baking dish.

2. In a separate bowl, combine bread crumbs, garlic, parsley, and remaining oil, and stir together until well moistened. Sprinkle mixture over beans and bake 30-40 minutes until bubbly and brown.

Suggestions: Serve this hearty dish with warm rye bread, and you've got a hearty meal.

 Kitchen Tips

Beans are an excellent source of protein, recommended for vegetarians. But meat eaters need them, too. The USDA recommends that adults eat at least three cups of beans each week as a subgroup of the vegetable category.

Fried Okra

Okra originated in Ethiopia and was grown by the ancient
Egyptians in the twelfth century B.C.

Serves 4
Prep time: 60 minutes
Cook time: 10 minutes

1 lb. okra, fresh or frozen, rinsed and sliced into wheels

1 qt. white vinegar

2 eggs

1 tsp. salt

2 cups whole-wheat flour

2 cups cornmeal

1 TB. cayenne pepper

4 TB. olive oil

½ tsp. kosher salt

1. Soak sliced okra in vinegar for 30-60 minutes. Drain and rinse
   thoroughly. In a small bowl, whisk together eggs and salt. In a
   separate bowl combine flour, cornmeal, and cayenne.

2. Heat oil over high heat. Working in batches, dredge okra in
   egg and then cornmeal. Shake off excess, and fry until golden
   brown, about 3 minutes. Drain on paper towels, and sprinkle
   with salt.

Kitchen Tips

It's the slime that turns people off to okra. The vinegar soak is
a great way to combat this. Slicing the okra in small rounds
releases more of the slime in the vinegar rinse. If you like the
slime, then by all means, omit the vinegar and leave the okra
whole.

Sautéed Artichokes

This simple dish accentuates the unique qualities of the artichoke.

2 TB. olive oil

4 cloves garlic, sliced

2 (15 oz.) cans artichoke hearts

2 sprigs fresh rosemary

1 bay leaf

Juice of 1 lemon (about 2 TB.)

½ tsp. kosher salt

Serves 4	
Prep time: 10 minutes	
Cook time: 15 minutes	

1. Heat oil in a large sauté pan over medium heat. Add garlic and cook until tender. Add artichokes, rosemary, and bay leaf, and cook until golden brown. Season with lemon and salt just before serving.

Suggestions: Chill it overnight for a simple homemade marinated artichoke.

Biblical Culture

The artichoke is related to the cardoon, another edible thistle. In the second century B.C., Greek philosopher Theophrastus discussed eating wild thistle and gave detailed instructions regarding its cultivation. The species clearly originated in the Mediterranean region but exactly where is unclear. Evidence of its growth can be found in Tunisia, the ancient Carthage, whose inhabitants, the Phoenicians, were a seafaring people who probably spread this thistle throughout the Mediterranean region.

Stuffed Zucchini

This recipe is easy, quick, and always a hit.

Serves 4-8
Prep time: 10 minutes
Cook time: 5 minutes

4 large zucchini

1 cup mayonnaise

1 cup Parmesan cheese

1 cup green onions, chopped

1. Preheat broiler. In a large bowl, mix together mayonnaise, cheese, and onions. Slice zucchini in half lengthwise, and place cut-side-up onto baking sheet. Spread cheese mixture generously across zucchini. Broil until golden brown and bubbly, about 5 minutes. Serve hot.

Suggestions: If you have giant zucchini, make one huge boat and slice it at the table like a loaf of bread.

Kitchen Tips

There are several low-calorie and reduced-fat mayonnaise products on the market, but all contain fat in some form. To do away with it all together, substitute sour cream. But be warned, the recipe then contains dairy and should not be eaten with meat.

Pilafs, Potatoes, and Pasta

In This Chapter

- ◆ Choosing and working with grain
- ◆ Potatoes boiled and baked
- ◆ Noodles in light, savory sauce

"Do not be deceived; God is not mocked, for whatever a man sows, that he will also reap." (Galatians 6:7 RSV)

Grains are the single most important food in the history of civilization. By learning to cultivate this highly nutritious food, man graduated from a migratory life of hunting and gathering to a life of farming. This led to the growth of villages, irrigation, engineering, and government—all thanks to the humble grain.

Get Your Grains

Grain is also the most underutilized food in the United States. We eat a lot of wheat, but it's made into highly refined flour and mixed with refined sugars and hydrogenated oils until it is no longer recognizable as grain. In this state, the nutrients God gave the grain are gone, and it does more harm than good.

The processed grains found in white breads, white rice, and white flour are a major culprit in the poor health of modern humans. Refined grains are, in part, responsible for the epidemic of weight gain, type 2 diabetes, and cardiovascular disease. In addition, lack of fiber in the modern diet leads to gastrointestinal disorders, including several forms of cancer.

Increased intake of whole-grain products reduces these risks dramatically. The average adult should consume 8-11 servings of whole-grain foods a day. The portion sizes vary, but you should aim for 4-5 cups of grains every day. Most Americans get nowhere near that amount of whole grains, which is a shame because many interesting and delicious grains are available. This chapter introduces you to some basic pilaf recipes, in the hope that you will branch out on your own and investigate the use of grains in your daily meal plan.

The basic method of cooking grain is to boil it in water. The ratio of water to grain varies, but it is generally $2^{1}/_{2}$ to 3 parts water to 1 part grain. Water is boiled, and then the grains are added and simmered with the lid on to trap the steam, which tenderizes the grain by encouraging absorption of water. You can also cook grain as you would pasta, in a huge pot of boiling water, straining out the grain when tender. This method loses some nutrients but is convenient if the optimal water-to-grain ratio is not known.

While simply boiling grains works to cook them, toasting greatly enhances their flavor. Sautéed in a small amount of oil until brown and fragrant, grain takes on a nutty, rich flavor.

Many health and whole food stores carry an assortment of grains, both packaged and in bulk. They are also widely available online (see Appendix B).

Use some of the following common grains to make pilafs similar to those in this chapter:

Amaranth   A tiny grain grown at high altitude, popular in the Andes and Himalayas, and commonly popped like popcorn.

Barley   Hulled barley has the bran intact, while pearled or polished has the bran removed.

Buckwheat   Actually the seed of an herb, native to Russia and known as *kasha* when toasted.

Bulgur   Wheat kernels that have been steamed, dried, and crushed.

Couscous   Coarse granular semolina, a flour made from protein-rich Dur wheat.

Cracked Wheat   Crushed wheat kernels with the bran intact, not presteamed like bulgur.

Kamut   An ancient strain of wheat, more than twice the size of modern wheat kernels with a greater amount of protein.

Millet   Used mostly as birdseed in the United States, this small grain is a staple food in much of the world, due to its high protein content and pleasantly mild flavor.

Oats   Available as *groats*, rolled, quick-cooking, and steel-cut.

Quinoa   Tiny grain, extremely high in protein, consumed by Incans and Aztecs.

def•i•ni•tion

Groat is the term used for a grain that is hulled and crushed.

Rye   Closely related to barley and wheat, available rolled and as rye berries, in which the grain is whole with the bran removed.

Spelt   An ancient relative of wheat, native to Southern Europe, which has more protein than common wheat.

Teff   A tiny grain from Africa, high in dietary fiber and iron and providing some protein and calcium.

Triticale   A nutritious hybrid of wheat and rye.

Wheat Berries   Whole grains of wheat stripped of their outer hulls.

Potatoes

The potato often gets a bad rap, mostly because of its association with french fries. But it packs a nutritional punch as it is high in vitamins C and B_6 and is one of the best natural sources of potassium and fiber. It is low-fat, low-calorie (100 calories in a medium potato), and cholesterol-free.

What mucks potatoes up is all the stuff we add to them. For that reason, these recipes include, along with traditional preparations, healthy suggestions to help you cut the fat, should you choose to do so.

There are two kinds of potatoes on the market: waxy and mealy. Waxy potatoes have thinner skins and hold their shape well during cooking, which makes them perfect to boil for salads. They include red- and white-skinned new potatoes, Yukon Gold potatoes, and Peruvian purple potatoes. Mealy potatoes, which include russet, Burbank, and Idaho brands, have thick brown skins and disintegrate with heat into soft, crumbly, fluffy potatoes, perfect for baking, mashing, and frying.

It is true that potatoes cook faster when they are cut smaller. But the more exposed surface area means more vital nutrients are lost in the water. Cooking them whole, with the skin on, holds them together and holds in all the good stuff.

Pasta

The origin of noodles is the subject of some debate, but the first noodles were likely nothing more than dried gruel. Grains mixed to a paste, rolled thin, and dried were the first attempts at grain preservation. Such foods were portable and nutritious, perfect for travelers.

Every culture has its own form of noodles, made from many types of grains, including rice, potato, buckwheat, millet, and soy. Italian pasta (meaning "paste") is made from high-protein Durham wheat and is the most widely available noodle.

While Durham has high protein, the processing of it, as with white flour, diminishes much of the nutritional value. Whole-wheat pasta is fairly common now and is available in a wide assortment of shapes and sizes. By making the switch to whole-wheat pasta, you can begin to reverse the effects of a refined food diet.

Cooking Pasta

The secret to cooking pasta properly is to use plenty of water. Choose a large pot that holds at least five quarts. Allow the water to come to a full rolling boil before adding pasta. When you add pasta, the water will stop boiling momentarily, so immediately stir the pasta around to keep it from sinking and sticking. Oil added to the water will only rise to the top and does nothing to prevent pasta from sticking. But tossing finished pasta with a little oil after draining will help keep it loose.

Brown Rice Pilaf

The key to this simple dish is toasting the grain in oil before adding the liquid. It takes on a rich, nutty flavor that plain, boiled rice never has.

2 TB. olive oil	1 bay leaf
1 large yellow onion, diced	½ tsp. kosher salt
1 cup brown rice	½ cup sliced almonds
2 cloves garlic, minced	½ cup raisins
2 tsp. ground cumin	1½ cup vegetable broth
1 tsp. dry mustard	1 cup water
1 tsp. cinnamon	

> *Serves 4*
> **Prep time:** 10 minutes
> **Cook time:** 40 minutes

1. In a large sauté pan over high heat, cook onion in olive oil until tender. Add rice and cook 8-10 minutes, stirring, until toasted and brown. Add garlic, cumin, mustard, cinnamon, bay leaf, salt, almonds, and raisins, and cook another 5 minutes. Stir in broth and water, and bring to a boil. Reduce heat to low, cover, and cook 30 minutes until liquid is absorbed. Fluff with a fork just before serving.

Suggestions: Add a can of beans with the water and this side dish becomes a healthy meal.

Kitchen Tips _____

If you're cooking for a crowd and your stove top gets crowded, finish this off in a 350°F oven. Just bring the liquid to a boil, then transfer to a baking dish and cover.

Barley with Wild Mushrooms

Barley is available in several forms. Hulled barley has the bran and is more nutritious, but it takes up to an hour or more to cook. Quick barley has been steamed and will take only 15 minutes to cook. I like pearled, which falls in between. If you substitute, time the dish accordingly.

Serves 4-6
Prep time: 15 minutes
Cook time: 45 minutes

2 TB. olive oil	½ tsp. kosher salt
1 yellow onion, chopped	1 cup pearled barley
3 cloves garlic, minced	½ cup red wine
1 lb. mushrooms, chopped	3 cups beef broth
1 TB. dried thyme	

1. Heat oil in a large sauté pan over high heat. Add onion and cook until tender. Add garlic, mushrooms, thyme, and salt, and cook until dry. Add barley and cook 5-10 minutes, stirring, until toasted brown. Deglaze with wine, and cook until evaporated. Add broth and bring to a boil. Reduce heat to low, cover, and cook 45 minutes until liquid is absorbed and barley is tender. Fluff with a fork just before serving.

Suggestions: The mushrooms add an earthy quality to this dish which nicely complements darker meats like duck, lamb, and beef.

Kitchen Tips

Increase the mushroom factor by using shiitake, crimini, portobello, morel, or chanterelle mushrooms. If you can't find them fresh, look for the dried form. You can easily reconstitute them in water, and add the soaking water to the dish to further intensify the mushroominess.

Mixed-Grain Pilaf

Timing is the trick to this recipe because each grain requires a different cooking time.

3 TB. olive oil	¼ cup barley
1 large yellow onion, chopped	½ tsp. kosher salt
1 carrot, chopped	3 cups chicken broth
1 stalk celery, chopped	¼ cup brown rice
3 cloves garlic, minced	¼ cup cracked wheat
1 TB. sesame seeds	¼ cup parsley, chopped
¼ cup wild rice	

Serves 4-6
Prep time: 15 minutes
Cook time: 60 minutes

1. Heat oil in a large sauté pan over high heat. Add onion, carrot, celery, and garlic, and cook until tender. Add sesame seeds, wild rice, and barley, and cook 5-10 minutes, stirring, until toasted and brown. Add salt and broth, and bring to a boil. Reduce heat to low, cover, and cook 15 minutes. At the 15 minute mark, stir in brown rice and cook another 15 minutes. Lastly, add wheat and finish cooking, 15 minutes, until liquid is absorbed. Fluff with a fork just before serving, and top with chopped parsley.

Suggestions: Add vegetables to this dish but only during the last 10 minutes of cooking. Try some asparagus or green beans cut into 1-inch pieces.

Kitchen Tips

A number of grains will work well in this dish, such as millet, quinoa, buckwheat, kamut, or spelt. They all require a different water-to-grain ratio, so check the package instructions. Some may be quick-cooking; others may still have their hulls. It's worth the effort, though, as these more obscure grains are all quite good and make a terrific change of pace.

Wild Rice with Almonds

Wild rice comes from a wild marsh grass native to the northern part of the United States. Chewier and nuttier than regular rice, it is commonly thought to be undercooked.

Serves 4
Prep time: 20 minutes
Cook time: 60 minutes

2 TB. olive oil

2 leeks, chopped thin

1 cup wild rice

Zest of 1 lemon

½ cup sliced almonds

3 cups water

½ tsp. kosher salt

1. Heat oil in a large sauté pan over high heat. Add leeks and cook until tender. Add rice, zest, and almonds and cook 5-10 minutes, stirring, until toasted and brown. Add water and bring to a boil. Reduce heat to low, cover, and cook 45-60 minutes until liquid is absorbed. Add salt and fluff with a fork just before serving.

Suggestions: The chewy texture of wild rice makes a nice accompaniment to the tender flakey meat of grilled or broiled fish.

Biblical Culture

Common rice and wild rice are in the same botanical family, *poaceae*, or true grass, but have separate genera. Wild rice is native to North America, while common rice came from the foothills of the Himalayas. Domestication of rice occurred very early, in the sixth century B.C., but it appears to have stayed east of the Fertile Crescent until the first century A.D. An African native variety, found along the Niger River, was grown as early as 1500 B.C., but it never caught on.

Biblical Culture

This dish, a staple of northern Italian peasants, is similar to dishes of the poor around the globe. Before corn was brought back from the New World, a number of other grains were used, including ancient wheat, millet, and buckwheat. This kind of mush is highly nutritious but not very elegant. Paste made from grain and water was first made by early humans when vessels made of pottery became available.

Mashed Potatoes

There is no denying the decadent flavor of these potatoes. If the cream is too much for you, replace it with nonfat yogurt, sour cream, or low-fat cottage cheese, puréed in a blender.

4 medium russet potatoes, peeled and quartered

3 qt. water

2 TB. olive oil

½ cup cream

Salt and pepper to taste

Serves 4	
Prep time: 60 minutes	
Cook time: 10 minutes	

1. Boil potatoes until tender, about 30 minutes. Drain them thoroughly and spread them out on a baking sheet to dry for 15 minutes.

2. Combine olive oil and cream in a saucepan and set over low heat until warm. Put cooled potatoes through a ricer and add to cream. Beat with a whisk until smooth. Season with salt and pepper, and serve immediately. Or transfer potatoes to a casserole, cover with thin layer of cream, and bake at 350°F until golden brown.

Suggestions: Turn these spuds into garlic mash. Sauté 4 cloves of minced garlic in olive oil until golden, then add with cream. You may also roast 2 whole heads of garlic in tin foil and bake for 30 minutes at 400°F, until soft. Cut in half horizontally and squeeze out the soft roasted garlic into the potatoes.

def•i•ni•tion

A **ricer** is an old-fashioned tool that is basically a handheld extruder. The potato goes into a small perforated barrel, and a plunger shoves it through tiny holes. The result is a fine purée of potato made without excessive beating. If you don't have a ricer, use a food mill, or force the potato by hand through a fine colander. An old handheld masher works, too, if you don't mind lumps.

Herb-Roasted New Potatoes

This easy dish is always popular. Serve it hot from the oven for best results.

Serves 4
Prep time: 15 minutes
Cook time: 45 minutes

8-10 small red new potatoes

2 TB. olive oil

2 TB. fresh rosemary, chopped

1 TB. fresh thyme, chopped

1 TB. fresh sage, chopped

½ tsp. kosher salt

½ tsp. ground black pepper

1. Preheat oven to 400°F. In a large bowl, combine potatoes, oil, rosemary, thyme, and sage. Toss together until well coated, and spread into one layer on a baking sheet or roasting pan. Bake 30-45 minutes, until tender and brown.

Suggestions: Try this recipe with some unusual potatoes. Farmers' markets offer unique heirloom varieties, including narrow fingerling and purple Peruvian potatoes.

Potato Pancakes

During Hanukkah, potato pancakes called *latkes* are fried in oil in celebration of the Miracle of the Oil, in which a menorah with only enough oil for one day miraculously burned for eight. There are many variations to the recipe, including pancakes made from straight potatoes or with added onions, eggs, flour, matzo meal, or bread crumbs.

3 eggs

2 TB. flour

½ tsp. salt

¼ tsp. pepper

2 large russet potatoes, peeled and grated

1 medium yellow onion, grated

4 TB. olive oil

Serves 4	
Prep time: 10 minutes	
Cook time: 15 minutes	

1. In a large bowl, combine eggs, flour, salt, and pepper, and mix well. Add potatoes and onion, and mix to coat thoroughly.

2. Heat 2 tablespoons oil in a large skillet, and drop in ½-cup-size patties of potato mixture. Do not crowd patties in the pan. Fry until browned, about 3 minutes per side. Drain on paper towels, and repeat with remaining potatoes. Serve immediately, or keep warm in a 150°F oven.

Suggestions: Serve hot, topped with sour cream and applesauce.

Kitchen Tips

Potatoes oxidize, or turn grey, when exposed to air. The color does not affect the flavor, but it looks bad. To prevent discoloration, soak potatoes in cold water.

Oven Fries

These potatoes are surprisingly satisfying, despite their lack of fat. Try mixing up the seasoning a bit, with Cajun or other seasoning salts.

Serves 4	
Prep time: 15 minutes	
Cook time: 60 minutes	

3 large russet potatoes, sliced in ¼-inch sticks

½ tsp kosher salt

½ tsp. granulated garlic

½ tsp. granulated onion

½ tsp. dried oregano

½ tsp black pepper

2 egg whites

1. Preheat oven to 450°F. In a large bowl, combine potatoes, salt, garlic, onion, oregano, and pepper. Add egg whites, and toss together until well coated. Spread into one layer on a baking sheet or roasting pan. Bake 10 minutes, remove from oven, and stir briefly. Return to oven for another 10 minutes, and stir again. Repeat his for another 30-40 minutes, until potatoes are crisp, brown, and tender. Serve immediately.

Suggestions: Turn this dish into home fries or chips simply by changing the way you slice your potatoes. However you slice them, keep them thin.

Baked Sweet Potatoes

This is a lightened version of the Thanksgiving favorite candied yams. These sweet potatoes are lusciously sweet on their own, without any marshmallows.

3 large yams or sweet potatoes

¼ cup honey

Juice and zest of 1 lemon

½ tsp. salt

¼ tsp. pepper

¼ tsp. nutmeg

¼ tsp. ground ginger

¼ tsp. cinnamon

2 TB. olive oil

Serves 4	
Prep time: 60 minutes	
Cook time: 20 minutes	

1. Coat a baking dish with pan spray. Boil yams whole, in their skins, until tender, about 30 minutes. Cool, peel, and slice into ½-inch thick coins, and layer in prepared dish.

2. Preheat oven to 350°F. In a small bowl combine honey, lemon juice and zest, salt, pepper, nutmeg, ginger, and cinnamon. Mix well, and distribute evenly over top of yams. Drizzle with olive oil and bake until golden brown and bubbly, about 20 minutes.

Suggestions: For a change of pace, replace spices with 1 tablespoon herbes de Provence.

Kitchen Tips

Yams or sweet potatoes? They're similar but are actually two different plant species. And unfortunately, markets often get the two confused. (Canned yams are frequently sweet potatoes.) The sweet potato is a nutritional powerhouse, outperforming other vegetables with fiber, vitamins A and C, iron, and calcium. Eating one sweet potato with its skin gives you more fiber than a bowl of oatmeal.

Potato Dumplings

Called *gnocchi* in Italian, which means "lump" or "knot," these are another example of an economizing dish easily made with leftovers. This recipe is plain and basic with luscious browned butter, but the options for toppings and sauces are endless.

Serves 4	
Prep time: 60 minutes	
Cook time: 30 minutes	

3 large baking russet potatoes	¼ tsp. pepper
1½ cup whole-wheat flour	4 TB. butter
1 egg	2-3 qt. water
½ tsp. salt	1 tsp. salt
½ tsp. nutmeg	

Kitchen Tips

The recipe for these tummy-warming dumplings reads "more flour as needed." The amount is variable because moisture inside a boiled potato is variable. Add flour until the dough is easy to handle and is no longer sticky.

1. Cook potatoes, whole, in boiling water until tender. While still warm, peel and pass through a potato ricer or food mill. Transfer to a large bowl and add flour, egg, salt, nutmeg, and pepper. Mix well. Transfer to a floured countertop and knead to form a firm dough, about 5 minutes. Add more flour as needed.

2. Melt butter in a large sauté pan, and cook 2-3 minutes, until it begins to brown. Turn off the heat and set aside. Bring water and salt to a full rolling boil. Divide dough into 4 sections, and roll each section into ½-inch thick ropes. Slice each rope into 1-inch wide pieces. Roll and pinch each piece across the back of a fork to form decorative fluting. Drop gnocchi into boiling water, and cook until they float, about 2-3 minutes. Transfer with slotted spoon to the browned butter pan. Repeat with remaining dough. Rewarm gnocchi in brown butter and serve.

Suggestions: Pesto is terrific with gnocchi. Buy it, or make it from scratch. Combine in a blender 4 cups of fresh basil leaves, 3 cloves garlic, ½ cup toasted pine nuts or walnuts, and ¼ cup Parmesan cheese. Blend and slowly drizzle in ¼-½ cup olive oil until it's the consistency of tomato sauce. Season with salt and pepper.

Spaghetti with Tomato and Herbs

This fast and fresh pasta dish is surprisingly satisfying.

1 TB. olive oil

1 small yellow onion, diced

3 cloves garlic, minced

1 TB. dried oregano

1 tsp. ground fennel seed

2 large, ripe tomatoes

1 tsp. salt

½ tsp. pepper

½ tsp. red pepper flakes, crushed

2 qt. water

1 tsp. salt

1 lb. spaghetti

2 TB. olive oil

1 cup Parmesan cheese

Serves 4
Prep time: 15 minutes
Cook time: 45 minutes

1. Heat olive oil in a large sauté pan over medium heat, and cook onions until tender. Add garlic, oregano, and fennel, and cook until golden brown. Reduce heat, stir in tomatoes, and cook for 5 minutes to warm through. Season with salt, pepper, and pepper flakes, and set aside.

2. Bring water and salt to a full rolling boil. Add spaghetti, stir, and cook *al dente*, about 12 minutes. Drain, add oil, stir to coat, and add to tomato sauce. Top with Parmesan cheese before serving.

Suggestions: Serve with a fresh green salad and crusty Italian Bread (Chapter 4).

def•i•ni•tion

The term **al dente** means literally "to the tooth," and despite popular belief, it does not mean chewy. Pasta, and often vegetables, are described this way when they are cooked through, with a little bit of texture. The purpose of the term is to remind cooks that they should not cook pasta and vegetables until mushy.

Fettuccini in Cream Sauce

This recipe is called Alfredo and was created in the early twentieth century at Alfredo's Restaurant in Rome.

Serves 4
Prep time: 30 minutes
Cook time: 30 minutes

2 qt. water

1 tsp. salt

1 lb. fettuccini

2 TB. olive oil

2 cloves garlic, minced

3 cups heavy cream

1 cup *Romano* cheese, grated

1 cup Parmesan cheese, grated

1 egg yolk

1 TB. milk, cold

1 tsp. salt

½ tsp. grated nutmeg

½ tsp. pepper

1. Bring water and salt to a full rolling boil. Add fettuccini, stir, and cook al dente, about 12 minutes. Drain and rinse with cold water.

2. Meanwhile, heat olive oil in a large saucepan over medium heat. Add garlic, and cook until golden brown. Add cream and reduce by ½. Add Romano and Parmesan cheese and stir until melted. In a separate bowl, whisk together yolk and milk, then add to sauce. Reduce heat and cook, stirring continuously 3-5 minutes to warm and thicken. Add salt, nutmeg, and pepper.

3. Add fettuccini to sauce and toss to coat. Serve pasta in large flat bowls, topped with more grated Parmesan.

Suggestions: Lighten this very rich dish by substituting low-fat cottage cheese or silken tofu puréed in a blender.

def•i•ni•tion

Named for the city of Rome, **Romano** cheese, like Parmesan, is a *grana* cheese, which means "grain" in Italian. Grana are hard, often salty, cheeses, perfect for grating.

Baked Ziti

You can use any pasta you like in this dish, but you'll have to change the name.

3 qt. water

1 tsp. kosher salt

1 lb. ziti

2 TB. olive oil

1 large yellow onion, chopped

3 cloves garlic, minced

1 TB. dried oregano

1 TB. dried basil

1 TB. ground fennel seed

1 (28 oz.) can crushed tomatoes

8 oz. mozzarella cheese, grated

½ cup grated Parmesan cheese

Serves 4	
Prep time: 30 minutes	
Cook time: 45 minutes	

1. Bring water and salt to a full rolling boil. Add ziti, stir, and cook al dente, about 12 minutes. Drain and rinse with cold water.

2. Meanwhile, heat olive oil in a large sauté pan over high heat. Add onion, garlic, oregano, basil, and fennel, and cook until tender. Add tomatoes, reduce heat, and stir 5-10 minutes to warm. Remove from heat and add ziti. Toss to coat.

3. Preheat oven to 350°F. Coat a baking dish with pan spray. Layer ziti in baking dish alternately with mozzarella. Top with Parmesan and bake 30-40 minutes until brown and bubbly.

Suggestions: Add layers of sautéed mushroom, spinach, or ricotta cheese.

def•i•ni•tion

Ziti is a popular pasta, shaped like little tubes. Its name is plural for *zito*, meaning "bridegroom." Tubular pasta works best in this dish to better hold in the sauce. Try it with the angled *penne* (meaning "feather" or "quill"), the larger, ribbed *rigatoni* (meaning "to draw a line"), or the shell-shaped *conchiglie* (meaning "seashells").

Baked Noodle Pudding

This dish is slightly sweet but is served as a main-meal side dish.

Serves 4
Prep time: 30 minutes
Cook time: 50 minutes

2 qt. water

1 tsp. kosher salt

1 (12 oz.) package wide egg *noodles*

2 cups cottage cheese

2 cups sour cream

¾ cup honey

5 eggs

2 TB. olive oil

2 tsp. vanilla extract

½ tsp. nutmeg

¼ cup bread crumbs

1 TB. cinnamon

1. Preheat oven to 350°F. Bring water and salt to a full rolling boil. Add noodles, stir, and cook until half done, about 5 minutes. Drain and rinse with cold water.

2. Meanwhile, in a large bowl stir together cottage cheese, sour cream, honey, eggs, oil, vanilla, and nutmeg. Add cooked noodles and mix well. Transfer to a baking dish. In a small bowl, combine bread crumbs and cinnamon, and sprinkle on top. Bake at 350°F until firm, about 45 minutes. Cool for 10 minutes before serving.

Suggestions: Lighten this rich pudding by using low-fat or nonfat versions of cottage cheese and sour cream.

def•i•ni•tion

This dish is called *kugel*, and historically it was a baked pudding made from bread, potatoes, rice, or any other leftover grains. But in the United States it has come to mean **noodles,** and noodles alone.

Part 6

Celebrating

Now that your daily menu is in order, focus turns to the occasions in which the same old meatloaf just won't do. For these events, these chapters provide sweet endings and distinctive menus. Celebrations do not have to include overindulgence, nor must they consist of poor diet choices. They can be nutritious and delicious. A body that lives year-round with an eye toward health can endure the occasional slice of well-deserved chocolate cake.

Chapter 15

Desserts

In This Chapter

- ◆ Basic baking techniques
- ◆ Fruits, nuts, and chocolate
- ◆ Cake, pudding, and pie

"Train yourself in godliness." (1 Timothy 4:7b RSV)

Dessert is the most beloved course at any table but is the worst one for us, providing our bodies little in the way of nutrition. We all know this, but still we all indulge because sweetness brings a little joy to our lives, and what's wrong with that?

The key to keeping dessert guilt-free is moderation. You can bake the world's best vegan-carob, whole-grain, flax brownie, but it's still not good for you if you eat half the pan.

Dessert is meant to be a celebration, not the close to every meal. Many people naturally crave sweetness after a meal, most often after one laden with simple carbohydrates. The healthful reaction to this is to enjoy a piece of fruit. Fresh or dried, the sugar in fruit is the same stuff as in candy, but it's natural, unprocessed, and loaded with fiber and other micronutrients that our bodies need.

That being said, you'll find the following chapter full of traditional desserts. Why? Because you have company and birthdays and occasions to celebrate. There are many recipes for healthy baked goods, using prune purée instead of butter and puréed tofu instead of cream. But most desserts worth eating need to have butter, eggs, and sugar to achieve the proper texture and consistency. There is no suitable substitute for chocolate or good pie dough or cream cheese frosting. Just remember, these are not meant to be eaten every day. They are special, and the only way to keep them special is to bake them only occasionally.

Mixing Ingredients

Many of these recipes call for adding dry and wet ingredients alternately. This means you add a small part of the sifted flour mixture, work it in completely, and then add a little bit of the wet ingredients. Do this two or three times until all ingredients are added to ensure that all blend thoroughly and easily. If you tried adding all the dry ingredients at once, you'd have trouble mixing it well and make a real mess.

Folding is a common instruction, which typically appears when a foam, like whipped eggs, yolks, or whites, is added into a batter. The intention is to incorporate the foam without deflating any of the air that you've whipped in. To accomplish this as efficiently as possible, I fold with a big whisk. The 30 or 40 wires of the whisk drag through the batter, pulling the foam along with it. The ingredients combine much faster and with fewer strokes than doing the same task with a rubber spatula.

When folding, I always use the same motion. I envision the bowl of batter as a clock and drag my whisk from 12 o'clock to 6 o'clock, turn the bowl counter-clockwise an inch or two, bring the whisk around to 9 o'clock, and repeat five or six times. Bringing the whisk through a different patch of batter each time gets your batter mixed as thoroughly as possible in as few strokes as possible. If, as you are folding, the batter loses its peak and becomes thin and runny, you have folded too much. Try to keep the volume full and thick.

Baking

Most recipes designate a specific pan for use, but you can bake cakes in any size pan, from cupcake size to sheet cake size and beyond. Smaller pans will bake faster and should be baked at a higher temperature for the best structure, usually 25 degrees hotter than indicated.

Large cakes benefit from a cooler oven, at least toward the end of baking
the cooking process carefully. If your super-size cake is browning faster than
is setting, turn it down and be patient. It takes the heat longer to enter the center of a
large cake than a smaller one.

Larger pans will, of course, need more
batter. You can simply multiply the recipes
as much as necessary. Keep the size of your
mixers and bowls in mind when increasing
recipes. Large recipes are sometimes hard
to mix thoroughly, so it is often better to
make a batter twice than to wrestle with an
overflowing mixer bowl.

To assure even cooking, I always rotate
my pans from front to back halfway through
baking. If I have more than one pan in the
oven, I rotate their positions, switching left
to right, top to bottom, or back to front.

Kitchen Tips

Beware! When rotating pans
in the oven, move quickly.
Reach in and slide things
around as best you can while
keeping the pans in the oven.
Removing the pans from the
oven, even briefly, will cause
a drop in temperature that can
cause a collapse.

Cutting-in Fat

The cut-in technique is a method of incorporating fat and flour together by crumbling. The butter and flour do not actually combine, but remain separate and should
never look like a paste. Little hunks of fat are the key to tender, flaky crust, or crumbly streusel. Use your fingertips, a pastry blender, or a couple of knives or forks to
break down the butter into pea-size pieces.

To cut-in successfully, follow one simple rule: keep the dough cold. Use cold
butter, cold flour, cold water, cold room, and cold hands. The thing that sets pie
dough apart from tart dough, cookie dough, or bread dough is its flakiness, and cold
is what makes flakiness possible.

Flakiness is achieved through the tiny pieces of butter suspended within the flour.
Butter contains water, and in the heat of the oven, that water turns into steam, which
creates pockets of air within the crust.

If the ingredients are not cold or are allowed to warm up, the tiny pieces of fat
will cream together with the flour, rather than remain in separate chunks. That creates
tough, hard crusts, not tender, flaky ones.

Forming

Remember fat softens with heat and gets soft and sticky as it warms. If you keep the dough cold while working with it, it will be easy to roll out. The warmer it gets, through room temperature or overhandling, the harder it is to roll. It sticks to the counter, the pin, your hands, and becomes the source of much frustration. To combat the problem, work quickly. As soon as the dough shows signs of warming, throw it in the fridge.

Blind-Baking

Bakers often forget that it takes time for heat to penetrate a pie, and that unlike a cake, a baked top does not necessarily mean a baked bottom. To assure your crust is baked on the bottom, prebaking is a must.

This technique is known as blind-baking and allows you to precook a pie shell, either fully or partially, so that once the filling goes in, it's only necessary to bake the pie as long as the filling requires. In some cases, like cream pies, the filling isn't baked at all, in which case blind-baking is essential.

To blind-bake a pie shell, form the dough in the pan, decoratively flute the edges, and chill until firm. Line the shell with foil, parchment paper, or heavy-duty plastic wrap (it shrinks, but doesn't melt), then fill it to the rim with dried beans or rice. The weight of this filling will keep the shell from melting, shrinking, and bubbling up. Bake at 350°F until the edges are golden brown. At this point the shell is half cooked and can be used for several recipes in which the filling needs only to be cooked a short while. To cook the shell completely, carefully remove the weights and return it to the oven until the bottom is browned.

Cooking Fruit

While the flavor of fruit remains fairly constant, the amount of sugar does not. Every supplier, farmer, and market offers drastically different qualities of the same product. A recipe may require more or less sugar as the sweetness of the fruit varies throughout the year. To combat this variant, eat the fruit raw and determine if it needs a lot or a little sugar. Taste it again after you add sugar to be sure you've got it right.

Basic Pie Dough

Keep all elements of this recipe as cold as possible. On really hot days, I freeze my flour. Every little bit helps.

½ **cup ice water**

1 **TB. cider vinegar**

3 **cups all-purpose flour**

1 **tsp. kosher salt**

2 **TB. sugar**

8 **oz. (2 sticks) unsalted butter, diced and chilled**

Makes enough dough for 3 (8-inch) circles
Prep time: 20 minutes
Chilling time: 1 hour

1. Combine water and vinegar, and set aside. In a medium bowl, sift together flour, salt, and sugar, and mix well. Cut-in butter to pea-size pieces. Add half water, and stir with a fork to moisten. Add enough additional water to just hold dough together. Press it into a disc, wrap it in plastic, and refrigerate for one hour. The dough should look marbled with visible patches of butter and flour. Refrigerate dough for two days, or freeze for up to one month.

2. To roll out dough, divide into three even pieces. Work with only one piece at a time, keeping rest refrigerated. Knead briefly to soften, and form into a disc. Place on a floured surface and, with a rolling pin, roll over center of dough in one direction. Turn dough 90° and roll in center again. Turn again, and repeat this pattern until dough is a 10-to-12-inch circle. Turning in this manner keeps it round and alerts you right away if it starts to stick to the counter. Spread flour under dough as necessary to prevent sticking. Work quickly to prevent dough from warming up.

3. Transfer dough to a pan by rolling up onto the pin or folding in half. Place lined pie shells in the refrigerator while rolling out remaining dough and preparing filling.

Kitchen Tips

Many bakers prefer to make pie crust with lard, which can be cut into the flour in smaller, thinner bits while still remaining separate. But lard is a pork product, and should be avoided in observant, health-conscious kitchens. I don't recommend using vegetable shortening or margarine in pie dough, either. Besides its adverse effects on health, it leaves a distinctive aftertaste that I find disagreeable. Butter is better.

Basic Graham Cracker Crust

Buy graham cracker crumbs or make your own by grinding crackers in a food processor or a blender or placing them in a zipper bag and crunching them with a rolling pin.

Makes crumbs for
1 (9-inch) pie shell

Prep time: 20 minutes
Cook time: 10 minutes

1½ cup graham cracker crumbs

2 TB. sugar

2 oz. (½ stick) butter

1. Preheat the oven to 350°F. Lightly coat one (9-inch) pie pan with pan spray. In a medium bowl combine graham cracker crumbs, sugar, and melted butter. Mix well and press into prepared pan, covering the bottom and sides. Bake at 350°F until lightly toasted, about 10 minutes. Cool completely before filling.

Suggestions: Replace graham cracker crumbs with finely ground nuts or your favorite cookie.

Angel Food Cake

This recipe calls for superfine sugar, also available as baker's sugar. It is finer than regular granulated, but it's not powdered. Make your own by grinding granulated sugar in a food processor. The recipe will work with regular sugar, too, but the texture will not be as fine.

1¾ cup superfine sugar, divided

1¼ tsp. kosher salt

1 cup cake flour

12 egg whites

⅓ cup warm water

1 tsp. vanilla extract

1½ tsp cream of tartar

Fills 1 (10-12") angel food pan	
Prep time: 30 minutes	
Cook time: 45 minutes	

1. Preheat the oven to 350°F. Triple sift 1 cup sugar with salt and flour. Whip egg whites together with water, vanilla, and cream of tartar. While whipping, slowly add remaining sugar, and beat to medium peaks. Sift flour over egg whites and fold in by hand, using a whisk. Transfer to an ungreased angel food pan, smooth top, and run a knife around batter to remove air pockets. Bake 35 minutes, until a pick inserted comes out clean. Cool completely, upside down.

Suggestions: Serve with a compote of fresh fruits. Combine slices of berries, stone fruits, citrus, lemon zest, and a tablespoon of honey. Stir together and let macerate while cake bakes.

Kitchen Tips

To judge the peak stage of whipping egg whites, spoon a bit out of the bowl and hold it upright. If it makes a peak that stands erect at the tip of the spoon, it is a *stiff peak*. If the peak bends over a bit at the tip, it is a *medium peak*. If the peak flops all the way over, it is a *soft peak*.

Chocolate Cake with Chocolate Fudge Frosting

It's chocolate cake. What more can I say?

Makes 2 (10") layers	
Prep time: 30 minutes	
Cook time: 60 minutes, plus 60 minutes cooling	
Finishing time: 30 minutes	

1¾ cups cake flour

½ cup cocoa powder

2 tsp. baking soda

½ tsp. salt

⅔ cup vegetable oil

¾ cup buttermilk

¾ cup cold black coffee

½ tsp. vanilla extract

1⅓ cups sugar

2 eggs

For the Frosting:

½ cup brown sugar

¼ cup water

2 TB. corn syrup

1 cup chocolate chips

3 TB. butter, softened

1 TB. vanilla extract

1 lb. box powdered sugar, sifted

2 TB. hot water

Kitchen Tips

Don't frost cakes when hot. The heat of the cake will melt the fat, and you'll have a runny mess on your hands. To speed up the cooling process, slice the cake into layers and refrigerate in sections. Be aware that by rushing this way, the crumb will dry out from uncovered refrigeration. To avoid this problem, plan ahead!

1. Preheat the oven to 350°F. Line two 10-inch round cake pans with pan spray and a circle of parchment paper. Sift together flour, cocoa, baking soda, and salt, and set aside. In a medium bowl combine oil, buttermilk, coffee, and vanilla, and set aside.

2. In a large bowl, use a whisk or electric mixer to whip sugar and eggs until light and fluffy, about 5 minutes. Fold dry ingredients into eggs alternately with wet ingredients. Divide batter between two pans, and bake for 30-45 minutes until a pick inserted at center of cake comes out clean. Cool 10 minutes before inverting onto a rack. Cool completely.

3. For frosting, combine sugar, water, and corn syrup in a large saucepan, and bring to a boil. When sugar is dissolved, remove from heat, add chocolate chips, butter, and vanilla, and stir to melt. Add powdered sugar alternately with hot water. Adjust frosting consistency with more hot water or powdered sugar as needed. Frost cake immediately. Cake must be cool, but frosting must be hot.

Suggestions: Add fresh raspberries, strawberries, or orange sections between the two layers for a pleasant, tart counterpoint to the sweet chocolate icing.

Fruit Cake

This is not the heavy, doorstop fruitcake of modern mythology. It is tender and light, with a delicate crumb. It's more like a cake and less like a brick.

4 cups dried fruits, such as golden raisins, currants, figs, dates, apricots, or dried cherries

Zest of 1 lemon

Zest of 1 orange

½ cup candied ginger, chopped

1 cup brandy

8 oz. (2 sticks) unsalted butter

1½ cups brown sugar, packed

4 eggs

3 cups cake flour

2 tsp. baking powder

1 tsp. cinnamon

1 tsp. ginger

1 tsp. nutmeg

½ tsp. salt

1 cup milk

Fills 1 (10-12-inch) bundt pan
Prep time: 30 minutes
Cook time: 50 minutes

1. Combine dried fruits, lemon and orange zest, candied ginger, and brandy, and set overnight to macerate.

2. Preheat the oven to 350°F. Coat a bundt pan with pan spray. Beat butter and brown sugar together until creamy and lump-free. Add eggs, 1 at a time. Sift together flour, baking powder, cinnamon, ginger, nutmeg, and salt, and add to batter alternately with milk. Drain excess moisture from fruit and fold in. Transfer to prepared pan and bake 35-45 minutes, until a toothpick inserted comes out clean.

Suggestions: Serve this cake plain, or drizzle it with icing. Combine 1 cup sifted powdered sugar, a pinch of cinnamon, 1 teaspoon vanilla or brandy, and 2-3 tablespoons milk. Beat well to achieve a thin, creamy consistency. Drizzle over warm cake and let cool.

Kitchen Tips

The pleasure of this cake is in the fruit. Create your own combinations from fruits you love. Soaking in brandy helps plump them up, but if you'd prefer to omit the alcohol, use fruit juice or plain water.

Carrot Cake with Cream Cheese Frosting

Just because it has carrots does not mean it counts as a vegetable. It's cake!

Serves 8-10
Prep time: 20 minutes
Cooking time: 45 minutes, plus 60 minutes cooling
Finishing time: 20 minutes

2 cups all-purpose flour

2 tsp. baking powder

1 1/2 tsp. baking soda

1 tsp. salt

2 tsp. cinnamon

2 tsp. nutmeg

1/2 tsp. clove

2 cups sugar

1 1/2 cup vegetable oil

4 eggs

2 cups grated carrot

1 (8 oz.) can crushed pineapple with juice

1 cup chopped walnuts, divided

For the Frosting:

2 oz. (1/2 stick) butter, softened

1 (8 oz.) package cream cheese, softened

1 TB. vanilla

1 (1 lb.) box powdered sugar, sifted

Kitchen Tips

Make this cake into cupcakes, or bake into a traditional cake form. Line two (10-inch) round cake pans with pan spray and a circle of parchment paper. Then, when cool, use the frosting to fill the center and ice the top.

1. Preheat the oven to 350°F. Coat a 9×13-inch rectangular pan with pan spray. Sift together flour, baking powder, baking soda, salt, cinnamon, nutmeg, and clove and set aside.

2. In a large bowl, mix together oil, eggs, carrots, and pineapple. Slowly add sifted ingredients, combine thoroughly, and fold in half the nuts. Pour into the prepared pan and bake for 30-45 minutes, until a pick inserted at center of cake comes out clean. Cool completely.

3. For the frosting, cream together butter, cream cheese, and vanilla with a sturdy spoon or electric mixer until lump-free. Slowly add powdered sugar, and mix until smooth. Spread on top of cooled carrot cake, and sprinkle with remaining nuts. To serve, slice into squares.

Suggestions: Add raisins, chocolate chips, other nuts, or bananas, or leave the garnish out completely and keep it pure carrot.

Pound Cake

This cake is so named because the original recipe called for a pound of each ingredient: eggs, sugar, flour, and butter. The batter was beaten vigorously (by hand) to incorporate air, which was the sole leavening before baking soda or powder was known.

2¼ cup cake flour	1 cup sugar
1 tsp. baking powder	1 TB. vanilla
¼ tsp salt	4 eggs
8 oz. (2 sticks) butter	2 TB. milk

> *Makes 1 (6×9") loaf pan*
>
> **Prep time:** 30 minutes
>
> **Cook time:** 60 minutes, plus 45 minutes cooling

1. Preheat oven to 325°F. Line a 6×9-inch loaf pan with pan spray and a strip of parchment paper. Sift together flour, baking powder, and salt and set aside. In a large bowl with a sturdy spoon or electric mixer, cream together butter and sugar until light and fluffy. Add vanilla and eggs, one by one. Add milk, and slowly add sifted ingredients. Pour batter into the loaf pan and bake for 45-60 minutes until a pick inserted at center of cake comes out clean. Cool 10 minutes before inverting onto a rack. Cool completely before slicing.

Suggestions: Jazz this pound cake up with any number of flavors. I like to use rose water in place of vanilla, which was a favorite flavoring of the Victorians. You can find rose water in Indian and Middle Eastern markets.

Kitchen Tips

Marbleize your pound cake by topping it with 1 cup chocolate sauce, caramel sauce, jam, or fruit filling. Use a spoon to fold the topping into the batter. Take care to use only a few folding strokes. If you overmix it, the cake will not be marbled.

Apple Spice Cake

Welcome your guests with the scent of this cake wafting through the house. But be careful: they may never leave.

Serves 8-10
Prep time: 30 minutes
Cook time: 45 minutes

5 eggs

1 cup granulated sugar

1 cup brown sugar, packed

1¼ cup vegetable oil

1 cup unsweetened apple-sauce

3 cups all-purpose flour

2 tsp. baking powder

2 tsp. baking soda

½ tsp. kosher salt

1 tsp. ground cinnamon

1 tsp. ground ginger

1 tsp. ground nutmeg

1 tsp. ground cardamom

½ tsp. ground clove

½ tsp. white pepper

1 cup grated apple

½ cup golden raisins

½ cup dried cranberries

½ cup pecan pieces

1 cup streusel

Biblical Culture

Spices were highly prized in biblical times. They perfumed the rich and powerful, healed the sick, and preserved the bodies of ancestors.

1. Preheat oven to 350°F. Coat a 9×13-inch baking pan with pan spray. Whip eggs with a mixer or whip until thick and pale yellow, about 5 minutes. Continue mixing and slowly add granulated and brown sugar, oil, and applesauce.

2. Sift together flour, baking powder, baking soda, salt, cinnamon, ginger, nutmeg, cardamom, clove, and white pepper, and slowly add to batter. Scrape sides of bowl periodically. Fold in apple, raisins, cranberries, and nuts, and transfer batter to baking pan. Top with streusel, and bake 30-45 minutes, until firm. A pick inserted into center of cake should come out clean.

Suggestions: Turn this into a pumpkin spice cake by substituting apples and applesauce with 2 cups pumpkin purée.

Chocolate Bread Pudding

Serve this warm and creamy dessert on a cold winter night. Or crank up the air-conditioner and pretend.

4 cups milk

1 (12 oz.) package chocolate chips, divided

4-6 cups cubed bread

4 eggs

1 cup brown sugar

1 TB. cinnamon

2 tsp. nutmeg

1 TB. vanilla extract

2 cups heavy cream

1 cup sugar

Serves 6-8
Prep time: 30 minutes, plus at least 1 hour resting time
Cook time: 60-90 minutes

1. In a small saucepan, bring milk to a boil and immediately remove from heat. Add half chocolate chips and stir until melted. Coat a baking dish with pan spray, and fill it with cubed bread and remaining chocolate chips.

2. In a large bowl, whisk together eggs, sugar, cinnamon, nutmeg, and vanilla. Slowly add chocolate milk, and whisk to combine thoroughly. Pour over bread cubes, and refrigerate for at least one hour or overnight.

3. Preheat the oven to 325°F. Cover top of pudding with cream, sprinkle sugar evenly over top, and bake until golden brown and firmly set, about 1$^1/_2$ hours. Serve warm with a dollop of whipped or ice cream.

Suggestions: Make this recipe fruity with 1-2 cups dried or fresh fruit tossed into the bread cubes. Raspberries work particularly well.

Kitchen Tips

The best part about a bread pudding is, of course, the bread. Challah, brioche, and Hawaiian bread are good choices for this recipe. Other exceptional options include day-old Danish, croissants, cinnamon buns, sweet rolls, and even donuts. The richer the bread, the richer the end product will be.

Indian Pudding

This is a New England classic. Historically, cornmeal was known as Indian meal and was used by colonists in the absence of wheat flour. The creamy texture and rich molasses flavor is the perfect remedy for cold winter nights.

Serves 6
Prep time: 15 minutes
Cook time: 90 minutes

1 cup half-and-half

1 cup cornmeal

3 cups milk

1 cup sugar

1½ tsp. ginger

1½ tsp. nutmeg

½ tsp. cinnamon

½ tsp. clove

1 tsp. salt

½ cup molasses

1 cup cream

1. Preheat the oven to 300°F. Generously butter a 9×13-inch baking dish. In a small bowl, combine half-and-half and cornmeal, mix, and set aside. In a large saucepan bring milk to a boil. Reduce heat and stir in cornmeal. Simmer, stirring, until thickened, about 5 minutes. Remove from heat. Add sugar, ginger, nutmeg, cinnamon, clove, salt, molasses, and cream. Mix well and transfer to your prepared baking dish. Bake until firm and browned, about 1½ hours.

Suggestions: Serve pudding warm, topped with additional cream, and sprinkled with raisins.

Biblical Culture

Molasses is the by-product of sugar processing. Juice from sugar cane and sugar beets is extracted and boiled, causing the crystallization of naturally occurring sugar. Both of these crops are New World in origin, but in the Fertile Crescent similar syrups were made from pomegranates, dates, mulberries, and carob.

Apple Pie

To guarantee your apples are not half raw in the center of your pie, precook them on the stove until they are caramelized and tender. This step prevents the filling from shrinking in the oven, causing a gap of air between the apples and the top crust as well as excessive moisture.

1 recipe pie dough	**1 TB. nutmeg**
8-12 Fuji apples, peeled, quartered, cored, and sliced	**4 TB. (½ stick) butter, divided, and more as needed**
1 cup brown sugar	**2 egg yolks**
1 tsp. salt	**2 TB. cream**
1 TB. cinnamon	**¼ cup sugar**

Makes 1 (9-inch) pie
Prep time: 40 minutes
Cook time: 60 minutes

1. Line a pie pan with a circle of pie dough, roll out an additional circle for a top crust, and refrigerate both.

2. In a large bowl, toss together apples, sugar, salt, cinnamon, and nutmeg. Mix well to thoroughly coat apples. In a large sauté pan over high heat melt 2 tablespoons butter. Add one layer of apples and cook, stirring often, until tender and caramelized. Transfer apples to a baking sheet to cool, and repeat with remaining apples. Do not crowd apples in the pan, or they will cook too slowly and won't caramelize. Cool apples completely.

3. Preheat oven to 350°F. Pile cooled apples into the pie pan lined with dough. Be sure to add all cooking juices. Lay top circle of dough over apples, and let dough warm to room temperature for 3-5 minutes, until it bends easily without cracking. With scissors, trim bottom and top crust together, ½ inch from edge of pan. Squeeze top and bottom crusts together around the rim, and crimp with fingers or score with a fork. In a small bowl combine egg yolks and cream, and brush over surface of pie crust. Sprinkle with sugar, and bake for 45-60 minutes until golden brown and bubbly. Assemble pies and freeze raw for up to 2 weeks. Bake directly from the freezer for 60-90 minutes.

Suggestions: All apples are not created equal, but they're close. Most are grown for the lunch box and will generally hold up to heat just fine. So pick the apple you like the best; the Fuji is my favorite.

Kitchen Tips

Blind-baking does not work for a double-crust pie because the top crust must be pinched and crimped to the bottom crust, which can only be done if the dough is raw. So to ensure the bottom of a double-crust pie is cooked, leave it in 5 minutes after you think it's done. Then, if your oven allows it, move the pie off the rack and cook it 5 more minutes directly on the floor of the oven. This final direct burst of heat is perfect crust insurance.

Rhubarb Crisp

Rhubarb, sometimes called pie plant, is a tart plant that looks like big red celery. It's similar to cranberries in tartness and needs lots of sugar.

Makes 1 (9-inch) pie
Prep time: 20 minutes
Cook time: 60 minutes

6 cups rhubarb, cut in 1-inch pieces

2 cups sugar

1 TB. cornstarch

1 tsp. salt

Grated zest and juice of 1 lemon

1 recipe streusel (recipe Chapter 3)

1. Preheat the oven to 350°F. Coat a baking dish with pan spray. In a large bowl, toss together rhubarb, sugar, cornstarch, salt, and lemon zest and juice. Mix well to thoroughly coat. Transfer to your baking dish, and top generously with streusel. Bake for 30-45 minutes, until golden brown and bubbly. Serve warm with whipped or ice cream.

Suggestions: Make with any number of fruits: apples, blueberries, peaches, nectarines, or cherries, or even combine a few.

Biblical Culture
Rhubarb has only been enjoyed as a food for a few hundred years. Its medicinal properties were well known since the third century B.C., treating ailments including gastrointestinal disorders. The species originated in China and grew prolifically along the Vogel River. Trade along the Silk Road brought it to the Fertile Crescent and beyond.

Lemon Meringue Pie

There are many tips and tricks to prevent the meringue on this pie from weeping. The best method I have found is this precooked Italian meringue. Sadly, all meringues break down after several hours, and weeping is inevitable. My advice: eat it fast!

½ **recipe pie dough**

6 whole eggs

5 egg yolks, reserve whites

1¾ **cup sugar**

Zest of 4 lemons

1⅓ **cup lemon juice**

¼ **tsp. salt**

8 oz. butter

For the Meringue:

1 cup sugar

½ **cup light corn syrup**

¼ **cup water**

½ **tsp. salt**

4 egg whites

1 tsp. vanilla extract

Makes 1 (9-inch) pie
Prep time: 45 minutes
Cook time: 20 minutes
Chilling time: 3 hours to overnight
Finishing time (for meringue): 45 Minutes

1. Preheat oven to 350°F. Line a pie pan with a circle of pie dough, crimp edges, and blind-bake for 30-45 minutes, until edges and bottom are golden brown. Cool completely.

2. In a large saucepan combine whole eggs, yolks, sugar, lemon zest and juice, salt, and butter. Mix well and cook over high heat, stirring continuously until mixture thickens to sour cream consistency. Pour immediately into precooked pie shell, and refrigerate until set, 3 hours or overnight.

3. For meringue, combine sugar, corn syrup, water, and salt in a large saucepan. Bring to a boil and cook over high heat until it reaches the firm ball stage, 245°F. Meanwhile, in a large bowl, using a whisk or an electric mixer, whip egg whites to stiff peaks. Continue whipping while slowly drizzling in sugar syrup. Add vanilla and whip until stiff peaks are formed. Spread evenly and mound high over top of chilled pie. Before serving set pie under a broiler briefly to brown meringue, about 2-3 minutes. Keep chilled.

Suggestions: For Key Lime Pie, replace lemon juice and zest with juice and zest of key limes (also known as Mexican limes). Omit meringue and top with whipped cream.

Kitchen Tips

When cooking sugar on top of the stove, the old-fashioned method of testing sugar stages with ice water is easy, and, in most cases, more reliable than a thermometer. As the mixture thickens, spoon out a small amount into ice water. Immediately feel its consistency. If the recipe calls for soft-ball sugar, you should easily be able to form the sugar into a ball. Hard-ball sugar will keep the ball shape once formed. Crack stage will harden immediately once it hits the water and then crack.

Coconut Cream Pie

This is a coconut lover's delight.

Makes 1 (9-inch) pie	
Prep time: 10 minutes	
Cook time: 60 minutes	
Chilling Time: 4 hours to overnight	

1 recipe graham cracker crust

4 egg yolks

1 cup sugar

⅓ cup cornstarch

2 cups half-and-half

1 (15 oz.) can coconut milk

1 tsp. coconut extract

2 TB. butter

1 cup whipping cream

1 TB. sugar

1 tsp. vanilla extract

½ cup shredded coconut, toasted

Kitchen Tips _____

Coconut milk comes in cans and is full of coconut fat, which rises to the top as the can sits on the shelf. Before opening, shake the can good to loosen and mix in the clumps.

1. In a small bowl whisk together egg yolks, sugar, and corn-starch, and set aside. In a large saucepan combine half-and-half, coconut milk, and extract, and bring to a boil over high heat. At the boil, ladle $^1/_2$ cup into egg yolks and whisk quickly to combine. Pour warmed yolks back into saucepan and, over high heat, whisk immediately and vigorously until mixture begins to resemble thick sour cream, about 2 minutes. Remove from heat, add butter, and stir to combine. Pour immediately into prepared graham cracker crust and chill until set, 4 hours to overnight.

2. Before serving, combine cream, sugar, and vanilla in a large bowl, and using a whisk or an electric mixer, whip to firm peaks. Spread evenly over top of pie, and sprinkle with toasted coconut.

Suggestions: Replace coconut milk with half-and-half, omit coconut extract and shredded coconut, and you have vanilla cream pie. Layer the bottom with bananas, berries, or fold in melted chocolate.

Strawberry Sorbet

Sorbet is an impressive dessert, and it's surprisingly easy. Once you try it, you'll be hooked!

2 pints fresh strawberries, washed and trimmed

¼ cup honey

¼ tsp. salt

Zest and juice of 1 lemon (about 2 TB.)

Serves 4
Prep time: 20 minutes, plus 90 minutes cooling and freezing time

1. In a large sauté pan over medium heat, combine strawberries, honey, salt, lemon zest, and juice. Stir and smash berries until liquid begins to run and resembles loose jam, about 10 minutes. Taste and adjust seasoning with more honey or lemon juice. Remove from heat, and cool completely.

2. Process cooled fruit in a blender to reach a very fine purée. Strain through a fine sieve to remove any lumps. Freeze in an ice cream machine according to manufacturer's instructions.

Suggestions: Add a bit of bubbly, 1 cup of champagne, sparkling cider, or ginger ale, just before the mixture hits the freezing machine for an effervescent sorbet.

Kitchen Tips

This method works with almost any fruit. The heat breaks down fibers and sets colors. Berries and stone fruits benefit most from this. Cook fruit, such as apples, pears, and pineapple, longer until softened. Some fruit, like exceptionally ripe mangos or bananas, need no cooking at all. Never cook melons and kiwis because heat causes the pulp and water to separate and colors to dull.

Chapter 16

Biblically Inspired Menus

In This Chapter

- ◆ Menus for every season
- ◆ Menus for special occasions
- ◆ Inspired variations of previous recipes
- ◆ New techniques to sample

"For the kingdom of God is not meat and drink; but righteousness, and peace, and joy in the Holy Ghost." (Romans 14:17 KJV)

The Bible uses food throughout its pages both symbolically and as metaphor in stories and parables. But some of the most memorable descriptions of food are when we find it used as a means to celebrate. Food brings people together in weddings, festivals, celebrations, and remembrance. In these instances we understand the power of food as an equalizer, an apology, congratulations, and sympathy. It is the way humans come together. Whether for a Passover Seder or a dinner date, food brings us together.

The menus in this chapter reflect biblical dietary laws, each presenting three or four courses. Each course enhances the others, playing off specific themes or flavors. You'll find vegetarian, seafood, and meat menus, the latter being devoid of dairy in every course, in accordance with Scripture.

Some menus contain new recipes, while others are simply a variation on dishes that appear elsewhere in this book. In such cases, chapters are referenced and additional instructions given.

Even if you are not entertaining, these menus provide some tasty options for meal plans throughout the year.

Three Menus to Celebrate Spring Renewal

◆ Grilled Lamb Chops with Mustard and Rosemary
Steamed Asparagus with Lemon
Grilled Whole-Wheat Flat Bread

◆ Grilled Tuna
Pasta Primavera
Peach Crème Brûlée

◆ Yellow Lentil Soup
Spring Vegetable Salad with Creamy Dill Dressing
Strawberry Ice Cream

Grilled Lamb Chops with Mustard and Rosemary

Lamb is a classic culinary sign of spring, but many Americans find the meat too strong, and it has never been a big seller. While lamb is available in the market, the selection is not as extensive as beef, pork, or poultry. However, tastes are beginning to change, and quality is improving. Imported lamb from New Zealand is leading the pack and raising the bar for American growers.

For lamb chops, you may need to leave your supermarket's meat case and seek out a butcher. For the best chops, look for loin, rib, or sirloin about an inch thick. You'll need to marinate or tenderize any other cut in some way for grilling over high heat.

½ cup Dijon mustard

Zest of 2 lemons

3 TB. fresh rosemary, minced

2 TB. honey

8 small lamb loin chops

½ tsp. kosher salt

½ tsp. ground black pepper

Serves 4	
Prep time: 20 minutes	
Cook time: 15 minutes	

1. Preheat a grill on high heat. In a small bowl combine mustard, lemon zest, rosemary, and honey, and mix into a paste. Using half the paste, coat chops on both sides. Reduce grill to medium heat and grill chops, with the lid on, for 3-5 minutes. Baste, flip, and cook another 3-5 minutes or to desired doneness. Serve immediately.

Suggestions: Make this recipe equally well in a 450°F oven, on a stove top grill pan, or in an electric countertop grill.

Kitchen Tips

For medium-rare, cook about 15 minutes per pound to 140°F. For medium, cook for 20 minutes per pound to 155°F. For well-done, cook 25 minutes per pound to an internal temperature of 165°F.

Steamed Asparagus with Lemon

The lemon-parsley mixture, when made with garlic, is known as *gremolata*, a classic lamb accompaniment. But garlic is too strong for this recipe. Here, the lemon is designed to simply brighten the already cheerful flavor of asparagus.

Serves 4-6
Prep time: 10 minutes
Cook time: 15 minutes

Zest and juice of 2 lemons, divided

4 TB. fresh flat-leaf parsley, minced

½ tsp. kosher salt

½ tsp. black pepper

4-6 cups water

2 lb. fresh asparagus, trimmed

2 TB. olive oil

1. In a small bowl combine lemon zest and juice, parsley, salt, and pepper. Set aside.

2. In a large saucepan bring water to a rolling boil. Insert a steamer basket or colander, add asparagus, and cover. Cook 3-5 minutes, until tender but still bright green. Drain, drizzle with oil, sprinkle with lemon-parsley mixture, and serve.

Suggestions: To make this dish in advance, plunge the steamed asparagus into ice water to stop the cooking, then rewarm in a sauté pan with a little olive oil just before serving.

Grilled Whole-Wheat Flat Bread

Follow recipe for Pocket Bread in Chapter 4. After dough has doubled, turn out onto a floured surface, divide into 8 equal portions, and roll each into a tight ball. Preheat a grill on high heat. Using a rolling pin, form each ball into a flat disc, ¼-inch thick. Brush with olive oil on both sides and toss onto a hot grill. Reduce heat to low and cook until firm, but pliable, about 3-5 minutes per side. Remove carefully with tongs, and wrap with a napkin to keep warm until ready to serve.

Mixed-Berry Summer Pudding

A summer pudding is not a traditional custard pudding, but a molded dessert of bread and fruit. The preferred bread for this recipe is French *pain de mie,* a rich, dense white bread. The dense crumb and the lack of holes make it a perfect choice. But when making this for a dairy-free meal, use challah (see recipe Chapter 4).

1 pint raspberries	Zest and juice of 1 lemon
1 pint blackberries	Pinch salt
1 pint blueberries	1 loaf sliced challah, crusts removed
1 pint strawberries	
½ cup sugar	2-3 cups whipped cream

Serves 6
Prep time: 45 minutes
Cook time: 12-24 hours of chilling

1. In a large bowl combine raspberries, blackberries, blueberries, strawberries, sugar, lemon juice, zest, and salt. Mix together gently, and set aside at room temperature to macerate for 30 minutes.

2. Line a 10×2-inch cake pan with 2 18-inch long pieces of plastic wrap, placed in the pan to form an X. Trim 3-4 pieces of bread into triangles and place them at the bottom of the pan in one layer, overlapping a little. Cut 3-4 pieces of bread into rectangles and line the edges of the pan, overlapping a little. Fill the bread-lined pan with berry mixture, including all juice. Trim remaining bread to fit across top of berries, overlapping a little. Wrap plastic up and across pudding. Top with a plate and a little weight, such as a can of tomato sauce, and refrigerate overnight. To serve, unwrap the plastic and invert onto a serving plate. Cut into wedges, and top with a dollop of whipped cream.

Suggestions: If you don't have a 10×2-inch cake pan, anything close will work. You can also easily adapt for smaller, individual molds. I like making these summer puddings in cupcake pans.

Grilled Tuna

Fresh tuna has a unique texture and flavor that welcomes any marinade or sauce. But the meat itself is loveliest when grilled simply. If quality is high, all you need is the flavor of the grill with a touch of acid to cut through the fish oils. Serve this simple preparation with a fresh vegetable dish for a taste of spring.

Serves 4
Prep time: 5 minutes
Cook time: 10-15 minutes

4 (5-6 oz.) tuna steaks

4 TB. olive oil

juice of 4 limes

½ tsp. kosher salt

½ tsp. ground black pepper

1. Preheat a grill over high heat. Brush fish with oil, drizzle with lime juice, and sprinkle with salt and pepper. Cook over high heat for 3-5 minutes, flip, reduce heat, and cook to desired doneness.

Suggestions: For grilling, choose bluefin or yellowfin (also known as ahi). Each has a firm texture that holds its shape.

 Kitchen Tips

Remember, when cooking fish of any kind, follow the 10 minutes per inch rule: 10 minutes of moderate heat for every inch of thickness.

Pasta Primavera

Alla primavera means "spring style." To keep in the style of spring, keep these vegetables vibrant in color, texture, and flavor. This simple dish can be easily ruined by overcooking. To get it right, cut the vegetables as uniformly in size as possible, blanch to the proper doneness, then chill and hold them until the pasta is ready.

3-4 qt. water	3 TB. olive oil
½ tsp. salt	2 shallot, minced
8 baby carrots	1 cup half-and-half
8 baby zucchini	¼ cup fresh flat-leaf parsley
8 baby yellow squash	¼ cup fresh basil
1 red bell pepper	1 cup cherry tomatoes
8 spears asparagus	½ tsp. kosher salt
1 cup baby peas	½ tsp. ground black pepper
1 lb. fettuccini	½ cup Parmesan cheese

Serves 4-6
Prep time: 60 minutes
Cook time: 20 minutes

1. Fill a large pasta pot with water, and bring water and salt to a rolling boil. Add carrots, zucchini, squash, bell pepper, asparagus, and peas, one type at a time, and cook 3-5 minutes, until tender but still bright. Transfer immediately to ice water.

2. Fill pot with water again and bring to a rolling boil. At the boil, add pasta and cook al dente. Drain, rinse with cold water, and toss with 1 tablespoon olive oil.

3. Heat remaining oil in large sauté pan over high heat. Add shallots and cook until tender. Add cream, parsley, and basil, and bring to boil. Add blanched vegetables, pasta, tomatoes, salt, pepper, and Parmesan. Toss to coat, and serve immediately.

Suggestions: Let your pasta shape determine the size of your vegetables. Make vegetables no larger than the pasta. Linguini and fettuccini are long and thin, so their vegetables should be in julienne strips. Small or medium dice should accompany shell or bow-tie pasta.

Peach Crème Brûlée

The name means "burnt cream" because the top of the custard is covered with sugar and caramelized. To do this, you need a torch. The sugar cannot be successfully caramelized any other way without damaging the custard beneath. Several good torches are available at cookware stores and on the Internet (see Appendix B).

Serves 6-8
Prep time: 30 minutes
Cook time: 60 minutes, plus at least 2 hours cooling time

Kitchen Tips _____

When baking is complete, the custards will be set but not browned or risen. Look for the Jello-jiggle. They will set completely when chilled.

1¼ cup heavy cream	½ cup sugar
1 tsp. vanilla extract	2 ripe peaches
1 tsp. ground cinnamon	1 cup granulated sugar
6 egg yolks	

1. Preheat the oven to 350°F. In a small saucepan, warm cream, vanilla, and cinnamon together to just a simmer. Remove from heat. In a medium bowl whisk together yolks and sugar. Add ½ cup warm cream, whisk immediately to combine, then pour back into pot of cream. Strain and set aside.

2. Slice peaches into thin wedges and place at the bottom of 6 custard cups, fill with custard, and set cups in a larger baking dish. Fill dish with water to reach halfway up cups. Cover with foil and bake until set, about 45-60 minutes. Remove carefully from water, cool to room temperature, and chill completely.

3. When cool, dust top of each custard with granulated sugar. Burn with a torch, moving the flame back and forth until sugar melts. Continue to torch as sugar turns amber. Do not burn sugar. Cool to harden sugar before serving, about 5 minutes.

Suggestions: Substitute any fruit for peaches.

Yellow Lentil Soup

Lentils come from a species of the legume family that is available in many colors, including green, brown, and black. Look for orange lentils, which is their color until they are soaked and cooked. This recipe works interchangeably with any color, but is particularly sunny when yellow.

1 lb. dried yellow lentils, rinsed and drained

2-4 qt. water

1 large red-skinned potato, diced

1 carrot, diced

2 TB. olive oil

1 large yellow onion, diced

3 cloves garlic, minced

1 tsp. ground cumin

½ tsp. kosher salt

2 TB. fresh parsley, chopped

Serves 6-8	
Prep time: 15 minutes	
Cook time: 60 minutes	

1. In a large sauce pan cover lentils with water by 2 inches, add potato and carrot, and bring to a boil. Reduce heat, cover, and simmer until tender, about 30 minutes. Skim foam as necessary. Strain, reserving liquid. Purée solids, adding reserved liquid as necessary for a smooth purée. Set aside.

2. Heat oil in a large saucepan over medium heat. Add onion and garlic, and sauté until tender and golden. Add cumin and lentil purée. Add reserved liquid as necessary to reach soup consistency. Simmer to warm through. Season with salt, and serve with a sprinkle of chopped parsley.

Spring Vegetable Salad with Creamy Dill Dressing

The tangy flavor of yogurt brightens the already fresh flavor of these spring vegetables.

Serves 6-8
Prep time: 30 minutes
Cook time: 30 minutes

2 qt. water

1 tsp. kosher salt, divided

1 bunch asparagus, cut in 1-inch lengths

1 cup fresh peas

1 cup fresh fava beans

8 oz. fresh green beans, cut in 1-inch lengths

6 cups ice water

1 TB. olive oil

1 shallot, minced

1 bunch chives, minced

1 cup plain yogurt

¼ cup fresh dill, minced

½ tsp. ground black pepper

3 cups baby lettuce mix

1 cup fresh flat-leaf parsley or chervil leaves

1. Bring water and ½ teaspoon salt to a rolling boil. Add asparagus, peas, fava beans, and green beans, and cook 3-5 minutes, until tender but still bright green. Drain and immediately add to ice water.

2. In a large bowl, stir together oil, shallot, chives, yogurt, dill, remaining salt, and pepper. Drain and dry blanched vegetables. Add to dressing, along with baby lettuce and parsley. Toss to coat. Serve chilled.

Strawberry Ice Cream

Crème Anglaise is the name of this ice cream custard. The eggs cook quickly, so stir continuously and be prepared to stop the cooking immediately when the sauce is ready. It is not terrifically hard, but it can easily be overcooked. Get yourself enough ingredients to make it a few times, in case you flub it. And for goodness sake, do not make it for the first time in front of people.

3-4 cups of ice

4 cups half-and-half

1 tsp. vanilla extract

8 egg yolks

1 cup sugar, divided

2 pints strawberries, washed, stemmed, and halved

1 TB. lemon juice

Serves 4-6	
Prep time: 15 minutes	
Cook time: 60 minutes	

1. Fill a large bowl with ice, and set another large bowl on top of ice. Have a fine strainer nearby, and set this all aside, but nearby, until custard is cooked. Bring half-and-half and vanilla to a boil in a large saucepan. In a small bowl, whisk together $^1/_2$ cup sugar and egg yolks. At the boil, temper $^1/_2$ cup hot half-and-half into yolks and whisk quickly to combine. Pour warmed yolks back into the saucepan and, over high heat, whisk immediately and vigorously until mixture begins to resemble thick cream, about 2 minutes. Strain immediately into the bowl sitting on ice, and stir until cool. Refrigerate until completely cool.

2. In a large sauté pan over medium heat, combine berries, remaining sugar, and lemon juice. Heat and mash until juices flow and mixture resembles jam, about 5 minutes. Cool completely.

3. When custard and berries are both cool, whisk them together and run through an ice cream machine, following manufacturer's instructions. Pack in freezer for 1-2 hours before serving.

Suggestions: Traditional Crème Anglaise is made with milk. I cheated here with half-and-half, which makes it thicker and richer. You can cheat even more by using cream.

 Kitchen Tips

Ice cream machines are available at many department and discount stores and wherever kitchenware is sold. (See Appendix B.) They can cost as much as $1,000.00 or as little as $17.00. I bought a $17.00 machine over a decade ago, and it's still going strong. If it shoould die today, I will have gotten my money's worth for sure.

Three Menus to Celebrate the Bounty of Summer

Summertime is a traditional time for outdoor eating and playing. These menus take full advantage of this fact, using the grill as much as possible and limiting the time over oven and stove.

- ◆ Grilled Rib Eye with Cajun Barbecue Rub
  Grilled Corn on the Cob with Chili Salt
  Apricot Crisp

- ◆ Chilled Marinated Salmon
  Heirloom Tomato Gazpacho
  Black Bean and Rice Salad
  Coconut Cake

- ◆ Grilled Vegetable Brochettes
  Chickpea and Wild Rice Pilaf
  Cherry-Lemon Shortcakes

Grilled Rib Eye with Cajun Barbecue Rub

Follow recipe for Grilled Rib Eye with Herb Rub in Chapter 9, but replace the herb rub with a Cajun rub. Buy a blend of Cajun seasonings, or blend your own.

1 cup bay leaves	¼ onion powder
1 cup paprika	¼ garlic powder
¼ cup dried thyme	2 TB. cumin seed
¼ dried oregano	2 TB. celery seed
¼ yellow mustard seed	2 TB. cayenne pepper
¼ white peppercorn	

> *Makes about 4 cups spice blend*
>
> **Prep time:** 10 minutes

Mix bay leaves, paprika, thyme, oregano, mustard seed, peppercorn, onion powder, garlic powder, cumin, celery, and cayenne together, and grind in a coffee mill or mortar.

Suggestions: Turn this spice blend into a barbecue sauce by combining 1 cup rub spice with 1 cup brown sugar, 1 cup tomato sauce, ¹⁄₄ cup tamarind paste and 3 tablespoons cider vinegar.

def•i•ni•tion

Tamarind is a sweet-sour pod in the legume family that grows in the tropics of East Africa, Madagascar, the Caribbean, Asia, Australia, and Latin America. The pulp is a key ingredient of several popular condiments, including Worcestershire sauce. Find it in Latin American stores in the raw beans or processed into a brick. Both should be soaked in warm water to remove pits.

Grilled Corn on the Cob with Chili Salt

Grilled corn is easy and delicious. Soaking the corn in water keeps the husks intact and creates steam to cook the corn. But if you like your corn with a smokier flavor, omit the soaking and let the husks burn.

Serves 8	
Prep time: 30 minutes	
Cook time: 15 minutes	

8 large ears of corn, husks intact

1 tsp. kosher salt

1 TB. chili powder

1 TB. ground cumin

1 TB. onion powder

8 oz. unsalted butter, melted

1. Peel back husks but don't detach. Remove corn silk and fold husks back into place. Soak in cold water for one hour.

2. Preheat a grill on high heat. Drain corn and put on the grill, turning frequently for 10-15 minutes, until husks begin to char. In a small bowl, mix together salt, chili powder, cumin, and onion powder. To serve, peel back husks, brush with melted butter, and sprinkle with salt.

Suggestions: Try an herb rub for your corn. In a small bowl combine 1 tablespoon each dried sage, thyme, parsley, and basil. Add 1 teaspoon salt and pepper, mix well, and sprinkle over buttered corn.

Apricot Crisp

Follow recipe for Rhubarb Crisp in Chapter 15. Replace rhubarb with fresh apricots, pitted and quartered. Reduce sugar to 1 cup, and add 1 vanilla bean, split and scraped. Proceed with the recipe as written.

Chilled Marinated Salmon

This dish is known as *ceviche*, and although it is often referred to as the raw fish dish, the fish is not raw at all. It is cooked by the acid in the marinade. The longer it soaks in the marinade, the more it cooks, so be careful not to chill it too long.

¼ cup lime juice

¼ cup orange juice

1 tsp. Dijon mustard

3 cloves garlic, minced

1 cup green onions, minced

1 cup cilantro, minced

¼ cup olive oil

1 (6 oz.) salmon filet, sliced very thin

½ tsp. kosher salt

½ tsp. ground black pepper

2 large ripe tomatoes, diced

2 ripe avocados, diced

1 large mango, diced

4 cups romaine lettuce, shredded

Serves 4

Prep time: 30 minutes, plus at least 3 hours cooling time

---

1. In a large bowl combine lime juice, orange juice, mustard, garlic, onions, cilantro, and oil. Add salmon and toss to coat. Cover and refrigerate at least 3 hours or overnight until meat turns opaque pink.

2. Just before serving, add tomatoes, avocado, and mango, and toss to coat. Serve chilled, on a bed of romaine.

Heirloom Tomato Gazpacho

Heirloom tomatoes are the fancy varieties you find at farmers' markets and produce stands throughout the summer. They can be red, yellow, green, purple, or striped. For this dish, pick one variety or the mix of colors can look pretty weird when blended. Chop all ingredients to a uniform size. Big or small, it looks best when they're the same.

Serves 8
Prep time: 30 minutes
Cook time: 15 minutes

6 large ripe tomatoes, seeded and chopped

3 cloves garlic, minced

2 cucumbers, peeled, seeded, and diced

2 red bell peppers, seeded and diced

1 yellow bell pepper, seeded and diced

1 medium purple onion, diced and soaked in cold water for at least 30 minutes

1 cup green onions, diced and soaked in cold water for at least 30 minutes

¼ cup lemon juice

¼ cup fresh flat-leaf parsley, chopped

½ cup olive oil

1-2 cups tomato juice

1 cup sour cream

1. In a large bowl combine tomatoes, garlic, cucumbers, red and yellow bell peppers, purple and green onions, lemon juice, and olive oil. Cover, refrigerate, and marinate for one hour.

2. Blend half the ingredients until smooth, adding tomato juice as needed for a smooth purée. Stir purée back into the bowl of chopped vegetables, and serve with a dollop of sour cream.

Black Bean and Rice Salad

This simple dish is remarkably satisfying.

2 TB. white wine vinegar

2 TB. lime juice

1 tsp. ground cumin

1 tsp. honey

½ cup olive oil

2 cups cooked brown rice, chilled

1 (15 oz.) can black beans, drained and rinsed

1 large ripe tomato, diced fine

1 (4 oz.) can diced green chilies

½ cup green onions, diced

¼ cup cilantro, diced

½ tsp. kosher salt

½ tsp. black pepper

Serves 4-6
Prep time: 30 minutes

1. In a large bowl, whisk together vinegar, lime juice, cumin, honey, and olive oil. Add rice, beans, tomato, chilies, onions, and cilantro. Toss well, season with salt and pepper, and serve.

Coconut Cake

The key to this recipe is the coconut extract. Replace it with vanilla if you're not a coconut fan.

Serves 8-10
Prep time: 30 minutes
Cook time: 45 minutes
Finishing time: 45 minutes

3 cups cake flour

1 TB. baking powder

¼ tsp. salt

8 oz. unsalted butter, softened

2 cups sugar

1 TB. coconut extract

1 TB. vanilla extract

4 eggs, separated

1 cup milk

2 cups shredded coconut, lightly toasted and divided

For the Frosting:

1 cup sugar

½ cup light corn syrup

¼ cup water

½ tsp. salt

4 egg whites

1 tsp. vanilla extract

1. Preheat oven to 350°F. Coat two (10-inch) round cake pans with pan spray, and line the bottom with circles of parchment paper. Sift together flour, baking powder, and salt, and set aside. In a large bowl, use a sturdy spoon or electric mixer to cream butter and sugar until light and fluffy. Add coconut and vanilla extracts and eggs, one by one. Add sifted ingredients alternately with milk. Fold in 1 cup shredded coconut. Divide batter between two pans, and bake for 30-45 minutes until a pick inserted at center of cake comes out clean. Cool 10 minutes before inverting onto a rack. Cool completely.

2. In a large saucepan, combine sugar, corn syrup, water, and salt. Bring to a boil, and cook over high heat until it reaches the firm ball stage, 245°F. Meanwhile, in a large bowl, using a whisk or an electric mixer, whip egg whites to stiff peaks. Continue whipping while slowly drizzling in sugar syrup. Add vanilla and whip until stiff peaks are formed. Fill and frost cooled coconut cake, and top with remaining coconut.

Grilled Vegetable Brochettes

Follow recipe for Shish Kebab in Chapter 9. Omit the meat, and marinate vegetables instead. Add more vegetables, including wheels of corn on the cob, asparagus, small new potatoes, and green beans. Proceed with the recipe as written. Use two skewers for asparagus and green beans, piercing through the top and bottom to form a "ladder".

~

Chickpea and Wild Rice Pilaf

Follow recipe for Wild Rice with Almonds in Chapter 14. Replace almonds with 1 (15 oz.) can of chickpeas, and add with them 1 teaspoon cumin, 1 teaspoon ground cinnamon, and ¼ cup sesame seeds. Proceed with the recipe as written.

~

Cherry-Lemon Shortcakes

Who says a shortcake has to have strawberries? Any delicious fruit will do. You can even used dried fruits in the winter.

Follow recipe for Currant Scones in Chapter 3. Omit currants and add grated zest of 4 lemons. Flatten out dough, and cut into circles with a cookie cutter. Bake as directed.

In a large bowl combine 4 cups cherries, pitted and halved, juice and zest of 1 lemon, ½ tsp. cinnamon, and 2 tablespoons honey. Toss to coat and set aside to macerate for at least 30 minutes. Using an electric mixer, whip 1 cup heavy cream to stiff peaks.

To assemble, slice scone in half horizontally, and sandwich a generous helping of cherries and a dollop of cream. Dust with powdered sugar to serve.

Serves 8
Prep time: 90 minutes
Cook time: 15 minutes

Three Menus That Utilize Autumn's Abundance

The menus in this section celebrate everything that is fall. Warm flavors and colors of squash, nuts, spice, and fruits are best appreciated when the temperature drops.

- ◆ Oven-Roasted Turkey Breast
  Roasted Butternut Squash and New Potatoes
  Pumpkin-Pecan Pie

- ◆ Beef and Barley Stew
  Broiled Cauliflower
  Walnut Bread
  Cranberry Sorbet

- ◆ Wild Mushroom Chowder
  Spinach and Arugula Salad with Raspberry Vinaigrette
  Gingerbread Pudding

Oven-Roasted Turkey Breast

This is a nice option when you feel like having turkey but don't feel like cooking an entire bird.

4 stalks celery, chopped

1 carrot, chopped

1 large yellow onion, chopped

1 (5-7 lb.) turkey breast, defrosted

2 TB. dried sage

1 TB. dried thyme

1 tsp. dried rosemary

½ tsp. kosher salt

½ tsp. ground black pepper

¼ cup all-purpose flour

2 cups turkey or chicken broth

Serves 4-6
Prep time: 1 hour
Cook time: 20 minutes per pound

1. Preheat oven to 450°F. Line the bottom of a roasting pan with celery, carrot, and onion. Wash and pat dry turkey, and set on top of vegetables. Sprinkle with sage, thyme, rosemary, salt, and pepper, and fill roasting pan with 2 inches of water. Reduce the heat to 325°F, and cook for 2-3 hours, until internal temperature reaches 165°F. Baste with olive oil drippings every 10-15 minutes throughout roasting time.

2. When bird is done, remove it from the pan and let it rest, covered in foil. Pour off all but ¼ drippings. Place the roasting pan on a burner over high heat. Add flour, whisking until all fat is absorbed. Slowly add broth, whisking, until gravy reaches desired consistency. Slice turkey, strain gravy, season with salt and pepper, and serve.

Roasted Butternut Squash and New Potatoes

Follow recipe for Herb-Roasted New Potatoes in Chapter 14, and add to it 2 cups diced butternut squash. Cut potatoes and squash in a similar size, and proceed with recipe as written.

Pumpkin-Pecan Pie

Why choose one over the other? Combine them into one fantastic explosion of pie goodness.

Makes 1 (9-inch) pie
Prep time: 60 minutes
Cook time: 60 minutes

For the Pumpkin Layer:

½ recipe pie dough (Chapter 16)

½ cup brown sugar

2 TB. cream

2 eggs

2 TB. peanut oil

1 TB. vanilla extract

½ tsp. kosher salt

1 tsp. cinnamon

1 tsp. nutmeg

1 tsp. cardamom

½ tsp. clove

½ tsp. ginger

3 cups pumpkin purée

For the Pecan Layer:

1 cup pecan halves or pieces

½ cup sugar

½ cup corn syrup

2 eggs

2 TB. peanut oil

1 TB. vanilla extract

½ tsp. salt

1 tsp. cinnamon

1 tsp. nutmeg

1 tsp. cardamom

½ tsp. clove

½ tsp. ginger

1. Preheat oven to 350°F. Line a pie pan with a circle of pie dough, crimp edges, and blind-bake for 20-30 minutes, until edges just begin to set. Cool completely and remove pie weights.

2. In a large bowl combine sugar, cream, eggs, oil, vanilla, salt, cinnamon, nutmeg, cardamom, clove, and ginger, and mix well. Add pumpkin, combine thoroughly and pour into pie crust. Top pumpkin filling with pecans.

3. In a large bowl combine sugar, corn syrup, and eggs, and mix well. Add oil, vanilla, salt, cinnamon, nutmeg, cardamom, clove, and ginger, mix well, and pour over nuts. Bake for 30-45 minutes until golden brown and just set. Chill completely before serving.

Suggestions: Make this pie with a variety of squashes, including butternut and acorn. Simply cut in half, roast, and purée. Also pretty-up the top layer by arranging half the pecans in a decorative pattern.

Beef and Barley Stew

Follow recipe for Beef Stew in Chapter 9. Add 8 oz. sliced mushrooms with onion sauté. Increase liquid to 8 cups broth, and add 1 cup barley with potatoes. Proceed with recipe as written.

≈⌐

Broiled Cauliflower

This recipe can turn anyone into a cauliflower fan.

1 large head cauliflower, cut into florets

2 TB. olive oil

2 TB. lemon juice

½ cup kalamata olives, pitted and chopped

2 TB. capers

3 cloves garlic

1 TB. dried thyme

Serves 4-6
Prep time: 20 minutes
Cook time: 45 minutes

1. Boil cauliflower in salted water until slightly tender, about 5 minutes. Drain, cool, and slice each floret in half.

2. Preheat the oven to 350°F. In a large bowl, whisk together olive oil, lemon juice, olives, capers, garlic, and thyme. Add cauliflower, toss to coat, and transfer to a baking dish. Bake until tender, about 35 minutes. Transfer heat to the broiler, and cook a final 10 minutes to crisp and brown top.

≈⌐

Walnut Bread

Follow recipe for Italian Rosemary Bread in Chapter 4. Replace rosemary with 2 cups toasted, chopped walnuts and 2 tablespoons freshly cracked pepper. Proceed with recipe as written.

Cranberry Sorbet

Make a cranberry purée. Boil 1 (12 oz.) package whole cranberries in $1^{1}/_{2}$ cups water, zest and juice of 2 oranges, and 2 cups sugar. When they pop, remove them from the heat, cool completely, purée, and freeze as in Strawberry Sorbet recipe in Chapter 15.

Wild Mushroom Chowder

Follow recipe for Southwestern Corn Chowder in Chapter 7. Omit cumin, and use vegetable stock. Replace chilies, peppers, and corn with 6 cups chopped mushrooms. Sauté mushrooms in oil with onions and garlic before adding flour and liquid. Proceed with recipe as written. Garnish with fresh chopped thyme and sautéed sliced mushrooms.

Spinach and Arugula Salad with Raspberry Vinaigrette

The slightly peppery flavor of arugula is a delicious counter to the sweet, tart raspberries.

¼ cup raspberry vinegar

½ tsp. kosher salt

½ tsp. ground black pepper

1 TB. Dijon mustard

1 pint raspberries

½ cup olive oil

1 bunch fresh spinach, trimmed, washed, and dried

2 cups arugula, washed and dried

Serves 4
Prep time: 30 minutes

1. In a large bowl, whisk together vinegar, salt, pepper, mustard, and raspberries. Slowly drizzle in oil while whisking. Add spinach and arugula, toss to coat, and serve immediately.

Gingerbread Pudding

Follow recipe for Chocolate Bread Pudding in Chapter 15. Replace chocolate chips with ¼ cup molasses, 2 tablespoons ground ginger, 1 table-spoon ground cinnamon, 1 tablespoon nutmeg, and ¼ teaspoon clove. Add ½ cup golden raisins and ½ cup candied ginger to bread, and sprinkle top with cinnamon sugar before baking. Fold in 1-2 cups gingersnap cookie bits for an extra gingery kick.

Three Menus to Express Our Winter Gratitude

When the sun goes to bed too soon, nothing cheers up the winter doldrums like surrounding ourselves with friends and family. These menus are just as welcome at a festive holiday gathering as they are at a casual Sunday dinner.

- ◆ Horseradish-Crusted Roast Beef
  Parsnip-Potato Purée
  Garlic Sautéed Mustard and Collard Greens
  Pear Cobbler

- ◆ Baked Salmon with Sesame-Ginger Butter
  Sesame-Flax Crackers
  Green Tea Ice Cream

- ◆ Spinach Salad with Pecans and Blue Cheese
  Hearty Bean Stew
  Caramel Swirl Cheesecake

Horseradish-Crusted Roast Beef

A prime rib of beef is truly a special treat. Count on a rib for every two people, unless you have big beef eaters or want leftovers.

6 cloves garlic, minced

½ cup prepared horseradish

1 TB. fresh rosemary, minced

1 TB. fresh thyme, minced

½ cup kosher salt

2 TB. ground black pepper

½ cup olive oil

1 (2-3) rib roast, about 6-8 lb.

1 cup all-purpose flour

Serves 4-6	
Prep time: 20 minutes	
Cook time: 2 hours	

1. Preheat the oven to 350°F. In a medium bowl combine garlic, horseradish, rosemary, thyme, salt, pepper, and oil, and stir into paste. Place beef in a large roasting pan, and rub paste over surface of meat. Dust with flour, and roast for two hours or to desired doneness. (140°F for rare, 145°F for medium rare, and 150°F for medium.) Rest roast for 10 minutes before carving.

Parsnip-Potato Purée

Follow recipe for Mashed Potatoes in Chapter 14. Boil 4 parsnips, peeled and cut into 2-inch chunks and 5 whole cloves garlic with potatoes. Omit cream, and add ½ teaspoon fresh grated nutmeg. Proceed with recipe as written.

Garlic Sautéed Mustard and Collard Greens

Traditionally, collard greens are cooked for hours. But when shredded thin, they cook quickly, retaining a little crunch and their bright green color. The addition of mustard greens adds a peppery bite.

Serves 4-6
Prep time: 15 minutes
Cook time: 15 minutes

3 TB. olive oil

3 cloves garlic, minced

4 cups mustard greens, trimmed, washed, and shredded

4 cups collard greens, trimmed, washed, and shredded

½ tsp. kosher salt

½ tsp. ground black pepper

Juice of 1 lemon

1. Heat oil in a large sauté pan over high heat. Add garlic and cook until tender. Add mustard and collard greens and sauté, tossing with tongs to coat with oil and garlic until wilted but still green, about 2-3 minutes. Season with salt, pepper, and lemon juice, and serve immediately.

Pear Cobbler

Cobbler topping is technically a dough, either biscuit or pie. Crumbs and crumbles do not a cobbler make. They are reserved for fruit crisps.

6 Bartlett pears, peeled, seeded, and diced

½ cup brown sugar

1 tsp. cinnamon

1½ cup almond flour

⅛ tsp. baking soda

¼ tsp. kosher salt

3 TB. peanut oil

2 TB. honey

1 egg yolk

1 tablespoon water

Serves 4-6	
Prep time: 60 minutes	
Cook time: 40 minutes	

1. Preheat oven to 350°F. In a large bowl, combine pears, sugar, and cinnamon. Transfer to a baking dish and set aside.

2. In a large bowl, combine almond flour, baking soda, and salt. Using a fork, stir in oil and honey, and knead into a firm dough. Wrap and refrigerate 30 minutes. On a floured surface, roll dough ¼-inch thick in the shape of your baking dish, and place loosely on top of pears. Mix egg yolk with water, brush over surface of dough, and sprinkle with sugar. Bake until dough is golden brown and pears are bubbly, about 35 minutes.

Baked Salmon with Sesame-Ginger Butter

This Asian-inspired butter adds a subtle exotic flair to a simple baked fish.

Serves 4-6
Prep time: 60 minutes
Cook time: 40 minutes

¼ **cup fresh ginger, grated**

1 TB. sesame seeds

2 TB. fresh chives, chopped

4 TB. unsalted butter, softened

4 (4 oz.) salmon filets

1 lemon, sliced in ⅛-inch wheels

1. Preheat the oven to 350°F. In a medium bowl, combine ginger, sesame seeds, chives, and butter. Cream together to a smooth paste. Place a large sheet of foil on a baking sheet. Place filets together on foil, top each with tablespoon butter and 2-3 lemon slices. Cover with second sheet of foil and seal edges tightly. Bake for 15-20 minutes, until fish is firm and cooked through (10 minutes per inch). Carefully transfer from foil to serving plate.

Sesame-Flax Crackers

Follow recipe for 5-Seed Crackers in Chapter 4. Replace poppy seed, dill, and caraway with an equal amount of flax and sesame seeds. Continue with recipe as written.

Green Tea Ice Cream

If you can't find loose green tea, buy the bags and simply cut them open.

3-4 cups of ice

4 cups half-and-half

¼ cup loose green tea leaves

1 cup sugar, divided

8 egg yolks

2 pints strawberries, washed, stemmed, and halved

1 TB. lemon juice

Serves 4-6
Prep time: 15 minutes
Cook time: 60 minutes

1. Fill a large bowl with ice, and set another large bowl on top of the ice. Have a fine strainer nearby, and set this all aside, but nearby, until custard is cooked. Bring half-and-half and tea to a boil in a large saucepan. In a small bowl, whisk together ½ cup sugar and egg yolks. At the boil, temper ½ cup hot half-and-half into yolks, and whisk quickly to combine. Pour warmed yolks back into the saucepan and, over high heat, whisk immediately and vigorously until mixture begins to resemble thick cream, about 2 minutes. Pour immediately into the bowl sitting on ice, and stir until cool. Strain and refrigerate until completely cool. Run cooled custard through ice cream machine, following manufacturer's instructions. Pack in freezer for 1-2 hours before serving.

Suggestions: Serve ice cream with a side of fortune cookies.

Spinach Salad with Pecans and Blue Cheese

This fresh, flavorful salad is as healthy as it is tasty.

2 TB. balsamic vinegar

1 TB. Dijon mustard

1 tsp. herbes de Provence

½ tsp. kosher salt

½ tsp. ground black pepper

6 cups fresh spinach leaves, trimmed, washed, and dried

1 cup toasted pecans

1 cup blue cheese, crumbled

Serves 4-6
Prep time: 15 minutes
Cook time: 60 minutes

1. In a large bowl, mix together vinegar, mustard, herbes, salt, and pepper. Slowly drizzle in oil while whisking. Add spinach and toss to coat. Serve topped with pecans and blue cheese.

Hearty Bean Stew

This dish will warm you to the core.

Serves 4-6
Prep time: 20 minutes
Cook time: 2½ hours

3 TB. olive oil

1 large yellow onion, diced

3 garlic cloves

½ tsp. nutmeg

½ tsp. cayenne pepper

¼ tsp ground clove

1 tsp. dried thyme

1 bay leaf

1 (15 oz.) can cannellini beans, drained

1 (15 oz.) can kidney beans, drained

1 (15 oz.) can black beans

2 TB. honey

1 (15 oz.) can diced tomatoes

2 cups vegetable broth

½ tsp. kosher salt

1. Heat oil in a large saucepan over high heat. Cook onion and garlic until tender. Reduce heat, add nutmeg, cayenne, clove, thyme, and bay leaf, and cook until golden brown, about 15 minutes. Add cannellini, kidney, and black beans, honey, tomatoes, and broth, and simmer for 1-2 hours, adding more water as necessary. Season with salt before serving.

Caramel Swirl Cheesecake

There are several styles of cheesecake, including New York style, Californian, and Italian (made with ricotta cheese). This recipe, based on the famous cheesecake found at Lindy's Restaurant on Broadway in New York City, has an egg white foam folded in, which makes it light and airy.

For the Crust:

2 cups graham cracker crumbs

2 TB. sugar

2 oz. (½ stick) butter, melted

For the Filling:

3 (8 oz.) packages cream cheese, softened to room temperature

1 cup sugar

1 TB. vanilla

Zest of one lemon

5 eggs, separated

½ cup cream

2 TB. sugar

1 cup caramel sauce

Serves 8-10
Prep time: 30 minutes
Cook time: 2 hours, plus 4-12 hours chilling

1. Preheat oven to 350°F. Brush one 10-inch springform pan lightly with melted butter and line with a circle of parchment paper. Mix together cracker crumbs, sugar, and remaining melted butter and press into prepared pan, covering the bottom and halfway up the sides. Bake until lightly toasted, about 10 minutes. Set aside to cool. Reduce oven temperature to 325°F.

2. In a large bowl with a sturdy spoon, cream together cheese, sugar, vanilla, and lemon zest until lump-free. Add egg yolks, one by one. Add cream, mix in well, and set aside. In a separate bowl, using a whisk or an electric mixer, whip 3 egg whites to stiff peaks, slowly adding 2 tablespoons sugar. Fold carefully into batter. Pour batter into crust and smooth. Drizzle caramel sauce on top and, using a spoon, swirl it into batter. Bake at 325°F for 1 hour. Turn off oven, open door slightly, and let cake sit inside another hour. Chill completely in refrigerator four hours or overnight before unmolding and slicing.

 Kitchen Tips

The key to a good cheesecake is in the baking. If you bake it too hot, the top will expand and crack. But if you don't bake it long enough, the center will be runny. The trick is to bake it slowly, giving the heat plenty of time to penetrate the center of the batter.

A

Glossary

al dente   An Italian term that means "to the tooth" and refers to the degree to which certain foods, usually pasta and vegetables, are cooked. These foods are cooked until done, but still have slight texture when bitten. They are not raw or crunchy, nor are they soft.

antioxidants   Molecules that slow oxidation of other molecules. Oxidation can produce free radicals, which trigger chain reactions that damage cells. In addition to preventing these reactions, antioxidants can inhibit them, once begun.

Apicius   A collection of Roman recipes compiled in the fourth or fifth century A.D.

aurignacian   An upper Paleolithic culture of Europe and Southwest Asia, which dates to about 8000 B.C.

balsamic   An Italian vinegar made since the Middle Ages from the trebbiano grape and aged for as long as 25 years.

baste   To coat food as it cooks with fat or liquid to preserve moisture. A bulb baster is a suction-based tool.

blanch   To boil briefly, then submerge in ice water to halt cooking. The process is used to loosen skin and intensify the color of vegetables and fruits. Also referred to as parboiling.

blind-bake   To pre-bake a pastry crust or shell with an artificial, removable filling, usually raw beans or rice. The crust can then be used to hold a low-bake or no-bake filling.

bok choy   Chinese cabbage or leaf vegetable.

candied ginger   Ginger root, cooked in sugar syrup, and coated in sugar, used in baked goods.

capers   Small buds from an evergreen shrub, pickled in salty, vinegar-based brine.

caramelized   To cook food until the sugar, naturally occurring or added, darkens to an amber "caramel" color. Caramelization brings out the food's deep, sweet, rich flavors.

celery root   The edible, bulbous root of the celery plant. Also known as celeriac.

chili paste   Toasted, rehydrated, and then puréed dried chilies.

chili powder   Dried ground chilies, sometimes combined with other seasonings, such as cumin, oregano, and garlic.

cheesecloth   A fine linen mesh cloth, traditionally used in cheese making to strain whey from curds. Used by chefs for fine straining of all foods, as well as covering, wrapping, or steeping foods.

chutney   A chunky condiment from Southern Asia and India, sometimes cooked and jamlike, made with fruits or vegetables and often spiced with chilies.

clarified butter   Pure butter fat, made by melting butter and removing the solids and salts. The lack of salts and solids allows the fat to withstand higher temperature.

clarify   The term means *to clear*, and refers to removing cloudy sediment from a stock, soup, sauce, or liquefied fat.

Cobb salad   A chopped salad created at the Brown Derby Restaurant in Los Angeles in the 1930s. It typically consists of lettuce, tomato, eggs, chicken, avocado, bacon, and blue cheese.

curry powder   A spice blend originated by the British during their colonial rule of India, so they could bring home the flavor of the regional curry dishes. The flavor of the powder found in supermarkets is fairly generic, but throughout India and other parts of Asia, there are dozens of unique curry sauce variations.

cut-in   A method of incorporating fat into dry ingredients by breaking it into small pieces. With heat, moisture is released from the fat, creating a flakey texture. Used in recipes such as biscuits and pie dough.

daily value   This percentage is the recommended daily intake of key nutrients based on a 2,000 calorie/day diet. Its listing on food labels is meant as a guide to help determine the relative nutritional value of foods.

deglaze   A method of removing cooked food, and flavor, from the bottom of a sauté or roasting pan, by adding liquid, heating, and scraping.

Devonshire cream   Thick cream from unpasteurized milk. Also known as clotted cream.

double boiler   Two pots fitted one on top of the other, designed to allow steam from the bottom to rise up and warm the ingredients of the top. It is used when direct heat is too severe.

einkorn   This species of wild wheat (*triticum boeoticum*) is one of the world's earliest cultivated crops.

electrolytes   This is the scientific name for electrically charged salt ions. They are what your cells use to maintain and conduct electric impulses. Kidneys help to maintain electrolyte balance, but through sweat and other body fluid loss, electrolytes are lost as well. Several beverages on the market, including sports drinks, contain added electrolytes.

Emmentaler   A Swiss, semi-hard cheese made from cow's milk. It has a slight tang and characteristic holes.

emmer   This species of wild wheat (*triticum dicoccon*) is one of world's earliest cultivated crops.

emulsified   The blending of two ingredients by suspension of small globules of one inside the other, so that the resulting blend becomes one homogenous substance.

fallow   A method of crop rotation that includes letting a field lay unplanted for a season, which allows soil to be maintained and restored to productivity.

feta   Fresh Greek cheese made from sheep or goat milk. It is white and crumbly, and stored in a salty brine.

filet of beef   Meat from the tenderloin, or eye fillet, of a cow. This muscle lies between the shoulder blade and the hip socket, and does very little work, which renders an extremely tender steak. Cuts from this muscle include the filet mignon, French tournedos. The porterhouse and t-bone include part of the tenderloin. Left whole, the cut is known as the chateaubriand, or filet de boeuf.

firm ball stage   A stage of cooked sugar, which describes its texture when dropped into ice water. When the syrup reaches between 244-248°F, cooled syrup can be molded into a ball, which will then remain firmly in its shape.

fish sauce   A liquid condiment and ingredient similar in appearance to soy sauce, made from fermented fish. Popular in Asia, fish sauce was known in ancient Rome.

foie gras   A French delicacy, foie gras is the enlarged liver of a goose or duck.

food mill   A tool used to grind and press cooked food through small holes in preparation for purée.

garam masala   The most common spice blend from Northern India. The word *garam* means "warm" or "hot," and while it can be spicy, the name denotes the toasting of the spices prior to grinding.

garum   The ancient Roman name for fish sauce, a condiment made from fermented, aged fish. Similar sauces are still made and used today throughout Asia.

Gorgonzola   Commonly referred to as a blue-vein cheese, this Italian cow's milk cheese has veins that appear more green than blue. Made since the Middle Ages, Gorgonzola can be creamy, crumbly, or firm. Its piquant flavor comes from the addition of bacteria, added and allowed to germinate into mold.

gougère   A French cheese puff, made of pâte a choux pastry dough and Gruyère cheese.

gratinée, au gratin   The melting and browning of the top of a dish.

gremolata, gremolada   An Italian garnish made of chopped garlic, lemon zest, parsley, and anchovy.

Gruyère   A nutty, semi-firm cow's milk cheese from Switzerland.

hard-crack stage   Sugar cooked to between 300°F and 310°F, used in candy and pastry making. When cooled, the sugar hardens and snaps or cracks easily.

herbes de Provence   A spice and herb blend commonly used in Mediterranean cuisine, including lavender, thyme, sage, marjoram, basil, rosemary, fennel, and savory.

hydrogenated   Unsaturated fat (vegetable based) that is artificially saturated by the introduction of hydrogen.

immersion blender   A handheld blender used to purée foods. It can be inserted directly into a pot, saving the step of transferring the contents into another appliance.

infuse   To steep two foods or flavors together.

Italian seasoning   A spice and herb blend commonly used in Italian recipes, including fennel, rosemary, basil, and oregano.

jicama   A sweet, crisp tuber, with white flesh and thin brown papery skin, usually eaten raw.

julienne   A classic knife-cut that looks like long, thick matchsticks.

kalamata   Greek black olives marinated in wine and olive oil.

macerate   To soak food, usually fruit, in liquid to infuse flavor.

madras   A mild to hot red curry sauce from India.

maize   The Spanish word for corn.

masa harina   Flour made from dried hominy corn, used for corn tortillas and tamales.

maytag   An American blue cheese, from the Maytag dairy farms in Newton, Iowa, made from pasteurized milk using a technique developed at Iowa State University.

millet   A tiny, bland grain packed with protein, which can be boiled like rice or ground into flour.

mirin   A sweet Japanese rice wine.

monounsaturated fat   A fatty acid whose molecule can support only one hydrogen atom. This lowers the fat's melting point, so that the fat remains liquid when refrigerated. These fats, in addition to polyunsaturated, are found mainly in grain, fish, and soy products. They are considered good fats, and should make up 25 percent of daily fat intake.

naturalis historia   Latin for "natural history," this encyclopedia of geography, anthropology, physiology, zoology, botany, agriculture, horticulture, pharmacology, and mineralogy, was written in 77 A.D. by Pliny the Elder.

nigella   A smoky, peppery spice used in Indian cuisine, often referred to as black cumin or black onion seeds, although unrelated to both.

Old Bay   A spice blend from Chesapeake Bay, used to season seafood, consisting of celery seeds, bay, mustard, cinnamon, and ginger.

omega-3 fatty acids   Polyunsaturated fatty acids that are considered essential, meaning the body needs them, but cannot manufacture them. The best sources are fish and flax.

opo squash   A long squash similar in flavor and appearance to zucchini, with whitish skin. Also known as the bottle gourd and calabash.

paella   Spanish rice dish, made in a pan of the same name, flavored with saffron, and filled with a variety of meat, shellfish, vegetables, and aromatics.

pain de mie   A dense white sandwich bread from France.

parboiling   *See* blanch.

pastry blender   A u-shaped tool consisting of several wires with a handle, used to cut fat into dry ingredients. (*See* cut-in.)

pâté de foie gras   The French word pâté (with an accent over the *e*) means pie, but usually refers to a fine-ground meat preparation, made in various styles, such as chunky or smooth, and with various meats. (*See* foie gras)

Pentateuch   The Greek name for the first five books of the Hebrew Bible: Genesis, Exodus, Leviticus, Numbers, and Deuteronomy.

pink peppercorns   Unrelated to white and black peppercorns, these dried berries come from ornamental trees native to Brazil.

polenta   Cornmeal mush from Northern Italy.

polyunsaturated fat   A fatty acid whose molecule can support only two or more hydrogen atoms. This lowers the fat's melting point, so that the fat remains liquid when refrigerated. These fats, in addition to monounsaturated, are found mainly in grain, fish, and soy products. They are considered good fats, and should make up 25 percent of daily fat intake.

purée   Any food pulverized to a smooth paste of varying consistencies.

quinoa   An ancient Incan grain, and one of the few vegetable sources of complete protein.

rancid   Oxidation of oil that results in foul flavor and odor.

raw cuisine   The promotion of the consumption of uncooked, unprocessed, and usually organic foods. It is generally believed that consumption of raw foods can prevent and heal many forms of sickness and chronic disease. Also known as raw foodism.

reduce   A culinary term meaning to cook the water out of a dish, reducing its volume, intensifying its flavor, and thickening its consistency.

Roquefort   A French blue cheese made specifically from sheep's milk, exposed to *penicillium roqueforte* mold spores, and aged in limestone caves in southwestern France.

rotini   An Italian pasta shaped like a corkscrew.

roux   A thickening agent made with equal parts melted fat (usually butter) and flour.

sake   A Japanese rice wine.

saturated fat   Fatty acids fully saturated with hydrogen. These fats are solid at room temperature and are mainly found in animal sources, although oil from coconut, cotton, and palm contain high percentages of saturated fatty acids as well. Intake should be limited to no more than 7 percent of total daily calories, as saturated fat has been shown to be a major cause of coronary heart disease.

sauté   To cook food quickly, over high heat, constantly stirring for even browning. The term means "to jump," and sauté pans are designed with a curved lip, making constant motion as easy as a flick of the wrist.

sear   To brown food, usually meat, on all sides at very high temperature, ostensibly to seal in the meat's juice. The ability to retain the liquid in food by this method is under some scrutiny.

seize   A term that refers to the thickening and hardening of melted chocolate that occurs when a small amount of moisture is added.

shallots   A milder cousin of the onion consisting of a few small bulbs that grow together, with a brown papery skin.

Shavuot   A Jewish holiday celebrating the day the Torah was given to the Israelites on Mount Sinai. It is the culmination of the Counting of the Omer, a harvest-related festival that counts 49 days from Passover.

sherry   A fortified wine from the Andalusian region of southern Spain. There are several varieties, ranging from dry Manzanillas to sweet Olorosos.

soft ball stage   Sugar cooked to between 234°F and 240°F, used in candy and pastry making. When cooled, the sugar can be formed into a soft ball.

soft crack stage   Sugar cooked to between 270°F and 290°F, used in candy and pastry making. When cooled, the sugar is hard, but still bends.

sponge   A thin pre-dough or yeast batter that is made prior to making bread in order to prolong fermentation for improved flavor and texture.

star anise   A potent anise-flavored spice from a star-shaped fruit from an evergreen tree.

Stilton   An aged English blue cheese made from cow's milk.

sweet anise   Another name for fennel, though the actual herb anise is unrelated.

syconium   A fruit whose edible portion is not the ripened ovary of a flowering plant, but some ripened adjacent tissue. Examples include the strawberry and the fig.

tahini   A paste made of ground sesame seeds.

temper   A method of controlling the temperatures of foods so that they can be combined easily. Usually used when eggs or delicate starches are added to very hot mixtures.

torta   A Spanish word with several meanings throughout the world, including cake, omelet, and sandwich.

tortilla   A Spanish word with several meanings, including flat bread in Mexico, and open-faced omelet in Spain

trebbiano   A grape used extensively in the production of white wine.

triple sift   Sifting dry ingredients three times to incorporate as much air as possible, resulting in light baked goods.

tzatziki   A Greek appetizer and sauce with ingredients including yogurt, mint, dill, and garlic.

unsaturated   Fatty acids whose molecules can support one or more hydrogen atoms. This lowers the fat's melting point, so that the fat remains liquid when refrigerated. These fats include polyunsaturated and monounsaturated, and are found in plants such as olives, avocados, soy, nuts, and canola.

vin santo   A very sweet Italian dessert wine.

zest   The colorful outermost rind of a citrus fruit, containing high concentration of the essential oils and flavor compounds that flavor the fruit itself.

Internet Sources

Herbs and Spices

When you can't find it at your local market, try these internet spots.

glenbrookfarm.com—bulk herbs, as well as essential oils and toiletries

gourmetsleuth.com—online food catalog offering ingredients from around the world, cookware, tableware, books, plus recipe resources

herbies.com.au—herbs, spices, and blends from down under

nirmalaskitchen.com—herbs, spices, grains, salts, plus prepared foods and organic products

penzys.com—herbs, spices, and seasoning blends from around the world

savoryspiceshop.com—herbs, spices, blends, sauces, and extracts

thespicebazaar.com—huge international array of spices and herbs, plus tea, coffee, chocolate, and prepared foods

thespicehouse.com—exquisite variety of spices with lots of choices arranged by cooking category for easy reference

Fresh Herbs for the Garden

For the freshest quality, grow your own with seeds and plants from these sources.

b-and-t-world-seeds.com—French seed company with hard-to-find varieties

mountainroseherbs.com—seeds for the home garden, plus bulk organic herbs, oils, teas, bath products, and herbal education

mountainvalleygrowers.com—organic herbs and perennials, plus garden mixes to help you plan your planting

wellsweep.com

International Groceries

Hard-to-find foods from around the world are just a click away.

importfood.com—Thai ingredients, cookware, and recipes

wifglobal.com—Caribbean ingredients, beverages, and prepared foods

ethnicgrocer.com—complete resource of food from 15 countries in Asia, Europe, Eastern Europe, the Mediterranean, the Middle East, and Mexico

ayhansmarketplace.com—Mediterranean foods and products focusing on good health

asiamex.com—products from Asia, the Middle East, West Africa, Latin America, and the Caribbean

asianfoodgrocer.com—hard-to-find Asian ingredients

Chilies

Feed the spice lovers authentic ingredients from these purveyors.

melissas.com—exotic fruits and vegetables

sweetfreedomfarm.com—Hispanic spices, chilies, seeds, and herbs

kitchenmarket.com—hot sauces, salsas, and groceries

Olives

More olives than you knew existed, plus olive oils and other related products.

olives.com—olive products and resources

olivesetal.co.uk—olives, nuts, snacks, and assorted olive products

olivehouse.com—olives, oils, and vinegars

Grain and Cereal

Find unusual grains and flours at these reputable sites.

bobsredmill.com—whole grains, flours, and baking mixes

kingarthurflour.com—flours, grains, baking ingredients, and equipment

arrowheadmills.com—all-natural, organic, whole-grain and gluten-free foods

Organic Groceries

When you're ready to go all-natural, you can stock your pantry with the help of these companies.

shopnatural.com—natural and organic groceries, pet care, vitamins, supplements, and beauty products

truefoodsmarket.com—over 5000 health food products for all areas of the kitchen, plus pet foods, vitamins, gardening supplies, herbal remedies, and literature

wholefoodsmarket.com—the grocery store chain's Internet store

Index

Q-R

Also by Leslie Bilderback, Certified Master Chef and Baker

ISBN: 978-1-59257-633-3   ISBN: 978-1-59257-674-6   ISBN: 978-1-59257-562-6